THE
IN-BETWEENS

ALSO BY MIRA PTACIN

Poor Your Soul

THE
IN-BETWEENS

🕈

The Spiritualists, Mediums, and Legends

of Camp Etna

MIRA PTACIN

LIVERIGHT PUBLISHING CORPORATION

A Division of W. W. Norton & Company

Independent Publishers Since 1923

Frontispiece: Entrance to Camp Etna. *Greta Rybus*

Copyright © 2019 by Mira Ptacin

For information about permission to reproduce selections from this book,
write to Permissions, Liveright Publishing Corporation, a division of
W. W. Norton & Company, Inc., 500 Fifth Avenue, New York, NY 10110

For information about special discounts for bulk purchases, please contact W. W. Norton
Special Sales at specialsales@wwnorton.com or 800-233-4830

Manufacturing by Lake Book Manufacturing
Book design by Chris Welch
Production manager: Beth Steidle

ISBN 978-1-63149-381-2

Liveright Publishing Corporation, 500 Fifth Avenue, New York, N.Y. 10110
www.wwnorton.com

W. W. Norton & Company Ltd., 15 Carlisle Street, London W1D 3BS

1 2 3 4 5 6 7 8 9 0

For my soul pack: Andrew, Theo, Simone, Huck, and Maybe

༄

In memory of Mickey Jackson
July 7, 1939–July 15, 2018

With respect to the requirement of art, the probable impossible is always preferable to the improbable possible.

—Aristotle, *Poetics*

I am incapable of conceiving infinity, and yet I do not accept finity. I want this adventure that is the context of my life to go on without end.

—Simone de Beauvoir, *La Vieillesse*

God looks suspiciously a lot like the ruling class. Religion is politics in the sky.

—Gloria Steinem

Contents

†⋮†

Introduction: When the Spirit Moves You   xiii

CHAPTER 1: Opening Season   1

CHAPTER 2: Bright Eyes   35

CHAPTER 3: Ghost Hunting 101   61

CHAPTER 4: Rosabelle, Believe   95

CHAPTER 5: Loyalty Lodge   113

CHAPTER 6: Water Witching, or Dowsing for Answers   143

CHAPTER 7: The New Generation   171

CHAPTER 8: The Powwow   203

CHAPTER 9: Church   217

Acknowledgments   245
Notes   249
Further Reading   259

Introduction

WHEN THE SPIRIT MOVES YOU

╪╪╪

When I guessed correctly that it was my brother, Julian, coming through, the licorice-colored coffee table rocked back and forth a couple of times before tipping, my knees catching the thing before it could fall to the ground.

"It's him," said Janice.

The heavy table pressed into me, hard. "He's giving you a hug," Janice continued, exhaling with steady assurance even though my brother Jules had been dead coming on twenty years.

Outside the cottage of Janice Nelson-Kroesser, chocolate-milk mud puddles booby-trapped the path to her front door. A thin April fog hovered over the slushy gravel driveway, ambivalent, like a shy snake. Beyond Janice's parked minivan, a gaggle of boarded-up cabins lined Pond Street: cold, dark, cockamamie and hibernating, waiting for their summer residents to wake them up come May, to have life zapped back into their old gingerbread-house bones. Behind them, the air sap-filled and sweet, a tall forest of pines with creeping bittersweet, chopped logs, and brush, made way for a little clearing in which sat a port-a-potty with a laminated note taped onto its door: BE AWARE! TOADS HANG OUT ON THE TOILET TISSUE ROLL.

It was spring in Maine and we were at Camp Etna, the 141-year-old Spiritualist community brought to life in 1876 and, compared to its explosive popularity back in its youth and teenage years, kept pretty much secret for the past fifty. It was a hard place to find, and if it hadn't been for a friend, Celia, mentioning it to me, I probably never would have really known that Spiritualism was an actual religion, nor would I have ever found this sleepy hollow. I was thirty-four years old, living in Maine, and until this year I had never heard of Camp Etna. Despite its Burning Man–sized popularity back in the nineteenth and twentieth century, most people I spoke to knew zilch about this place either. When I asked the gas-station clerk a quarter mile down the road from Camp Etna if she had any idea of what happens up the street and behind the rusty iron gates at 77 Stage Road, she handed me my change and my bag of Cheetos, looked at me blankly, and supposed that the place was just a summer camp for Cub Scouts. She wasn't entirely off in her guess—the enchanted hamlet did build lots of bonfires, and it was for scouts, it's just that Spiritualists were the kind of scouts who ventured into the afterlife rather than into national parks. They spoke to the dead rather than earned merit nature badges, so that's what I told her: Camp Etna is a magical living organism of a community of clairvoyants, mediums, psychics, flute-playing shamans, table tippers, trance channelers, mind-readers, dousers, Reiki healers, angel painters, past-life readers, hypnotists, paranormal investigators, and other like-minded Spiritualists.

By Spiritualist, I don't mean "spiritual," as in, *I'm not religious, I'm spiritual* or *I'm trying to meditate more, eat more vegetables, and be more spiritual.* No. Camp Etna is legitimately a religious camp, and Spiritualism (with a capital *S*) is a legitimate, organized, officially recognized, tax-exempt religion. Unlike most religions, Spiritualism is fairly young. Like most religions, Spiritualism was founded by humans who believe in a higher power and life after death, as well as living life with purpose, and have dedicated that purpose to their religious pursuit. But what makes Spiritualists different from the most popular American religions (a poll by the Public Religion Research Institute estimated that 69 percent of Americans are Christians, 45 percent professing attendance at a variety of churches that could be considered Protestant, and 20 percent professing Catholic beliefs) was that Spiritualists believe each and every living human has the power and was born with the tools to access and communicate with that great unknown *directly*, as well as talk directly to people who have passed and gone back to the big white light. In other words, Spiritualists have two major beliefs in their faith: that it is our duty to practice the Golden Rule, and also that we humans can talk to the dead if we want to. They trust that ghosts are not facile, are not hoaxes, and are much more than white sheets with eyeholes cut out. Spiritualists believe that the human spirit is with us always, even after people die, and that we have the tools to reach these spirits. Spiritualists believe that somewhere within our flesh, our eyeballs, our brain, our muscle, fingernails, bone marrow, hair, and heart is an organic phone line from which we can chat with God, access angels, and converse with the departed if we want to. Spiritualists are also willing to provide scientific evidence to prove what many people may otherwise believe to be a bunch of bullshit.

And as for the rest of us? Some people believe them, and in them. Many are on the fence. Others laugh in the face of the Spiritualist belief system. Regardless of what the outside world thinks of it, the religion lives on. Since its birth in the late 1800s, Camp Etna, the tiny rugged hamlet in the middle of rural Maine, has served as a sacred meeting ground for the mystical evolution of many of these Spiritualists—a place for them to meet regularly to sharpen their swords, learn new skills, heal others by accessing the great beyond, tighten their worldwide community, and eat some really good homemade pie and pot roast. Despite efforts to shut the religion down and shut the women up, to shove them into the corner under the label "hysteria," despite all this, a century and a half after its conception, the camp still remained a living and breathing community. Today, as summer neared, Camp Etna was yawning and stretching, once again about to open its gates for peak Spiritualist season.

The inside of Janice's cottage was snug and calm and smelled like roasted vegetables and melon-scented candles. This was their summer place; Janice and her husband, Ken, called it Phoenix Rising. Small wooden signs with words like "Laugh" and "Love" and "Welcome" hung on the walls, the font painted in curled, feminine letters. *Believe in Magic. Welcome to the Funny Farm.* On the kitchen counter: Dr. Bronner's lavender soap. Chia seeds. Fresh sunflowers in a vase. It was a pleasant place. A lit brass lamp rescued from one of the abandoned Etna cottages made the small, warm room dim and intimate. Actually, sitting there in chairs with Janice felt like we were in a funeral-home parlor, which, in a way, we were, because we were about to visit with the dead: a séance was about to commence. Specifically, we'd be doing a certain type of séance called "table tipping."

The route from my home to Camp Etna is two hours on the dot. I live on a tiny island just off the coast of Portland, Maine. After kissing my children and husband goodbye this morning, I took a twenty-minute ferry ride, got in my car, and merged onto I-295 north. Pine tree, birch tree, hemlock, pine. The farther north I drove, aside from the handful of Subarus that passed me on the road, there was no indication of what era or decade I was in; years ago, Maine outlawed billboard advertisements on all of her highways, making the roads pleasant, timeless, and meditative.

Pine tree, birch tree, hemlock, pine. Public radio was playing a podcast called "Clever Bots," in which the hosts explored ways computers and technology were reshaping our ideas of what it meant to be human: nowadays, even a most basic computer chat program could mimic human emotion and intelligence. As I pulled off the highway into the teeny town of East Newport, the host spoke of a man who had inadvertently fallen in love with a chatbot on an online dating site. The host then recounted the true story of a man who coded "Cleverbot," a sentient software program that goes by the name of Al that learns from people, in context, and imitates them. Al the robot had figured out how to have empathetic conversations with humans and had been acting as a bit of a therapist to more than 3 million humans each month. Finally, as I pulled into Janice's driveway at 16 Sunset Acres, and right before I shut off the engine and walked up the steps to meet my medium, the radio host posed two questions to the listeners: (1) was it actually possible for machines to think and feel? and (2) if they could, how could we humans ever prove it?

"The table is very old, so it has lot of energy in it," said Janice as I placed my nervous fingers on the table. I tried to remember to relax my body, as she'd instructed me. Table tipping, she explained, was a type of spirit communication in which we, women, people, the bereaved, whomever—whether it be one to twenty-one humans—would sit around a table, place our hands on it, breathe, relax, believe, and wait for movement from the table. The table might rock. It might rotate. It might spin, it might elevate. Before it happened, you wouldn't know what to expect other than that the table's movement would be coming from the dead. Through the table was how they would talk. Table tipping was Janice's specialty. In the Spiritualist community, it was what she was known for. I was new to it. In fact, I was completely new to all of this.

Music wafted throughout the cabin. Gentle, New Age, and techno-ish, like a funkier version of Kenny G's "Sax by the Fire," but still soft. Music with no words; the kind you'd hear in the lobby of a recently renovated hotel. "The table goes where it wants to go," she said, and although I didn't understand, I nodded. The table itself was about three feet tall and two feet wide, maybe a foot and a half. Hard, heavy, wooden, vintage.

"I found this table at Elmer's Barn of Junk and Dead Things," Janice explained, "in Cooper's Mills, Maine. She was in bad shape. But she had character. The top was all loose and she had square nails and pegs in her." Janice rubbed the surface of the table. "But I took her home anyway, and asked Ken to fix her up, so, voilà!"

"Is this going to be like a Ouija board?" I asked. "But with a table instead? Exactly how big of a movement is actually going to be going on here?"

Janice had soft, feathered red hair that smelled like it had just been shampooed. A dab of makeup here and there with just a bit of shimmer to it, a spritz of perfume. Janice was vampy. She was voluptuous, feminine; her form was like the human embodiment of a hug—a cherubic face, apple cheeks, doe eyelashes, and a bosom that made you want to rest your head in it while she raked back the hairs on your scalp with her precise red fingernails. Bangled wrists. Hoop earrings. Self-aware and self-nurturing; a *woman*. A Gerry Goffin/Aretha Franklin/Carole King "You-make-me-feel-like-a-natural-woman" kind of woman. She was rather gamey, and she was rather attractive.

"I'd tried them all," Janice sighed. "Pentecostal, Catholic, Methodist, Episcopalian. Nothing resonated with me."

The electric fireplace popped on and off and on again, making me jerk my head around as if it were a sign, as if I'd got lucky on my first day in the field and spotted a ghost, but my hostess didn't flinch.

She continued, "I got kicked out of Sunday school at the Baptist church for arguing with the Sunday school teacher because she said animals didn't have souls. But I knew they have souls because I could see them. I can see dead people, and I can also see dead cats." I looked down from my notebook onto the floor, thinking I might see a ghost cat in the room too.

"When we're born," said Janice, "we're connected to Spirit, right? I mean, that's where we come from. When we're young, well, children have that psychic ability. Imaginary friends? They aren't imaginary. And then we socialize it out of them, and then they—we—stop exercising that muscle, and it just goes *meeeeeerp*. When I was a kid, I would tell my dad what I could see and he'd say, 'No, no you didn't. You didn't see anything, shut up, you're nothing but a witch.'"

Outside, a tractor stuttered then came to life. It was Ken, Janice's husband. He was sharply handsome, like a game-show host, much taller than Janice. Fit, masculine.

"What does *spiritual* mean to you, Janice?" I asked.

"To be connected to a higher power," she answered.

Another loud pop and a bang, and Janice rolled her eyes and grinned, motioning to the kitchen window. Outside, Ken was sitting on top of the tractor, jerking it out of a big mud hole.

"He's doing one of his man projects," she said. "Building a new shed. When we're at Etna, he does his thing and I do mine, and it works." Ken was Janice's second husband; her first was abusive. "Those scars don't show," she'd laid out. "I went from a father who was physically abusive then I married a man who was verbally abusive, and I thought that's just what things were like. That's just what men were like." Eventually, after her kids were grown, Janice left her husband—she said she was evolving and he wasn't—then met Ken through a friend, and around this time in her life she'd begun attending a Spiritualist church, and that's when everything clicked. "Until then, I was a closet medium. And when I found Spiritualism, I found Ken, I found my people, I found my religion, and I was released."

In the coming months at Camp Etna, I'd learn what she meant. Soon I'd learn about what Spiritualism provided for its followers and practitioners since its conception, as well as what it provided for those who were just curious about it, those who had twenty bucks and a wild idea to go see a medium or psychic. I'd engage in the practices, go on a ghost hunt, release trapped spirits, access my Akashic records. I'd water witch, read some auras. I'd be introduced to the metaphysical explanations and the science and the realms of our souls, the difference between an angel and a spirit guide (and how to get them to find you a parking space, and fast—it's been working for me without fail ever since). I'd also learn that even in this religious community, you can find the same kinds of fierce ideological, political, and even personal disputes that you might find at a corporate shareholder meeting. But on this first day, the spring afternoon of table tipping at Janice's, I knew nothing about Spiritualism's past or present, or of its value and the space within death culture and grief that it filled, nor was I concerned about its future. I was a complete neophyte, just a journalist eager to see a ghost, and so in the beginning and for a good bit of my time at camp, I'd cling to my superficial knowledge about those who believed in and coexisted with what they believed to be the supernatural. But before all this, our hands were on the table.

"You know," said Janice, "I'd like to think I just stumbled upon all of this, but I also think my spirit guides were responsible for it too. They brought me where I am today. We all have them."

I smiled at Janice then squinted, trying to see or feel a glimpse of something—smoke or vapor or a shadow or anything that could be an extra presence. I was trying to locate my own spirit guide. Nothing came of it, or at least nothing that I myself could see.

"You meet them through meditation," said Janice. "We all can do it. I used to meditate every day before I met my husband. I found my best meditations were in the bathtubs. Candles around the tub, that kind of thing. And some kind of classy music is on and I just drift. And I've had some of my best, best, best communications that way."

"Can you see *my* spirit guides?"

"I can't," admitted Janice. "I'm not that good. Some people will tell you, 'Oh yeah, you have an Indian standing right there,' but I've heard that medium describe it to ten other people that way. People who do that aren't mediums; they're shysters."

Janice scooted to the edge of her chair and lifted her spine, making herself more erect, and described one of her guides.

"Sam," she said. "He has me call him Sam, but I think it was Samuel. He's probably from the sixteenth century. He's dressed in that kind of garb. Shows himself to me that way. He's around me a lot. Not 24/7, but he could be if he wanted to."

"What about during 'intimate moments'?" I asked. "Like sex. Is Samuel around then or does he give you . . . privacy?"

Janice's mouth made a curved line. "Actually, I had Spirit help me once. And there are spirits out there that do have sex with you, and that's happened to me once. Just once, though. I was paralyzed when it happened. I couldn't move. I wasn't asleep but I was totally aware of what was happening."

The front door opened and in walked Ken. He stepped into the kitchen, paying us no mind, opened the fridge, bent over, stuck his head inside.

"I was single at the time," said Janice, not lowering her voice. She looked over at Ken then back to me. "It was a weird sensation."

"Myra?" Ken sang sweetly, mispronouncing my name. "Can I offer you some filtered water or organic tea?" I shook my head no, smiled, then turned back to Janice.

"And that's what happens," said Janice. "We get so busy with our personal and work life that we don't slow down and connect with Spirit."

"When you die," I asked, "what will you do with your body?"

"Probably cremation. I find this body so hard to maintain . . ." She trailed off, sighed, and looked down. This was followed by a tricky silence. "So," said Janice, finally breaking the quiet. "Should we table tip or what?"

My parents worked hard to instill a faith in me. I grew up in a household that valued peace, love, compassion, empathy, selflessness, consequences, and so forth, and religion was a way about it. As a young man, my father attended a Catholic seminary and was studying to be a priest until he hit his twenties and quit to follow his dream of being a banjo player (he's now a family doctor). My mother, a Polish immigrant and physicist-turned-restaurateur, was raised in a religiously conservative country—Poland under the Iron Curtain—and her upbringing involved plenty of priests and nuns, strict and disciplinary, front and center. My brother Julian, sister Sabina, and I went to a Catholic school from kindergarten up through junior high, memorizing Bible stories alongside multiplication tables. We attended church twice a week at least. But it fizzled relatively fast. When I hit junior high, my parents decided we'd learn more about the real world from attending public schools. They felt there was more to life than religion, and there was more to religion than men in robes chanting in Latin and reminding us of how guilty we should feel about the human mistakes we made, or how we could repent by saying the same memorized prayers, now empty of meaning. For some reason, I stuck with the Catholic Church for a while. Perhaps it was because I was too lazy to commit to something new, or maybe it was the sound of prayers I'd heard so many times—that their words meant nothing to me but were soothing and calmed me, let me turn off my brain and listen to what was really coming through. To me, the physical building of the church itself was a shelter to keep me warm, the service a distraction from my inability to sit still. I'd memorized the service just like I'd memorized my drive home.

Before coming to Camp Etna, I was not a true believer in anything. It'd be most accurate to say I'm riding the fence of faith, further away from being an atheist and closer to a "you never know" kind of a hope. I did not come to Camp Etna seeking proof that life beyond death exists, nor to debunk some deception. I came to Camp Etna to learn about how a strong, independent, faith-based subculture of women (and a few men) live and have lived for centuries, unbeknownst to most of us, in a specific way that is exquisitely fulfilling to them.

One of the most absurd things about the human mind is that it can reason unreasonable things. Faith is unreasonable—that's the nature of it: it's unscientific, unprovable, and it relies on itself. It requires devotion. What makes Spiritualism different from many religions is that it believes it does have proof: the tipping of the tables, the messages from the dead. At Camp Etna, the proof is embedded into a culture completely its own. The women at Camp Etna were living a life that was the polar opposite of the world most of us live in: theirs was a matriarchal society. An altruistic community. Some might say it's an unreasonable place, an illogical one—a place in the woods where women were still running with the wolves, living in accordance with nature, with the seasons, making important decisions not based on money but according to their own personal instinct, intuition, and faith. They were their own priestesses. The women of Camp Etna, living and deceased, were women who, for centuries, had broken through the chains of a patriarchal society, stepped over the boundaries of expected domesticity. They'd been living for hundreds of years in the photo negative of my world that I never knew existed.

Every day I was at Camp Etna, the Spiritualists laid themselves bare. At the end of the day and at the beginning, every time I showed up, more than anything they just wanted me (and everyone they served) to be fulfilled and find peace. This was a camp of healers. Healing others was essentially their main goal in life. Answers, and love, is what they offered to me, tirelessly.

This is a book about the people of Camp Etna, past and present, as I have come to understand them. This is a book of nonfiction, but it is not a book that will attempt to suspend a certain set of beliefs. This is not a book that is going to try to convince you that life beyond death exists, or that it does not, but rather it is an exploration of the ecosystem of Spiritualists at Camp Etna—the quirky underworld of fringe characters whose stories defy conventional narratives about American life. Beautiful and complex and larger-than-life characters who are real people with immense (and diverse) convictions. People grasping for meaning in humanity beyond the basic biological fact that we're just a bag of chemicals, eating and farting our way from birth to death. This is a book simply about faith.

"Please place your hands on the table," said Janice. "First we will do a prayer."

I bowed my head and closed my eyes but then peeked up at her.

"Infinite Intelligence," she prayed, "we ask that you put your white light of protection around us. We ask that the highest and best come to us, we ask that angels, descending masters, guides, our families and our loved ones, that they come to us and help us to guide us throughout life as we walk down our path. Amen." She opened her eyes and looked at me.

"Amen," I agreed, and took a breath.

"Next, we are going to use our chakras," said Janice. "You know about chakras, right?"

I'd heard of them.

Janice began to explain, but the table had already started moving. It was moving hard. And fast. She stood up, pushing her chair quickly out of the way. I stood up as well, trying to keep up with her, or the table. It was up and running without warning, immediately rocking around the room like a clodhopper, rotating on its four legs, tipping hard and so fast, but it stayed under Janice's three or so fingers like a piano's keyboard.

I basically galloped in order to keep up with Janice and the table as they spun into the next room. They were dancing together. Despite the fast movement of the furniture and my fumbling around to stay with them, it seemed to me that it was Janice who led the duet. The thing wasn't floating on its own, because her fingers were on it the entire time, and that's the only way I can explain it, because that's the only thing I could make sense of, given the quickness of it all, and my befuddlement. Then, when we were closer to its original position in the living room, the table stayed in one location but began rocking faster and harder, my hands slipping off the table again and again, all the while Janice with her hands on it, then just one hand, then both again, then just a couple of fingers, her face smiling calmly down at the table and then back at me, cool as a cucumber. It rocked and rocked smaller and smaller as Janice lifted all her fingers but one—her pretty painted index finger, now right smack down in front of her on the table pressing down, as if she were pushing down on a child's forehead.

Finally, the rocking slowed, the table rocked to the left then to the right then stopped into the position a table should be in. A two- or three-second pause, and then it tipped once more to the right, leaving us unsure what it would do next. Janice laughed at it a little, lovingly and permissibly at its minor rebellion.

"So basically," said Janice, "now we are gonna just sit here with our hands slightly on the table."

I put my hands back on, hesitantly, as if the thing could possibly bite.

"And you say, 'is there anybody here for—' and then you put your name out, because it gives off your vibration."

I did as I was told. "Is there anybody here for Mira?" I asked.

The table rocked to the right.

"Yes," said Janice. "Right off. It rocked to the right. Yes is to the *right*. Is there anyone you think it might be? She'll tip to the right now if it's a 'yes,'" said Janice.

I had known people who had died, just as much as anyone else did. The closest to me had been my younger brother. I asked, "Is it anybody I've lost, like a relative? Like, maybe direct family member?"

The table rocked right. "Yes."

"Could it be . . . is it a boy?"

It rocked to the right again. "Yes," said Janice.

"Oh, OK. Well, then could it be Julian?"

And that's when the big heavy black table leaned forward, pressing itself into me and Janice smiled.

"A hug," she said. "He's giving you a hug. Now. Close your eyes, feel the energy. He's hugging you so tight. Can you feel it?"

I closed my eyes. I told myself to think of my brother. I tried to feel him. I saw the memory of his face in my head, a memory I hadn't intentionally dedicated a moment to open up at and explore consciously for more than a minute in quite a while. Julian had died in 1997, at age fourteen, after he was hit by a drunk driver. I was seventeen at the time. After he died, I had trouble remembering anything about him, as if the trauma had shut down a certain part of my brain where the memory of Jules lived. But during this moment, I did feel what it felt like when I thought of him, or what it was like to be around him, or what he felt like. But the moment was fleeting, because the voice in my head returned to the queerness of the situation. I opened my eyes.

"What do you want to ask him?" Janice asked. "Remember, it can only be a yes-or-no question," she said. "Back in the olden days, table tippers would use the alphabet, but it ended up taking too darn long to spell out the answers. So now we just use the yes-or-no questions."

A hug. Your brother is giving you a hug. It was a euphony I wanted to hear, regardless of the context. Under pressure, I had no questions for my dead brother. Or maybe I was just too confused in the spur of the moment, so Janice suggested some questions. She went ahead and asked the table. They told me he didn't suffer when he died. That his death was planned, it was all part of life's plan, and that he was happy. I was told that I wouldn't have any more children, and that I needed more strict boundaries for my son and daughter, and that both my father and I needed to take more time to talk to Jules. These words were given to me, followed by the sound of Janice's breathing, and then, in somewhat stunned reflection, I said clumsily, as if ending an awkward job interview, "OK, then. I guess those are all the questions that I have!" and took my hands off the table.

"Wait," said Janice, still calm and somewhat trancelike. "Before we close up the session, I myself want to ask a couple of questions." Janice closed her eyes, inhaled, exhaled. "The two ladies I just hired. Will they be good employees?"

The table rocked right.

"I had that good feeling in my gut," said Janice, "and I just wanted to confirm. And am I going to find someone to buy my facility?" She opened her eyes and turned to me as an aside, and said, "It's a non-profit, and I don't know how to back out of it. It's hard to sell and I'm hoping to retire, find someone to take over and give me a nice severance package, just enough to live on . . . also, is this Sam?"

Yes, the table tipped.

"OK, good," said Janice. She paused another beat, inhaled and exhaled again, and said, "And now it's time to close the session. Thank you so much for coming and doing your best, spending your time and energy so that we could communicate with our loved ones and be in a safe environment, protected and loved. Thank you so much for that."

"Hallelujah. Can I say that?" I asked. "Amen?"

"Amen."

We closed the session, chatted a little longer, just the two of us, and then Janice invited me to the upcoming Camp Etna board meeting. She walked me to the door and Ken to my car and we all waved goodbye.

After leaving the gates of Camp Etna that first day, I swung by Country Corner Variety for some soda water and homemade fudge, packed myself back into the car, and hit the highway back to the land of the living. I drove in silence the whole way, concentrating on thoughts and memories of my brother, which was something I hadn't done in a long time, and thinking about the radio hosts' questions about things that were not alive. Was it actually possible for them to think and feel and communicate with the living? If they could, how could we ever prove it?

Soon I would arrive home and jump back into my fast-moving, modern life. And soon, I would pick dates on my calendar to return to Etna. The snow would melt, spring would pass and the warmth would arrive, and Camp Etna's Reverend Gladys Laliberte Temple, the cobalt-colored Healing House, and the Ladies' Auxiliary would be up and running. Someone would flick on the lights to the Camp Etna Museum, with all its artifacts unsorted but saved, kept secure in plastic bags. A key would be inserted to unlock the doors of the Rotary Room and the Visiting Mediums' Cottage, the Hot Spot Café, the kitchen and chow hall. Soon, the enigmatic mediums would breathe life back into the summer cottages, pull up their shades, dust off their steps, and hang their tin shingles. As the summer seekers arrived, the Spiritualists of Camp Etna would rock and rock and rock on their porch chairs, and, once again, their story would begin.

❧✦❧

CHAPTER 1

Opening Season

Spiritualist Suffragettes
Come to Camp Etna, we have a message for you.

Since the dawn of their religion, Spiritualists have
always had their boots on the ground in the
fight for women's rights.

They believed they would live forever.

After our bodies were stiff and buried under rosebushes, we humans—in fact, all creatures—would awake as more advanced beings. In the afterlife, our souls would gain not only the ability but also the inclination to provide truths for the living, clues and insights into all their quandaries. Once we were dead, we would finally understand life. This had always been possible and always would be. Those left breathing just had to listen.

Despite the eternity of it all, they set the date of March 31, 1848, as their beginning. A Friday. It began with a sound: a tapping. A coded conversation between two sisters and an unknown third party: a ghost in the wall. "Mr. Splitfoot" the two sisters had called him. The three of them talked. Folks witnessed—first parents, then neighbors. Word spread. Next came the chin-wags and the believers, the opportunists and the newspapermen. This led to more demonstrations, conversations— séances, if you will—that unearthed glimmers of hope. Faith.

The turbulent decade about to unfold—the railways unfurling across the continent, the glittering promise of gold in the west, the slow hurtle toward a war that would rend the country—made the timing just right; an ancient longing was released into the air and blown like a thousand seeds soon to take root in cities and towns large and small, known and not, across the country. It would grow into a cultural revolution that challenged then changed the established American institutions of patriarchal authority and the Christian Church. It was the conception of a religion that by 1897 would spread across the United States and Europe, sprouting more than 8 million disciples. And at the dead center of all those believers were two sisters, Kate and Margaret.

In Hydesville, a small town in upstate New York, Kate and Margaret Fox, ages twelve and fifteen, lived in a house that had always felt sinister to the townsfolk, even before their family had moved to town.

One night, their parents started hearing things. First some small taps, then harder knocks that sounded like apples dropping off the dresser in the girls' room. Soon, those noises grew more and more sophisticated, stronger, like the scrape of a bed foot being dragged across the plank floor. But when Kate and Margaret's mother would rush upstairs and fling open the door to their room, her daughters would both be asleep. Finally, after much confusion and questioning, the sisters called their mother into the room.

Mother, watch.

Margaret, the eldest, snapped her fingers once—*tik*—and was immediately answered by a tap in response. She snapped twice, and something snapped twice. Little Kate's hands were in her lap, unwavering. There was something in that room.

> I asked the noise to rap my different children's ages, successively. Instantly, each one of my children's ages was given correctly, pausing between them sufficiently long enough to individualize them until the seventh, at which a longer pause was made, and then three more emphatic raps were given, corresponding to the age of the little one that died, which was my youngest child.
>
> I then asked: "Is this a human that answers my questions so correctly?" There was no rap. I asked: "Is it a spirit? If it is, make two raps." Two sounds were given as soon as the request was made. I then said: "If I was an injured spirit, make two raps," which were instantly made, causing the house to tremble. I asked: "Were you injured in this house?" The answer was given as before. "Is the person living that injured you?" Answered by raps in the same manner. I ascertained by the same method that it was a man, aged thirty-one years, that he had been murdered in this house, and his remains were buried in the cellar. . . . I asked: "Will you continue to rap if I call my neighbors that they may hear it too?" The raps were loud in the affirmative . . .
>
> —*SIGNED, MRS. MARGARET FOX 1848 [Mother of the girls]*

Two days later, the evening before April Fools' Day, it happened again. Picture young Kate and Margaret in long, pearl-colored night-gowns and bouncy hair, dangling their feet from the edge of their unmade bed, this time surrounded by their parents, huddling neigh-bors, and flickering candlelight. Soon enough, the spirit spoke, com-municating in the coded language the girls and the ghost had already established: One tap meant yes. Two taps, no.

The next morning, neighbors left the Fox girls' bedroom believing they'd spent a night with an apparition and two girls with mystical powers, and by the end of the next evening, the night of April Fools', they were excavating the Fox family's cellar, digging and digging and digging and digging until water pooled up in a hole and they had to put down their shovels.

The story might have ended then, or maybe after the sisters were sent to Rochester by their parents to protect them from a potential witch-hunt. There, the girls could live under the eye of their older and more responsible sister, Leah, and move on from what they'd started and live a normal life. But the ghost—Mr. Splitfoot—seemed to follow them, and Leah turned out to be more opportunistic than she was reli-able, a better publicist than guardian. Leah booked her younger sisters as the headliners in a four-hundred-seat theater in New York, where the sisters took questions for the dead from the audience. Thus marks 1849 as the first public demonstration of Spiritualism, in Corinthian Hall, Rochester. Kate and Margaret Fox emerged as mediums.

Within a few years, the girls became the talk of antebellum New York and were drafted to serve as clairvoyants for rich believers. On the cor-ner of Broadway and Maiden Lane, the Fox sisters booked a suite and began showcasing their work in a parlor at Barnum's, a swanky hotel owned by a cousin of the famed showman and huckster P. T. Preemi-nent New Yorkers frequented the scene, mostly inquiring about "the state of railway stocks or the issue of love affairs," which soon brought forth the attention of other notables and luminaries to Spiritualism: Elizabeth Cady Stanton, Frederick Douglass, William Cullen Bryant,

George Bancroft, Sojourner Truth, James Fenimore Cooper, Nathaniel Parker Willis. When William Lloyd Garrison, an eminent abolitionist of the time, sat through a Fox sisters session, he recounted a ground-breaking session in which the spirits rapped in time and tempo to a popular song of the era, and spelled out a message: *Spiritualism will work miracles in the cause of reform.*

In the Fox sisters' hotel parlor, séances were held daily, starting in the morning at ten then in the evening at five and eight, each session thirty hopefuls deep, humid and breathy, the audience pregnant with expectation or maybe disbelief, their gaping eyes on the two girls at the head of an egg-shaped table. Admission was a dollar.

Dollars added up. In time Kate and Margaret were wealthy and famous, touring and filling auditoriums. People swarmed from mansions and flophouses, waiting for hours for the chance to hear a simple yes-or-no answer through the mediums.

— Did you die peacefully?
— Will you forgive me?
— Do you love me?
— Are you at peace?

Some believed. But for many, the sisters were a diversion, a curiosity of the times: there were no televisions, no movies or recorded music. Entertainment wasn't as ubiquitous as it eventually became; these female mystics were the reality show. The young women were captivating—even if their audiences didn't believe in ghosts or spirit communication, this was the first time they'd ever witnessed a female— let alone two—speak in public, on a stage, not just with permission but by popular demand. At the time, women speaking in public was essentially unheard-of. And on top of that, these girls were offering not only hope but proof: there was life after death.

However, although Spiritualism marks its birth with the emergence of the Fox sisters and Mr. Splitfoot, the trio was not the first to bring forth such messages. Years before they entered the limelight (yet with-out as much razzmatazz and fanfare) a New York visionary had put forth an explanation and proof of spirit manifestations as well as meta-physical account of his experience in the other realm. His name was Andrew Jackson Davis, aka "John the Baptist of Spiritualism," aka "The Poughkeepsie Seer."

He, too, came from humble beginnings. Born in Blooming, New York, in 1826, Davis grew up poor as dirt. In Poughkeepsie, where he spent his youth, his mother died when he was still very young. His father was an uneducated alcoholic shoemaker and weaver. Despite what may have been a depressing and limiting home life, from a young age Davis claimed he'd always been a clairvoyant, that he'd heard voices from those not alive. A few years into his adulthood, Davis's belief in metaphysics and mediumship was fueled after an encounter with a traveling mesmerist (that is, one who practices and teaches the work of Franz Anton Mesmer, a seventeenth-century physician and visionary who believed cures could be effected by having patients sit with their feet in a fountain of magnetized water while holding cables attached to magnetized trees). Soon, after attending a series of these mesmerist lectures in Poughkeepsie, Andrew Jackson Davis the Medium arrived (or so he claimed): on the evening of May 6, twenty-two years of age, Davis felt suddenly and completely overwhelmed by a compulsion to take a "rapid journey" from Poughkeepsie to the Catskill Mountains. He said he was obliged to fly. When Andrew Jackson Davis traveled that fateful night in 1844, he did so miraculously—he swore that he got to the Catskills via levitation, also referred to as astral travel, in a semitrance state. That the next day, upon gaining full consciousness some forty miles from his home and not quite recalling how he got there, Andrew Jackson Davis did recall perfectly that he had partaken in a deep philosophical discussion with the Swedish seer and mesmerist Emanuel Swedenborg as well as Galen, a prominent Greek philoso-pher, physician, and surgeon during the days of the Roman Empire. Both men, according to Davis, had engaged with and enlightened him directly. Both men, of course, were dead. For the three years following this episode, Davis passionately continued to explore magnetic healing, dictating his knowledge about life after death to a scribe while in a trance state.

Then in 1847, just one year before the arrival of the young Fox sisters onto the mystic scene, Davis published *The Principles of Nature: Her Divine Revelations, and a Voice to Mankind,* which not only explained the workings of the other side, but, in his work, predicted the advent of Spiritualism that would soon be delivered by the sweet and unassuming and wet-behind-the-ears Fox sisters. Soon after the Foxes' debut, Davis and a small group of Universalist ministers began to spread his books and doctrines and his new journal, *The Univercoelum and Spiritual Philosopher,* throughout the nation. Davis invited Kate and Margaret to his home in New York, and, having investigated their claims of spirit communication, accepted them and went on to explain them to the public in terms of his own expertise and study. Soon after, Davis would lecture and preach and create a six-volume encyclopedia, as well as twenty-nine other books. In one title—*The Philosophy of Spiritual Intercourse*—Davis provided step-by-step instructions for the formation and implementation of séance circles, a ritual that would become the very basis for much of Spiritualist practice in the years to follow.

Aside from Davis's book of séance instructions, the rest of his literature didn't quite take. In fact, it barely held on. Compared to the popularity of the Fox sisters, the majority of Americans might not have been reading Davis's *The Principles of Nature* any more than the average American today might be curled up with a blanket and cup of tea reading Thich Nhat Hanh, let alone Deepak Chopra. The Fox sisters, however, continued to build a following. They continued to fill theaters and auditoriums because they brought with them more zest and shimmer and a palpable excitement. They offered a *physical* show. Why would one read about the impossible when one could see it happening onstage? And because they were young women, the Fox sisters also delivered an additional kind of radicalism. Kate and Maggie's exhibition struck at something vital in a certain kind of seeker. For those who felt shack-led by the mores of the times, the very beings of the teenage sisters were revolutionary. While seeking a higher power was nothing new, the Fox sisters' message rode on the American yearning to go it alone, to live one's life in accordance to self-guidance and one's individual intuition without needing someone's permission, without hierarchy, without interference of the Church or any other institution. The Fox sisters represented something that had been feared by many, yearned for by others, and only imagined by the patriarchal American society at the time: a woman's right to self-sovereignty. Each time the Fox sisters addressed a crowd, they were also shedding their Victorian sensibili-ties and their assigned gender roles, breaking the ossified boundaries between classes, ages, sexes. Each time they stepped onto the stage, they were inspiring a silent but large segment of the nation that was hungry for change and for someone to start it. Unlike their Christian contemporaries, the Fox sisters proved that Americans no longer had to rely on speculation or even revelation for information about the ulti-mate fate of the soul; we would continue to evolve after death, even if we weren't baptized. You didn't need a deacon, priest, bishop, pope, or any man, for that matter, to connect you to the higher power; Spiri-tualism eliminated the need for a savior. As they continued to dazzle the crowds, the sisters planted the seed of new religion—what would soon be named Spiritualism with a capital S—kindling the individual's request for individual truth, and permission to believe in it with a fear-less tenacity.

Around the same time, another group of radical American reformers was gaining momentum. Just down the road from where the Fox sisters first publicly demonstrated their séances with Mr. Splitfoot, the very first women's-rights convention was held in Seneca Falls, New York, in July of 1848. Many of those who attended the Seneca Falls Conven-tion had already caught wind of the two sisters, and these feminists lent their support to the young women and their cause. These girls were not powerless, mute observers, and this convinced the feminists of their authenticity. They praised the girls for their bravery and pro-gressiveness, for defying their roles as politically, financially, sexually, and socially repressed second-class citizens. Women's-rights advocates quickly and fully joined forces with the Fox sisters, backing them and building the bridge that linked Spiritualists to the suffragettes, thus adding a strong foundational element of feminism to the Spiritualist movement at its outset, with both movements calling for the "emanci-pation of women from all legal and social disabilities."

"Spiritualism has promoted the cause of woman more than any other movement," proclaimed adamant women's-rights activist Mary Fenn Love, who eventually met and married Andrew Jackson Davis. It was even reported that, as Elizabeth Cady Stanton and Lucretia Mott drafted the Seneca Falls Convention's resolutions, spirit raps tapped their table.

The collaboration wasn't just limited to protofeminists. In fact, before the support from women's-rights advocates, it was a small group of abolitionists who first took the Fox sisters seriously. Upon the initial boost from big sister Leah Fox, and before Kate and Maggie hit their stride, it was a group of abolitionist Quakers who helped establish and endorse the girls' first public séances for smaller crowds. The merging of the sisters and the Quakers was quite natu-ral: Quakers believe in self-sovereignty, that no human should rule over another; they don't have much use for religious authority. They believed that when a white person controlled the life of a person with darker skin, or when a husband exerted authority over his wife, he was usurping the place of God. The Quakers soon realized that this new practice of Spiritualism eliminated the place of a male author-ity and replaced it with new and more "feminine" qualities. That is to say: harmony replacing forcefulness, acceptance replacing domi-nation, individualism replacing hierarchy. Radical individualism. The women's-rights movement, the abolitionists, and the Fox sisters, all guided by their common credo, merged like railroad cars hitched to a locomotive belief that each human being has the capacity to do good and to right the world's wrongs, in whatever shape, form, or plane they may appear.

> The first conditions to be observed relate to the persons who compose the circle. These should be, as far as possible, of opposite temperaments, as positive and negative in disposition, whether male or female; also of moral characters, pure minds, and not marked by repulsive points of either physical or mental condition. The physical temperaments should contrast with each other, but no person suffering from decidedly chronic disease, or of very debilitated physique, should be present at any circle, unless it is formed expressly for healing purposes. I would recommend the number of the circle never to be less than three, or more than twelve. The use growing out of the association of differing temperaments is to form a battery on the principle of electricity or galvanism, composed of positive and negative elements, the sum of which should be unequal. No person of a very strongly positive temperament or disposition should be present, as any such magnetic spheres emanating from the circle will overpower that of the spirits, who must always be positive to the circle in order to produce phenomena. It is not desirable to have more than two already well-developed mediums in a circle, mediums always absorbing the magnetism of the rest of the party, hence, when there are too many present, the force, being divided, cannot operate successfully with any. Never let the apartment be overheated, or even close; as an unusual amount of magnetism is liberated at a circle, the room is always warmer than ordinary, and should be well ventilated. Avoid strong light, which, by producing excessive motion in the atmosphere, disturbs the manifestations. A very subdued light is the most favourable for any manifestations of a magnetic character, especially for spiritual magnetism. . . . I recommend the séance to be opened either with prayer or music, vocal or instrumental; after which, subdued, quiet, and harmonising conversation is

better than wearisome silence; but let the conversation be always directed towards the purpose of the gathering, and never sink into discussion or rise to emphasis; let it be gentle, quiet, and spiritual, until phenomena begin to be manifest. Always have a slate, or pen, pencil, and paper on the table, so as not to be obliged to rise to procure them. Especially avoid all entering or quitting the room, moving about, irrelevant conversation, or disturbances within or without the circle room, after the séance has once commenced. The spirits are far more punctual to seasons, faithful to promise, and periodical in action, than mortals.

—From *"Preparing for a Séance,"* 1875

By the 1850s, Spiritualism had spread across the nation, with women front and center of the anti-official, anti-figurehead, anti-organization organization. Citizens were holding séances and gathering to talk to spirits as casually as we gather for Sunday brunches. By then, Spiritualism wasn't just limited to audience members or activist leaders anymore. It appealed to people on many levels: as a reformation—a dismissal of Calvinism or Christian evangelicalism; as a quest for a more liberal theology; and as a desire to overcome mourning through not just prayer but communication with departed loved ones, and with empirical evidence to boot.

It's impossible to know how many times during this era the séance ritual was performed—Spiritualists hardly kept any courtly authoritative documentation. But the movement grew, and as it did, Spiritualism found more and more ways of disseminating information, organizing, and keeping believers united.

In 1852, *The Spiritual Telegraph* began circulation to support the more than 150 séance circles meeting regularly in New York City, more than 60 in Philadelphia, and thousands of others popping up across the United States. A year after that, the snappy and upbeat song "Spirit Rappings" was published and became a nationally popular tune. More and more Spiritualist newspapers, periodicals, and journals were conceived: *The Carrier Dove. Spirit of the Age. The Battle Creek Idea.* And *The Banner of Light*, which was, hands-down, the most popular Spiritualist periodical, and the favorite publication of abolitionist and bestselling author Harriet Beecher Stowe. She urged her publisher to send them a review copy of her hot-off-the-press book *Old Town Folks.*

By the mid-1850s, almost anyone could find a venue to attend progressive Spiritualist lectures on life after death just as easily as they could take part in orchestrated séances at which the dead materialized by tipping tables, levitating tin trumpets, or simply by writing in shorthand: composing messages themselves on sealed slates to give answers to human seekers. More evidence of life after death came forth. Slimy stuff started to appear: filmy and disconcerting substances—said to be the clear outer layer of the cytoplasm in amoeboid cells—would be emitted from mediums' bodies during a séance (come 1894, psychical researcher Charles Richet would give ectoplasm its official name). Spiritualists called themselves "investigators" (still do) and were asserting the belief that Spiritualism was a science just as much as it was a religion (still are). Soon, one could even pose for spirit photographs; photography was just as miraculous a breakthrough. All the while, skeptics and critics of Spiritualism said the movement, which they nicknamed "Rapplemania," was just a passing trend. They couldn't have been more wrong.

Then came 1861 and the Civil War, a nationwide tsunami of grief taking out at least 620,000 souls, nearly all at once. Never before had so many Americans at the same time been hit with such death and sorrow and mortality. Surprisingly, most antebellum Americans did not belong to a church, and only about 25 percent belonged to a Christian denomination. Mourners needed an outlet and they needed hope, something different from the you're-born-a-sinner, fire-and-brimstone afterlife they'd been told to fear and respect. Spiritualism offered the perfect balm. It rejected traditional Christianity. It demanded less and promised more. Spiritualism promised that if you died before you were baptized, you would not suffer in the eternal flames of hell. Spiritualism offered not only the hope of life after death in a heavenly realm, it offered proof of immortality through conversations with dead loved ones—all of this offered with no commitment or financial obligation.

During her husband's tenure as our nation's president, a devastated Mary Todd Lincoln brought countless mediums to connect her (and Abe) to her late sons William and Edward, but she wasn't the first FLOTUS to bring Spiritualism into the White House. Jane Pierce, wife of Franklin Pierce, had already hosted the young Fox sisters after losing her son Benjamin in a train crash. By now, the attempt to communicate with the dead was neither taboo nor was it a trend; it was becoming the norm.

Prominent men got on board as well. Consider the conversion of Judge John Edmonds, president of the New York Senate (who later resigned to become a full-time medium and advocate). Consider Alexander N. Asakof, imperial councilor to the tsar of Russia, who, immediately upon reading Andrew Jackson Davis's work, launched into a new role as a Russian Spiritualist pioneer. Consider Pierre Curie, Nobel laureate, French physicist and husband of Marie Curie. Consider Sir Arthur Conan Doyle, known for penning *The Adventures of Sherlock Holmes,* who went on to write the mammoth multivolume work *The History of Spiritualism* and create the "Ghost Club" (which was frequented by Charles Dickens). Consider Dr. Russell Wallace, co-discoverer of the theory of evolution with Charles Darwin, who, after much research, concluded and declared widely that spirit phenomena could be proven scientifically. Or consider the well-respected but little-known East Coast farmer and preacher Daniel Buswell, who, in 1858, along with his wife, Lizzie Francis Mosley, at the top of the hill on the east line of Etna-Bangor Road in a Maine settlement called Crosbytown, hosted the very first of many Spiritualist gatherings on their land. These camp meetings would eventually bloom into one of the largest Spiritualist communities in the nation: Camp Etna. By 1875, fewer than thirty years after the young Fox sisters had made their debut, Spiritualism had more than 1 million practitioners in the United States and Europe. All was well.

All was not well. The temple was cold. Cold and dark and dead, and even though the tips of our toes were beginning to burn with numbness, no one would be going anywhere for the next few hours. We were seated around two tables pushed together. Space heaters were cranked up high, and we all still had on our gloves, our hats, scarves, parkas. The woman next to me wore a blanket wrapped around her legs and one around her shoulders too. Her name was Cathy McIntyre. She was knitting a hat.

"Call to order!" Deftly, Janice Nelson-Kroesser rose from her seat. Janice's red hair rested on her shoulders, framing her face like a beauty queen. She put her fist to her lips and cleared her throat twice, standing at the head of the church, officially named the Reverend Gladys Laliberte Memorial Temple of Camp Etna, after one of its more prominent and dedicated mediums from the 1960s. With Janice at the helm, today's Camp Etna board meeting was about to commence. "Call to order," she said again, her voice excessively diffident. She was the board president.

Behind us, an empty basilica. Unoccupied orange chairs had been arranged to face the stage of the temple; there was no priest's pulpit in front, just a few steps up to a raised platform. In the third row of the congregation, a printout was taped on the backs of the chairs: THIS ROW RESERVED FOR HEALING. There were no pews. Toward the back of the room, a long table had been pushed up to the wall and covered in a tablecloth stamped down by a smorgasbord of snacks— comfort foods—the same medley of dishes that people drop off at the homes of the recently bereaved: crockpots of chili, mac-n-cheese casseroles, sugar cookies, deviled eggs, and two massive square cardboard containers of Dunkin' Donuts Box of Joe coffee. Today's meeting would end up clocking in at about four hours and change.

"Call to order," Janice said a third time, even louder to quiet the rest of the chatter from the board members. Despite the mandatory obligation to be here on a Saturday morning, the group was cheerful and chatty and needed a cowgirl to wrangle their focus. There was an incredible amount of work to do before camp opened for her 141st summer season. Mediums Day, Janice reminded her team, was less than two months away.

Below her gaze sat the cast of characters: the 2017 Camp Etna Board of Directors. "Roll call," said Janice, pulling out a purple pen. Sue Jalbert. *Here.* Ernie VanDenBossche. *Present.* Krista Wright. *Yep!* Angie Butler-Welch. *Present.* Marcia Ruland, James Kidder, Cathy McIntyre: all present, all in attendance.

"Ernie, would you like to give the invocation?"

A very tall man began to stand. Ernie had hair as white as birch bark, large round glasses, a pale yet genial face and winter lips, and as he stood, Ernie wobbled a bit—he didn't have his crutches nearby at the moment; he'd had polio. Ernie VanDenBossche had also been trained as a Reiki master, was a verified medium, a psychic, a board-certified hypnotherapist and instructor with the National Guild of Hypnotists, and was currently the Camp Etna Board vice president, with a term ending in 2018. "Let us pray."

We lowered our heads and Ernie blessed the group briefly, thanked the divine, our spirit guides, our loved ones passed, and we agreed. The prayer was quick. Ernie sat back down. I'd later be told (and on multiple occasions by multiple Spiritualists) that the ability to compartmentalize and stay present and focused on the task at hand was essential to mediums and psychics and those who can speak to the dead, who have no concept of time.

Today's meeting began like this: a board member discussion of former camp member Rosy D'Elia's "Dear John" email about leaving the community and selling her cottage (for $10,000) as well as Janice reading

aloud the section of Rosy's letter that thanked the camp for enlighten-
ing her on her life journey. A membership application for Sherwood
Denham ("did he complete the questionnaire and the requirements of
volunteering?"), who would like to become a member of the nonprofit,
live here, practice here, and so on and so forth. This was followed by
the board discussion and decision on who is responsible for turning on
the water for the summer ("not too soon, because we don't want the
pipes to burst"), the ongoing saga of the pumping and vacuuming of
the ground's cesspool. The testing of water. The cost of building a storage unit for yearly maintenance tools. The plowing of the roads. The
contract of the Healing Light Church's camp rental membership. The
idea of a mobile potluck. The lot fees. Temple donations. Roof repair.
The garden committee budget. The call to increase the price of message circles and the gallery readings and the séances from $15 to $20.
And most important, pulling the final thread to hold taut the definitive
schedule of camp's summer events.

Next to me, a metallic *click, click, click*. Cathy McIntyre, or "Cathymac"
as members called her affectionately, continued knitting. Cathymac was
one of the longest-attending members of camp, one of the matriarchs.
Click, click, click. Her head was folded down and her body had shrunken
with it, folding into itself. Cathymac's skin was wafer-thin and wrinkled
in a new kind of pretty from years and years and years of Earth's gravita-
tional pull, from the expression of emotions, from being a human on this
planet. Around her, there was continued talk of cesspools and Cathymac
knitted onward, knuckles rising and lowering like piano keys, looping
and stitching. She spoke very little despite having been at Camp Etna
since 1980, which, to me, was an indication that she'd become wise in
her years, despite having a strong opinion about what happens at and to
the camp, and its fate. There had always been battles at the camp, and
by now she had learned what battles were worth picking or backing, what
words of hers were worth giving and when. Cathymac didn't live here
year-round anymore—few people did now—but she was still committed
to the place and had driven up here by herself in the New England winter

from her home in Gloucester, Massachusetts. To her, Camp Etna was not a novelty or a pet project. These grounds were sacred.

Still not lifting her head, Cathymac leaned over and whispered into my ear. "Our port-a-potties *flush.*"

Behind Cathymac, the walls of the Gladys Laliberte Temple were an art gallery of portraits and relics of those who came before her. A prominent photograph of a mustachioed man, black suit, white shirt, white bow tie, regal. Harrison D. Barrett, 1863–1911. Underneath him, his words: *Spiritualism is a religious science and a scientific religion, a religious philosophy and a philosophical religion.* Farther down, a framed periodical. Headline: *What Spiritualists Demand.* The publication: *The Progressive Thinker,* a late-1800s Spiritualist journal that ran until the mid-1900s and was dedicated to "Spiritualism, Biology, Electro-Psychology, and its differentiations, Mesmerism, Animal Magnetism, and Hypnotism; Somnambulism, natural and induced, as presented by Dr. Fahnstock; Telepathy; Visions while awake, in sleep, or in Trance; Psychometry; cremation, a Spiritual and Sanitary necessity; Brain Waves, Psychic Waves, or Soul Force; Ethics as a Factor in Religion, and as annunciated by the Philosopher and Seer, Hudson Tuttle; the Various Stages of Death, in the Transition of the Spirit to Higher Spheres; the signs of Death; the Danger of Premature Internment, etc."

Ghosts of the past covered the space like wallpaper—more clippings, more headlines, paintings, postcards, pictures, collages. In particular, a framed sepia photo of hundreds and hundreds and hundreds of souls, some men and mostly women gathered in the woods, facing the camera and not smiling, all dressed in dark clothes: tailored dresses, long jackets and skirts, bustles, topped with small hats and bonnets. White beards, dark beards, seated, hats resting on their laps. Several children in the picture as well, dressed in tidy white gowns with lots of frills. The caption: *Group at Camp Etna, 1885. Donated by the Sylvia Dean Family, descendants of Mary Drake Jenne.* A little farther from that hung a large, happy yellow banner in pretty good shape, adorned with sunflowers

A salvaged banner still intact from the original Sunflower Success Club. *Greta Rybus*

and a cheerful font declaring the "1926 Camp Etna Sunflower Success Club. Organized October 5th by Spirit-Force." Next to that, an American flag.

"I have organized a printout of Spirit Sampler Week," said Ernie, passing papers to the group.

JUNE–JULY SPIRIT SAMPLER DAYS
- — Table Tipping. $20. Janice Nelson-Kroesser.
- — Psychic Self Protection, or Defense Against the Dark Arts. $20. Dr. Barbara & Steve Williams.
- — Ghost Hunting 101 and Beyond: more than a walking tour. $40. Dr. Barbara & Steve Williams.
- — Church. Guest speaker Reverend Candace Nadine Breen.
- — Dowsing for Answers. $30. James Kidder.
- — Late Night Transfiguration. $20. Laurie Xanthos.

— Private Readings. Kelly Dawn Purington and Chris Smith.

— Test the Medium. Chris Smith.

— Primal Empowerment. Chris Smith.

Lectures ranged from "Psychic Self-Protection" to "Finding Faces in Nature." Topics varied from "Discovering the Power of the Third Eye" to "Trance Healing" to "Upgrading your Mediumship." Janice laid out the rest of the schedule: the summer sessions would be punctuated by a new weekly host—a visiting medium from outside the camp, a Spiritualist guest lecturer and teacher. The visiting hosts were usually bigwigs, nationally recognized healers, the more famous the better. Once they were booked and given a down payment, come summer they would, too, heal and lead workshops for a week, in a rotation, and they charged a pretty penny. "We really should make them feel special, gang," Janice said. "You know, gussy up their rooms, greet them in person upon arrival, give them an organized info packet, leave a small care package in their room. Make them feel special, and also make us look professional."

The board was hopeful that these more renowned mediums would bring in more warm bodies to camp, bodies that would pay admission. Outsiders, even nonbelievers, were welcome to attend; everyone had always been welcome to come to Camp Etna, but lately few have been coming. In the past, and despite its remote location, the summer had brought thousands upon thousands of visitors to Camp Etna. Now, camp was lucky if attendance got to double digits. But this would not deter the camp's board or the camp's members. Neither had it deterred the bigwigs from coming in, because they all understood: religions will ebb and flow. Spiritualism went through phases. This year, the camp was thrilled to add Dr. Raymond Moody to the top of its list of summer guest speakers. The Big Kahuna, as Janice called him. To the general public, Dr. Raymond Moody was lesser known by his own name and more for the famous term he coined in his line of research on dying: "Near Death Experience." The Big Kahuna, indeed.

Upon the fortunate news of Dr. Moody's booking at Camp Etna, nearly everyone on the planning committee and board was thrilled, but a few members remained reticent. This kind of thing was common in small, organized communities, societies, churches, groups wherever they were: members pledged different allegiances and preferences to different practitioners and mediums, but no one made the rules. Everyone at Camp Etna (and in Spiritualism overall, as this is one of the more important components of the religion) composed their own belief system under the larger heading of "Spiritualism"—what fit, what belonged for *them*. Everyone, whether they admitted it or not, had an opinion about what other practitioners' beliefs were. Allegiances could get hot and testy, especially when there is no way to prove what another believes or sees or claims to be able to prove. Was a medium more of a Spiritualist than a Spiritualist who did not have the ability to see the dead? Or was a clairvoyant a better leader than a clairaudient? There was no rulebook or magistrate to speak to these questions and concerns, because Spiritualism is and has always been a religion without a figurehead or set of commandments. The boundaries are self-appointed by one's self to one's self and no one else.

Since its inception, Spiritualism has been anti-authority, because authority was tyrannical: masters over slaves, husbands over wives, clergy over congregations. Spiritualism argues that individuals have direct access to divine knowledge. But when an individual does step up to share their beliefs, and spreads out the results of their investigations, or teach their truths, it can rub other believers the wrong way. Dr. Moody wasn't a certified medium, so some Spiritualists and members of the camp had already chosen to skip his lectures. But others argued that he was legit, a big name, famous, even, and the camp was lucky to have him. Plus, they'd already paid his $500 deposit. Money wasn't pouring down like manna from heaven, and the board definitely would hate to leave Dr. Moody with a bad impression of their beloved Camp Etna.

"We'll host a continental breakfast at the Hot Spot Café," said Janice.

"The guest presenters will stay at the Medium's Cottage, which I hope we can all agree to pitch in and gussy it up."

Outside the temple window, cedar trees shivered. Two brave squirrels made U-shaped hops in search of food on the rock-hard parking lot, a long smear of frozen tan sand. A few bags of salt had been scattered along a walking path, a few cars dotted the parking area. There were no birds overhead. Wind shook the purple front doors of the temple, making the sanctuary shimmy. On the porch of the cabin adjacent, a pile of snow weighed down an otherwise empty rocking chair. Down the steps of the cabin lay the remains of a midsummer gardening bed now brown and yellow and melancholy, a plot of composting kale, lurched lavender stalks, and frozen brown sunflower stems, all quiet and still beautiful beneath a sulfur-colored sky.

Hard to believe that just over a hundred years ago in summertime this place had been elbow-to-elbow. That if you walked onto Camp Etna's great lawn, you'd think you'd walked into the World's Fair. To your right, on Bishop's Row, vehicles would be bumper-to-bumper, the footpaths of Barrett Square would be stomped solid from spiritual pilgrimages, Temple Court and Pond Street would have a steady influx of campers and coaches and bonnets and walking sticks, suitcases and parasols and mustaches and horses and buggies and top hats and trunks and picnic baskets and open, yearning hearts. At the other end of these grounds, down by the lake-sized Etna Pond, people would arrive by packed trainloads from the Maine Central Railroad, which sliced straight through the surrounding agricultural town. Visitors came from as close as Boston or as far as California, all hopping out at the depot in front of the pond, then hiking up the footpath and through the woods, the soil a light loam grounding the pine, spruce, and hemlock, leading visitors uphill to the great lawn, tent platforms, and mediums. Sojourners, still smelling of coal and train engine and eagerness, now getting acquainted with this slice of heaven on Earth where they'd be staying for maybe a day or a weekend or a week, and eventually for the entire summer, soon having a séance, pitching a tent, pitching in on a potluck, the air scented with the faint smell of last night's meandering skunk. All thanks to the Maine farmer Daniel Buswell, most likely led by his wife, Lizzie.

The year of the United States Centennial and the twenty-third quadrennial presidential election, 1876; the year Heinz Ketchup was invented; the year the first crematory was built in the United States (followed by the United States' first legal cremation); the year Alexander Graham Bell made his first successful phone call. *Mr. Watson, come here, I want to see you.* The Indian Wars were under way, and *The Adventures of Tom Sawyer* was published. Despite the Civil Rights Act being passed a year before, Southern state legislatures ushered in the first Jim Crow laws. The year also brought the moment when the all-star lineup of founding feminists Susan B. Anthony, Matilda Joslyn Gage, Lillie Devereux Blake, Sara Andrews Spencer, and Phoebe Couzins firmly presented, in Philadelphia, a "Declaration of Rights of the Women of the United States" on behalf of the National Woman Suffrage Association while standing atop an empty platform to a crowd gathering below that included a rather dumbfounded Sen. Thomas Ferry. Susan B. then preached the following:

> And now, at the close of a hundred years, as the hour hand of the great clock that marks the centuries points to 1876, we declare our faith in the principles of self-government; our full equality with man in natural rights; that woman was made first for her own happiness, with the absolute right to herself—to all the opportunities and advantages life affords to her complete development; and we deny that dogma of centuries, incorporated into the codes of nations—that woman was made for man—her best interests, in all cases, to be sacrificed to his will. We ask our rulers, at this hour, no special favors, no special privileges, no special legislation. We ask justice, we ask equality, we ask that all the civil and political rights that belong to citizens of the United States, be guaranteed to us and our daughters forever.

You'd think that Spiritualism might have been mentioned in that speech somewhere, as by the time the 1870s arrived, both movements had already become comrades with the other two most progressive reform groups of the time. But by the time of Anthony's speech, paradoxes and tensions had spilled over among the groups and set Spiritualists a bit adrift from their former cohorts. Essentially all Spiritualists were women's-rights advocates, but not all women's-rights advocates were Spiritualists, and it didn't take long before the women's-rights agitators peeled away from the Spiritualist movement. Their primary mission was and had always been equal rights for women, but the Civil War prompted the reformers to temporarily set aside their feminist agenda of equality with men until *basic human rights* were secured by African Americans and the soldiers fighting for them, thereby making women's rights their secondary objective. Powerhouses Susan B. Anthony and Elizabeth Cady Stanton had formed the Women's Loyal League to lobby for a constitutional amendment outlawing slavery, while most other Spiritualists zoomed in their focus on *women's* rights as the preeminent reform, and Spiritualists and the women's suffrage movement began to grow in different directions.

It's quite awful how, at the time, some Spiritualists in Southern states still hadn't gotten on board with antislavery. "Even if it was acceptable to us on the subject of slavery, *which it is not* . . . it is against both the law and public sentiment here to distribute or circulate incendiary and Abolitionist publications," wrote two correspondents upon canceling their subscription to the *Spiritual Telegraph*. Most likely fearing further loss of subscriptions, the leading Spiritualist publications (which were, aside from séances and traveling trance lecturers, the main method of dissemination of Spiritualist communications to its communities) began to grow weak on their stance for antislavery and strong in impartiality. In 1866, in response to its now neutral stance on the movement to end slavery, the publication *Banner of Light* broadcasted, "The Banner shall continue to wave until all humanity are completely disenthralled, and WOMAN, the brightest gem in the human galaxy, placed on an equality in every respect with her . . . companion MAN!"

Despite all of this, the number of Spiritualists in the United States and Europe soared, but the religion still hadn't maintained total cohesion and was still working without formal organization, official leadership, or canonical text. But that was the point. Spiritualists feared that organization would routinize their religion, as it had done to all the others that had come before it. Attempts had been made. For instance, an endeavor in 1864, when a group of Spiritualists in favor of forming a structured national organization rallied enough of a congregation and held the First National Spiritualist Convention in Chicago, but the debate over whether Spiritualism should formally organize evoked so much controversy that not much else got done during the five-day convention. Out of this, only one woman engaged in the frenzied debate (she spoke in opposition of formal organization, and she did so while in trance). Otherwise, the convention was essentially men arguing, and little came of it aside from commotion and frustration, with the majority of the nation's Spiritualist community continuing to resist formal organization.

In 1865, a Second National Convention regrouped. This year, it was held in Philadelphia, and unlike the previous year's assembly, the Philadelphia convention was by invitation only, with attendance open to designated representatives of local Spiritualist groups. But as with the first convention, this year's delegates were overwhelmingly male. Eighteen officers resided over the convention—seventeen of them men, and one woman, a non-medium. The majority of mediums in Spiritualism were women, as were as the majority of Spiritualists. Despite the convention's majority of pro-organization male delegates, the women delegates stood their ground, explaining to their male cohorts, as they'd done so many times before, why official governance was a threat to them all, and that formal authority in Spiritualism equated to qualities of dominance and supremacy rather than their religion's original true feminine essence. Mediums were gentle channels, not roaring rapids. "This is man's work, the production of men's brains," passionately declared Lizzie Doten, a well-respected trance medium at the convention. "I see nothing of woman about this plan . . . we are acting from policy, not principle." And yet the principle and passion of Lizzie and the rest of the opposition weren't enough. When it came time to fight, the pro-organizing delegates had arrived at the battle better prepared. They dominated in sex and in number, which led to a control over the ballots, which then passed the motion that voted the American Association of Spiritualists into existence. Years passed, and more conventions were held. Disappointed adherents of the anti-authoritarian Spiritualist belief system had their fears borne out when, in 1869 in Buffalo, New York, at the sixth National Convention of the American Association of Spiritualists, attendance records revealed that the Spiritualist delegation from Ohio sent a twenty-one-member fleet containing only one woman. And it wasn't only happening with Ohio. As efforts to define and tame and organize Spiritualism lurched forward, female leadership within the religion declined nationally, and rapidly.

More attempts to systematize Spiritualism came in fits and starts, spearheaded by the more formally educated of the bunch, but not long after the Buffalo convention, the majority of Spiritualists went ahead with an outright boycott of the American Association of Spiritualists, making it clear that the AAS would not hold based on grit alone. The group of self-appointed leaders lacked a majority of followers, thus proving incapable of becoming institutionalized, and after a bit of time floundering, the AAS eventually folded. To the true believers, the Spiritualists and mediums the AAS had knocked down and stepped over, it didn't matter. In the grand scheme of the universe, none of it really mattered. The AAS was just a brief episode, a blip, a temper tantrum of mankind's ego that served as a reminder to them to stay the course. When the AAS came into power, it hadn't conquered its opposition. Instead, its opposition was actually thriving. Despite Philly and the damage it left in its wake, devoted mediums like Lizzie

Doten and other true Spiritualists remained unfettered, buoyed by their hope of finding a bastion of right-thinking. When they were told to give up and give in to authority and dominance by their own congregation, their faith did not waver nor did principles fold. Instead, Spiritualists simply just took to the woods.

While some artifacts declare the year was 1876 and others 1877, that detail is inconsequential. The fact of the matter is it happened: the first official meeting of the Etna Spiritualist Camp on Buswell's Farm. Folks were invited to arrive on the east line of the Etna-Bangor Road and congregate in what was known as Buswell's Grove "under a tent that Daniel Buswell, Jr. had purchased for such an occasion. Mrs. Buswell, his wife, a practicing Spiritualist and fine home medium, was the talent. Admission was ten cents a day, from which a certain Mr. Buswell, Jr. took a percentage." The template of the event was similar to, but no less significant than, what was taking place in other Spiritualist camps across the East Coast, places like Lake Pleasant, Cassadaga, Lily Dale, Salem, and Silver Lake, with more summer camps to soon emerge throughout the rest of the nation.

Rather than focusing on reform, development, or how to further the Spiritualist agenda, summer-camp gatherings, called "meetings," provided a place where Spiritualists could enjoy themselves, with intermittent communion with the dead. Meetings were held near lakes or ponds, beaches, forests, gardens, and arboretums, and attending these early Spiritualist summer meetings was a lot like taking a July road trip to a festive vacation campground, but with a séance or two sprinkled in. They were fun, celebratory, and despite the focus on the dead, full of life and "with few implications for the conduct of the living."

In the beginning, summer meetings at Buswell's Grove lasted less than two weeks and featured less serious philosophical discussion and more entertainment. One would expect to mingle with Spiritualist pilgrims, meet new people, receive a private reading by a medium, attend a concert performed by a musical medium, attend a lecture or two that "gracefully mingled sensationalism and sentimentalism," and, at the end of the excursion, be shipped back home recharged and refreshed, possibly with a souvenir photograph or portrait of a departed loved one "painted by a medium who had never seen a likeness of the subject than a subscription to a reform periodical."

The camps grew in size and in charisma. Some had merry-go-rounds. Others, hot-air balloon rides or a bowling alley. Most Spiritualist summer camps had their own restaurants, perhaps a dance hall, a full band, you name it, making their atmosphere more carnival than church and turning religion into a party where everyone was invited. Attendance was astounding: in 1869, 12,000 people turned up to the Spiritualist summer gathering in Abington, Massachusetts. Another in Melrose counted 8,000. In 1874, the *Boston Globe* reported that 2,500 people visited the Silver Lake, Massachusetts, Spiritualist camp on a summertime Friday, and then clocked in with a head count of 10,000 the following Sunday.

By the summer of 1880, the Buswells had outgrown their plot. The family needed more room to accommodate the throngs of Spiritualist pilgrims trekking to their property, so a pavilion was built for approximately $500, with a seating capacity of more than 1,000 human bodies at a time, and another seventy-eight cottages were constructed on the grounds. Eventually, the Buswells constructed a fifty-room hotel with a livery. Later would come a ladies' auxiliary, and a boardinghouse. An ice-cream parlor. A restaurant. A barbershop. A dance hall. A photography salon. Boats for your enjoyment, available down at Etna Pond. The little camp meetings that had first sprouted up as a response to authoritarians in Spiritualism were now triumphant, having evolved into functioning seasonal Spiritualist epicenters of their own. The circus-like atmosphere of these camps horrified many prewar reformers, who felt that Spiritualists were again losing sight of their original objectives—personal sacrifice and spiritual evolution. They had a point. While the summer camps were opening and affirming, they were also vacationlands saturated in pleasure, rest, socialization, and sensationalism, which made the Spiritualist religion come across as less hallowed and more entertaining—the mediums merely performers, and Spiritualism the big-top show.

"Who needs a coffee break?" asked Janice. She'd clearly read our minds. At a sleepwalker's pace, several board members stood up from the table and walked over to the buffet to pour themselves some Box of Joe. I joined them too. As we sipped our stimulants—a tonic to the incessant cold—steam rose from the mugs, warming our hands and our chins. Next to the box of coffee, a proud display of business cards and brochures topped the table. *"Dee Powers, RSCT, PP, Akashic Records." "Rev. Janet I. Decker, C. Ht. Psychic Medium, Clinical Hypnotherapist, Serving Spirit for 30+ Years."* The pamphlets and adverts were brightly colored, mostly shades of purple: ultraviolet, lilac, amethyst. "Purple is the palate of choice for Spiritualists," someone said. It was Angie, one of the younger mediums on the board. "Violet is the color of spirituality, the color of the crown chakra. Purple represents spiritual awareness." Angie took two doughnut holes and several long strides back to the meeting, which was starting up again. More cards: *"Psychic Mediumship with Bonnie Lee Gibson." "Maine Tourmaline. Crystals. Fine Gifts at Bennett's Gems & Jewelry—Route One, Belfast, Maine, next to Perry's Nut House. Look for our famous pink dinosaur!"* I grabbed Angie's card out of the pile then rejoined the board.

There were decisions to be made: when the message circles would be (on Wednesdays), when the podium-driven gallery readings would run (Fridays). Next, the fine-tuning of the programming: disclaimers for the hypnosis-journey workshops. Time slots for crystal meditation. Time slots for orb photography. Time slots for trance channeling, for candle meditation. Release forms for the kinesiology classes and the emotional release sessions. Items were checked off the board's agenda with little fanfare, and they forged ahead with a stern and professional attitude. Once the summer program was finalized it could be posted on the Camp Etna website, and once that was done, this year's brochures could be printed and distributed, the Facebook page updated and shared. Everyone had a role in making this come together; Ernie even volunteered to teach himself how to use Twitter. Raising his hand slowly so as not to disrupt the fast flow, he asked gently, "Excuse me, Angie? Will you be doing angel paintings this year?"

Just then, around noon, a tall man stumbled into the temple with a blast of air cinematically following behind him, the door slamming shut. He plodded down the aisle of the temple until he reached the front of the sanctuary, stopping just short of the board's table, and then plopped into a chair in the front row of the empty congregation seats. A few members looked up nonchalantly, then turned back to the discussion at hand.

The man was possibly fifty. Or sixty. Or seventy. His hair was tousled and his nose was bulbous and clay-red, but underneath his mug were the remains of some kind of handsomeness from back in the day, despite his pockmarked clay-red skin. Right now he was looking pretty bristled in his flannel shirt and jeans, no coat, smelling of tobacco or maybe the smoke of a woodstove. He said nothing; neither did he wait for any kind of recognition. With his long legs spidered out in front of him, the man looked like a giant sitting in a toddler's chair.

"Welcome, Duey," someone from the table finally said.

"Ayuh," the man—Duey—responded.

This was Dwight "Duey" Grant. Husband to medium Arlene Grant, a longtime Camp Etna–dweller/medium-on-hiatus. Duey did some maintenance on the grounds; I'd heard about him before. His name had come up in conversation about the operations of camp. But this place was also Dwight's home. Maybe even more so than others', depending on your perspective, because long before Camp Etna proper was even built, and even before Buswell's Farm had been here, it was Dwight Grant's ancestors who occupied the land. Dwight, or Duey, was a Native American. This land had always belonged to Duey (or he had always belonged to the land). I'd been told that Duey was also a great medium, that it came incredibly easily to him. Duey could see members of his tribe long dead but walking among the grounds all the time, and he could hear them drumming in the middle of the night in the woods down by Etna Pond, and he could talk to his ancestors effortlessly.

"Duey," Board Secretary Sue Jalbert asked sweetly, "will you be leading the drum workshop this summer?"

In a low and barely audible mumble, he responded, "Ayup."

"And what's the date on that again, Duey?" she continued, her pen hovering in place over a notepad.

"June twenty."

"Great," Sue replied, recording it in her notes. "And the cost?"

"Two hundred thirty."

"And does this include supplies?"

"Ayup."

"Materials for the drum and beaters?"

"Ayup."

And with that, and just as unceremoniously as he came in, Duey Grant rose up and left the temple. Drumming was added to the summer program, and another note was checked off the Camp Etna Board of Directors' scrupulous agenda.

1–4 PM DRUM MAKING W/DWIGHT GRANT $230
($35 non-refundable deposit by June 20th)

Make your own 13″ drum and drum beater with a Native American from the Passamaquoddy Bear Clan. Materials for the drum & beater are included. Dwight will bless the drums in a Native American Ceremony once assembled.

One last item on the list and then we'd break for lunch. The ballot: should the board raise the price of séances from $15 to $20?

"All those in favor?" asked Janice.

Aye, the chorus echoed, then said Ernie: "All those awake?"

I regard Spiritualism as one of the great-
est curses that the world has ever known.
—Katie Fox Jencken, New York Herald, *October 9, 1888*

By the late 1880s, Kate and Margaret Fox, the now-grown childhood celebrity stars and founders of the Spiritualist movement, had hit rock bottom. They were broke and had major alcohol problems. Margaret had convinced herself that her powers were diabolical and was planning to return to the Catholic Church to redeem, or exorcise, herself. That same year, the girls' older sister, Leah, held an intervention with Kate, citing that her sister was killing herself with the booze and was drinking too much to take care of her own children. Whether they needed money or because they wanted to punish Leah, or it was their truth, when a reporter offered Kate and Margaret $1,500 if they'd expose their Mr. Splitfoot methods and give him an exclusive on the story, the two sisters accepted. On October 21, 1888, at the 4,000-seat New York Academy of Music opera house on the northeast corner of East Fourteenth and Irving Place in Manhattan, Margaret stepped forth and demonstrated to the crowd how she could produce, and had produced, by cracking the joints of her toes, the rappings of Mr. Splitfoot. Her signed confession was printed in the *New York World* that very same day:

> My sister Katie was the first to observe that by swishing her fingers she could produce certain noises with her knuckles and joints, and that the same effect could be made with the toes. Finding that we could make raps with our feet—first with one foot and then with both—we practiced until we could do this easily when the room was dark. Like most perplexing things when made clear, it is astonishing how easily it is done. . . .

It was a gut punch, but it wasn't a deathblow. Many Spiritualists simply refused to hear the confession or to ever abandon their faith. True believers remained committed to their religion. Like clockwork, when spring drew near and summer sprouted, they returned to their beloved Spiritualist camp meeting, in multitudes.

On December 5, 1890, farmer Daniel Buswell Jr. finally let go of the grove and deeded ownership of his land—approximately 300 acres—to the First Maine Spiritualist State Camp Meeting Association. The group of Spiritualists coming to his land had grown larger than he could lead, so he sold it off for $2,500. In addition to the transfer of ownership, the deed had two covenants on it: that the farmer's medium wife would be able to have a cottage on the lot and could keep the cottage as long as she lived, and that a path would be left open for cows to cross back and forth on the property.

Two years later, both Fox sisters were dead: Kate, in 1892, having passed away at her home in New York City on 609 Columbus Avenue, and then Margaret a year later, having perished deeply alcoholic and living on charity as the sole inhabitant of an old tenement house on West Fifty-Sixth Street.

Four years before her death, in November 1889, Margaret renounced her confession in writing, saying she had been scraping the barrel—she was a now pauper with no other options. By then, both Kate and Margaret were in abject poverty and nearly forgotten by the world who had once so loved them, now nothing more than hazy ghosts of a story that had long since eclipsed them. After the concrete had been poured and hardened over the graves of the Fox sisters, the movement they'd created during the beginning of their lives was still in its infancy.

There had been plenty of times—bad board, bad budget, bad luck, bad press, or no press—that Camp Etna nearly folded. Keeping the people happy was tricky. Keeping the peace wasn't easy. Keeping this place running wasn't cheap.

"She's paying rent, isn't she? With the table tipping?" Janice asked no one in particular, then waited until she got her answer. Camp needed to pay the bills, and the place was in some ways a low-budget enterprise. Even with the summer scheduling now in place, a mild atmosphere of stress still hovered over the heads of the board. The looming concern: How are we going to bring people in? How can we make this place appealing to outsiders? How are we going to keep this place alive?

"Camp Etna belongs to the Chamber of Commerce," said Sue Jalbert, "which brings us to the next item on the agenda: getting us listed on the National Register of Historic Places."

With each season, each board meeting, and each camp meeting that passes, the Spiritualists of Camp Etna did what they have to keep the big iron gates open, dreaming as ever of perfect self-sufficiency, in addition to world peace. But for now and in the short term, Janice would shift the group's focus to the topic of housekeeping duties and room rentals. After that, the board would review the annual budget. And after that, we would all hold hands, lower our heads, and close our eyes as Ernie delivered the final benediction.

✝✝✝

CHAPTER 2

Bright Eyes

A group of Etna campers in the early 1880s.

"My husband died," whispered the woman next to me. She lowered her voice and, folding her hands into her lap, continued, "while we were making love."

It was springtime now and we were perched on a prickly orange velour sofa in the lounge of the Etna Inn on Bishop's Row, waiting for the unofficial-official camp opening kick-off historical tour to start. About seven people, this woman and me included, were in attendance.

"It was my late husband, Fiddlin' Red. We had been making love for about thirty minutes when he gasped then stiffened and all of a sudden I heard this big *oomph*!" She lifted her hands into the air—strong, muscular, tan hands with long fingers and crescent-moon fingernails, the hardworking hands of a person who dug into the soil. "After that, I felt Red's spirit fall through me." She flickered her fingers like dropping rain. "Like the spirit of the bird I had hit with my truck and killed just a few weeks before—that's what it felt like." After her husband collapsed, she threw off Red's body and called out his name, then picked up the phone and dialed 911 while simultaneously performing CPR. "But Red was gone, my husband was gone." Though, as his widow saw it, Fiddlin' Red hadn't left completely—she swears part of him still lingers within her.

I looked at her, not knowing what to say, and settled on "Bless you."

"*Thank you*," she mouthed back.

From the front of the room, a familiar voice boomed. "For those of you who are new here, welcome." It was Janice, and she stood facing our small yet eager group of now eleven participants. We'd settled into a half-circle of rocking chairs and loveseats in a large living room that smelled like pinecones and attic and listened attentively as Janice formally introduced herself.

Throughout the room were framed prayers, paintings, and framed photographs—dignified portraits of important-looking women and men. The entire building felt not haunted, but not quite not, either.

Janice dabbed a tissue to her forehead a couple of times—despite the floor and table fans, the room was muggy as hell, with the summer solstice still more than a month away—then cleared her throat.

"Diane?" Janice queried our group. "Diane, are you ready to begin?" With that, the widow seated next to me softly patted my knee, rose, and took Janice's place.

"My name is Diane Jackman Skolfield." She paused confidently and grinned. "I am a proud Spiritualist, intuitive healer, yoga instructor, mother, businesswoman, author, and Camp Etna historian. I believe I was put on this Earth to help others find peace, and I will be your tour guide today."

Perky and fresh, Diane was sixty-one but seemed ten years younger. She was Maine-bred but Californian-looking, with bright blue eyes and silvery mermaid hair, gray locks that rested on her sculpted gymnast's shoulders. Diane had immediately emerged warm and wide-open, and when she acknowledged our group of camp tourists, she did so with the affection of a golden retriever and the enthusiasm of a college orientation leader. She wore a mauve tank top paired with a long, flowing floral skirt. Today, Diane was shoeless. Janice backed away and exited the room.

"So," said Diane, rubbing her palms together then placing them over her heart chakra. "Anyone know who the first mediums were?"

Crickets.

"Oh, come on. Any brave soul care to take a guess?"

A young guy in Carhartt dungarees and a Red Sox cap called out, "The Fox sisters!" and Diane shot him down by making the exaggerated sound of a game-show buzzer. *Ehhhhht.*

"WRONG," said Diane. "Sorry. Anyone else want to take a stab at it? Because the answer is the Native Americans. The Native Americans were the first mediums."

She walked to the back of the adjacent room and stuck her head under a sink basin while continuing her lecture. "Surprised?" she asked. "Because the history of Spiritualism is delicious, vast, and I've been working on this timeline, which I'm about to—" She rummaged around for a minute, then emerged with a bag, reached inside it, pulled out a large long roll of construction paper, and unfurled it, revealing a paper scroll containing Diane's handwritten rendering of the timeline of Spiritualism. It was presented in chronological order and written in Crayola marker.

"It was really the Native Americans, the *first* Spiritualists," said Diane, "who believed that the thoughts coming into our heads were not our own. That these thoughts came from spirits."

A few heads in the group nodded knowingly. Diane had centuries to cover, so she quickly plowed through the events on the chart, essentially a world history, starting with the Paleolithic age and the early hominids, blasting through the Hermetic Kabbalah, the Greek oracles, Jesus, the Akashic records of the 1400s, the tarot cards of Italy, Joan of Arc, Martin Luther, and the Swedenborgs. With bazooka-fire speed, Diane shot us through the Shakers and Mesmer and Andrew Jackson Davis until we finally landed at the feet of the Fox sisters. All significant dates and events had been hand-plucked and sketched by Diane onto her paper chart in royal blue, with proper names in red, descriptions in black, and a few recent edits in lime green. The underlying point of her chart was clear as crystal: medium and spirit communication has been here always, and everywhere, since forever.

"Oh rats!" cried our historian. "I can't believe I skipped over one of the most important moments of the timeline!" She lowered her voice dramatically, almost to a whisper. "The year was 1859, when along came a super geomagnetic solar storm known as the Carrington Event." Diane lifted her arms like a symphony conductor and widened her eyes. "It brightened night skies around the world for seven days— *seven days!*—causing many humans to question life as they knew it." Diane leaned onto a bookshelf and placed a hand on a jutted-out hip. "One can only imagine the conversations that took place about God, about life, about life after death after the Carrington Event."

Yes, of course, we all nodded in agreement as if to avoid ourselves being questioned.

"And in the northeast part of the country," Diane continued, "our very own Camp Etna drew scores of scientists, physicians, and reputable men and women to investigate this new science where people seemingly could talk to other dimensions." She put down her timeline, bringing the story to a sudden halt.

"Now," said Diane. "If there are no further questions about this part of the tour, I will invite you to join me in exploring what is now the beginnings of our new Camp Etna Library and Historical Society."

Our squad stood up, stretched, and migrated to a petite cove adjacent to the living room. Above its doorway was a wooden sign that read A LIL' BIT OF HEAVEN. Underneath that, Scotch-taped to the wall, were two sheets of white paper with motherly cursive that read *Library and Historical Section.*

Inside, the room was an explosion of artifacts: glass bottles and pearl necklaces, leather-bound handwritten diaries—centuries-old secrets and observations. Ivory faded handkerchiefs and Victorian jewelry of clear stones and colored gems, black-and-white photographs of women posing alongside other women, postcards and dentures and handheld mirrors and church service programs. Silverware. Hand-stitched dolls. Banners and flags and toaster ovens and nearly 150 years' worth of ephemera from thousands of people, most likely 100 percent of them now deceased.

Diane invited us to snoop around. I drifted over to a bookshelf and read off the titles to myself: *The Little Red Book. One Day at a Time. Metaphysical Meditations. Death of an Angel. I Know This Much Is True. In Search of Historic Jesus. The Grapes of Wrath.*

The Camp Etna Museum was still being sorted, still in its fetal stages, but it was tremendous. For the past decade, Diane had been working like a manic archaeologist, ceaselessly salvaging whatever remnants of Camp Etna's past she could find. She'd combed through boarded-up cottages, scrutinized hazardous dump sites, shoveled out and sifted through old fire pits and burn piles. Some stuff had been handed over from relatives now de-junking their attics. Other artifacts, like the seventeenth-century pamphlets and camp program notes, had been used as insulation covers on ceilings until Diane looked up and pulled them down. While the pieces of Camp Etna's history were scattered and entropic, Diane was giving them order and meaning, breathing life into the inanimate objects, like that butter dish and that heart-shaped locket, those corn-on-the-cob skewers and at least twenty strands of pearl necklaces and coral earrings and the World Word II–era folding canvas bathtub and the rest of the things in this room that were giving off a palpable feeling that they'd been waiting for us.

I picked up a pair of false teeth, and Diane spoke up. "I found these when I opened up a box in the little old cottage on Pond Street, and I could feel the owner standing beside me, laughing hysterically with me." Across the room, a member of our tour group lifted a corsage of dried dead carnations off a bench, and, for some reason, smelled it.

Diane ran her fingers over a peeling black suitcase that had been sealed shut. Behind it was a desk with at least fifty filled storage bag-gies stocked upon it, and just as many overstuffed binders and thick envelopes. ITEMS DONATED BY SYLVIA DEAN FAMILY, 2013, read one sign. "Discussing our past and the importance of Spiritualism helps bring its original purpose to fruition, proving the continuity of life," said Diane, pressing a tin teacup of water to her lips and taking a sip. "And also the healing of humanity."

It was two years after the death of her third husband, Red, when Diane arrived at Camp Etna. She'd just fled Florida, with its frosted tips, Jet-Skis, and bikinis. Up until then, Diane's life was filled with workshops on qigong, yoga, medical intuition, and energy medicine. She was a volunteer carpenter and taught yoga. She was a success-ful businesswoman and entrepreneur, owned a good bit of property, and was quite happy with the woman she'd become: financially independent, spiritually enriched.

Before Red died, their marriage hadn't always been easy for her, because when you have a live iguana dressed in a top hat and coat-tails as the best man at your wedding ceremony, it's possible that these particular nuptials may not end up being the most mundane or conventional. Red was a musician. He'd toured with Captain & Tennille and was often on the road if not on the stage; being wed to a professional musician meant Diane was also married to the jukebox scene. In the beginning, she traveled gladly with her husband everywhere, lending him her support by sitting in the Suburban for hours, practicing being very patient while Red rehearsed, then went to pawnshops to buy, sell, or repair musical instruments, and then to gigs with lots of adoring fans and lots of booze.

Diane herself had ended what she called her "days of Diet Cokes and dyeing my hair" and had instead been standing on her soapbox of hope, faith, and good nutrition as a way of life. Red countered this with taverns and alcohol, and Red could get angry. There was verbal abuse against which to bob and weave. But Diane was all in and stayed simultaneously committed to her husband as well as her soapbox. As dissonant as things seemed during that period of her life, Diane firmly believed that she was exactly where she was supposed to be, even if she didn't like or understand it. She referred to Red as her mir-ror, a funhouse-like tool that reflected back to her what she wanted to embody and what she didn't. She believed these mirrors were every-where, and they were all part of life's obstacle course—a puzzle that she had to figure out how to solve, and that she was being guided and protected by a force greater than Diane or her husband, and for this she was grateful. But then Red went ahead and died.

Despite the trauma of witnessing Red's sudden death, Diane says it made her softer, more appreciative rather than longing, more empathetic rather than defensive. After Red died, Diane knew she had a choice, and decided to perceive all the moments preceding and following her husband's death as things that were happening for a reason, like her clues in her own personal treasure map. Red was dead and his death led her to take another step forward. A stop to visit a psychic in Florida, which introduced her for the very first time to the religion of Spiritualism, which led her to the Spiritualist camp called Cassadaga—a tiny unincorporated community in Volusia County, Florida, just north of Deltona, which led her to seek out other Spiritualist camps, and eventually landed her in Etna, Maine, and the beckoning arch of 77 Stage Road. Diane stepped toward it, just as so many women seekers had done before, and lifted the veil of her new life. Now here she was, digging deeply into moldy, dusty boxes, fingering through abandoned cottages, dumpster diving, and sifting through burn piles with a mission to make Etna known again, and in turn, not forgotten.

"But I cannot communicate with the dead." Diane didn't hesitate to share this fact. She was a Spiritualist—a member of the Spiritualist religion—but just because a person was a Spiritualist, that didn't mean they were a medium. Not all Spiritualists could see the dead. And not all mediums out there belonged to the Spiritualist church, either. The two could coexist independently. Diane wasn't psychic, wasn't a medium, could not talk to or hear or see the dead, try as she had through meditation and workshops and classes and mentors, to no avail. It was disappointing, but after years of trying, she'd finally come to accept it. She had faith in her own intuition, and she had faith in fate. Plus, Diane had gumption, with a side order of enthusiasm and a hippie heart the size of Milwaukee. Clairvoyant or not, what Diane did hold on to (and hold up) were the basic values that were the founding principles of Camp Etna. She was like a silver-haired Golden Rule.

As we continued to snoop around her museum, Diane moved into the center of the room and straightened her posture. She placed her hand across her chest, took a breath, and pledged:

I will start anew this morning with a higher fairer creed.
I will cease to stand complaining of my ruthless neighbors' greed.

I will cease to sit repining while my duties' call is clear.
I will waste no moment whining and my heart shall know no fear.
I will look sometimes about me for the things that merit praise.
I will search for hidden beauties that elude the grumblers' gaze.
I will try to find contentment in the paths that I must tread.
I will cease to have resentment when another moves ahead.
I will not be swayed by envy where my rival's strength is shown.
I will not deny his merit but I'll strive to prove my own.
I will try to see the beauties spread before me rain or shine.
I will cease to preach your duty and be more concerned with mine.

"That's the poem 'I Will,'" said Diane, disengaging her spine, "written by former camper Estelle Dudley and presented through Camp Etna's Pollyanna Club in November 1916. Just lovely, isn't it?"

Nearly one hundred years prior, the Pollyanna Club was established. One hot day in July, a handful of women at camp decided to form a small society within their Spiritualist community, a group whose sole purpose was to "promote sociability, good cheer, and the general advancement and upliftment of all." Diane swooned. "Its constitution was incorporated on July 25, 1916, and each member pledged themselves in all sincerity to seek gladness, help others 'Play the Game,' and to *try* to have a motive for good in all they do and say." In the more recent decades, the Pollyanna Club had wilted and decomposed completely. But Diane had taken it upon herself to resurrect it. On July 25, 2016, on the club's hundredth birthday, a meeting of the Pollyanna Club of Camp Etna was once again called to order, with Diane gleefully driving the bus. "We invite you to join us in spreading good cheer around the world!" she chirped, handing me a document.

Across her neck I could see a faint liquid-blue shadow cast by a small glass angel perched on the windowsill. Behind the figurine, the sun streamed through the window, cooking the uncooled room enough to bring forth the ancient smells from a timeworn rug and the musty odors of a piano's keys in the adjoining room. The smell of old fingertips.

The lounge area of the Camp Etna Inn. *Mira Ptacin*

Outside it was warm and the grass verdant. Indoors, something caught my eye: a brass-framed photograph perched upon a doily-topped table. Within the frame, a peculiar portrait, now canary-colored and faded with age, of a young woman with the face of a Native American and the hairdo of an upper-class white girl of that time period. The yellow bow on her head was enormous.

"That's Bright Eyes," Diane whispered fondly, then reached her arm forward and, with the tip of her index finger, grazed the photo affectionately.

I had retired but was wide-awake. I became aware of a
human form in the room, near the bed.
—Mary Ann Scannell

The year was 1882, and a fifteen-year-old orphan by the name of Mary Ann Scannell had a vision. The young girl, daughter of a broom-maker, had been living in Happy Hollow, Massachusetts, with her aunt for some time after the death of her mother. On that particular day, Mary and her foster mother had gone to visit friends in Narragansett, Rhode Island. These friends were recent converts to Spiritualism and only accustomed to receiving spirit messages by means of table tipping—at the time it was all the rage—and had planned on doing some tipping during the evening of the ladies' visit. As the day's sun descended, the families took their seats around the table, ready to tip, when out of nowhere, young Mary began uncontrollably spitting out letters of the alphabet. To the stunned group, the letters dribbling out of Mary's mouth seemed random, but letter by letter and within minutes, they came to realize the girl had spelled out the name of her late mother, leaving everyone, Mary especially, dumbfounded. Later that night, after she'd retreated to her room to rest, Mary saw something. "There was something about it that differed from the persons I knew . . . and I screamed. When I described the person I had seen, the family there said I had described one of their relatives who had died—a person I never had seen, nor even heard of."

The rest of the night carried on like an acid trip. Mary delivered more messages that evening, ones that went even further in depth, explaining that it wasn't actually Mary who was speaking but the "spirit of a little Indian girl named Bright Eyes" who had taken over Mary's body. Bright Eyes proposed that Mary, her young human vessel, remain in the home of her family friends for the next three months to be groomed as a medium. All of this terrified Mary, and she vigorously fought back, vowing that she wouldn't remain in the house one hour beyond the scheduled departure time.

The next day, when the moment came when Mary and her aunt were to head home, Mary couldn't be persuaded to go. She unpacked her bags and began her training, thus marking the beginning of the career of Camp Etna's most famous medium, Mary Ann Scannell Pepper Vanderbilt, and her spirit guide, Bright Eyes.

Early training consisted of validity tests and private séances until Mary graduated to public and platform séances—séances performed on stages or in theaters for larger audiences, as opposed to the small, intimate groups in home parlors. Her messages were delivered in a voice described by a newspaper of the time as "a curious dialect, half African, half Indian, wholly ungrammatical, but spoke with great fluency: 'You squaw in de corner,' she would say, 'I know you wants I to speak to you awful bad. You don't feel half as shiny as you pretends you does.'"

Not long after Mary's first public appearances, a well-educated Spiritualist offered to lend his efforts to Mary and Bright Eyes. His name was Abram H. Dailey, and he was a retired judge of the Surrogate Court of New York. For a considerable time, Dailey would keep appointed hours at his offices with the duo in which he worked to shape Bright Eyes's utterances into grammatical sentences, annunciations, and pronunciations. Once primed, and thanks to Judge Dailey, inspirational speaking was then added to Mary and Bright Eyes's repertoire.

While living in New York, Mary met George William Pepper, a well-regarded lawyer and professor. He was also a Republican and staunch Christian activist, married with children, and despite all of it, he fell in love with Mary, and she with him. Soon George left his wife and children for her. George and Mary never officially wed, because George never legally divorced his wife, but Mary added his last name to her own, thus becoming Mary Ann Scannell Pepper.

Following their unofficial marriage, Mary passionately continued her work and evolution as a medium. George wanted to be a part of Mary's foremost devotion (which took up the greater chunks of her days and nights), and what could be better, he believed, than a financial sponsorship? He began a weekly contribution of $40 of his salary to sponsor her professional needs. But money wasn't enough, and George couldn't purchase Mary's time, gaze, or focus. He grew impatient and jealous, and it was shortly after Mary and George (and Bright Eyes) relocated to Brooklyn that the unofficial marriage dissolved. The new addition to her last name, however, Mary would keep.

Now it was 1893, nearly forty years after the Fox sisters stepped onto the scene. Camp Etna was in its third year, Mary and Bright Eyes were still in New England, and in Chicago, a great group of Spiritualists was gathering. It was September 27, and a three-day Spiritualist convention had just commenced. Until then, the majority of attempts at consolidating and classifying the religion had all failed and Spiritualism was still running loosely. But it was now less free-floating and shape-shifting and more like a human with no bones—a sack of skin. The religion needed some work, and that's when the two hundred delegates from all over the country got together in Chicago to brainstorm. Among them: Harrison D. Barrett, a medium from Maine.

Harrison Delivan Barrett was born in 1863 to Levi P. and Lucetta Barrett, two lifelong residents of Canaan, Maine, a small town forty-five miles east of Bangor. When Harrison's sister Ollie passed to spirit at the age of twelve, she began communicating with her brother through rappings to let him know she was still there. Harrison had been interested in Spiritualism since he was seventeen, after Ollie died, and although he was already an ordained Unitarian minister (in his mind it had been impossible to reconcile the religion of Spiritualism with the beliefs of the Unitarian Church), Harrison switched teams and became a dedicated Spiritualist, attending summer sessions at the nearby Camp Etna.

Fast-forward to 1893. Legend has it, Diane told me, that a Spiritualist woman was on trial for witchcraft, and Harrison stepped in to defend her. The judge—a man—said to Harrison that if he could prove that the woman's practice was a "true" religion—one with some kind of creed or structure—he might let the woman go free. That's when Harrison asked for a recess, during which he wrote the first three Spiritualist Principles as they stand today.

1. We believe in Infinite Intelligence.
2. We believe that the phenomena of Nature, both physical and spiritual, are the expression of Infinite Intelligence.
3. We affirm that a correct understanding of such expression and living in accordance therewith constitute true religion.

Thus, the National Spiritualist Association of Churches, or NSAC, which is now one of the oldest Spiritualist organizations in our country, was established. At the Chicago convention, the committee composed the NSAC's first list of objectives:

1. Organize Spiritualists in the United States into one working organization.
2. Open a permanent business office so the Secretary to be elected can collect and compile statistics pertaining to Spiritualism.
3. Furnish Spiritualists everywhere a simple but uniform practical plan of organization.
4. Build temples and lecture halls.
5. Provide a competent core of organized lecturers.
6. Provide uniform and effective methods for teaching lecturers and speakers by instituting one General Conference at the same time each year.
7. Apply practical business methods to the promotion of educational and other special interests of Spiritualism.
8. Raise revenue.

Despite Spiritualism's anti-organization heritage, there was a flip side to this establishment: forming the NSAC meant the prevention of persecution and legal prosecution of mediums and Spiritualists—those attacked as fortune-tellers or witches or Satan's spawn—which was happening. The more order and structure in the religion meant the more Spiritualists could help nonbelievers or persecutors distinguish genuine mediums from frauds, magicians, and tricksters. It meant protection from counterattacks by orthodox ministers, or slander in the press. It meant power.

Then in 1899 three more Spiritualist Principles were added, establishing a six-article "Declaration of Principles" soon to be adopted by most Spiritualist practitioners, churches, and organizations (and, in the years that followed, would continue to be revised and expanded):

1. We affirm that the existence and personal identity of the individual continue after the change called death;
2. We affirm that communication with the so-called dead is a fact, scientifically proven by the phenomena of Spiritualism;
3. We believe that the highest morality is contained in the Golden Rule: "Do unto others as you would have them do unto you."

Shortly after Harrison formed the NSAC in 1893 and was appointed president, he in turn appointed Mary Ann Scannell Pepper to be a "state agent" to promote the religion. By now, she and Bright Eyes were well known, delivering platform readings and inspirational messages to great crowds throughout New England, their reputation and popularity growing by the day.

On October 13, 1897, Harrison married his sweetheart, Margarite M. Coffyn, of Grand Rapids, Michigan, and together they merged into a Spiritualist power couple, taking over and running the publication *The Banner of Light*, the longest lasting and most influential of the hundreds of Spiritualist newspapers. In addition to covering the Spiritualist movement that was sweeping the country, the *Banner* also contained columns with messages received by its resident medium (as well as letters from relatives confirming the authenticity of these messages); book reviews; transcripts of lectures; notices of meetings; and letters from its readers, of whom there were many. The *Banner* claimed to have a readership of 30,000—doctors, judges, scientists, researchers, clergymen, and people from all walks of life.

Readers who viewed Spiritualism as a religious science and a scientific religion, a religious philosophy and a philosophical religion.

Spiritualism claimed, and still claims, to be a science, because Spiritualism asserts that it can offer proof—proof of life after death, and proof of communication by the spirit world with those still living on the earthly plane. Proof like a public séance in New Bedford, Massachusetts, when Bright Eyes's true identity came forth. The year was 1898 and Mary was up onstage, in the middle of pointing out a skeptic in the audience, when Bright Eyes took over Mary's body and chimed in to help.

Why hello Mister So-and-So, Bright Eyes said to the skeptic, addressing him by his name. *We've met before.* But the skeptic said he knew nothing of her. *Yes, you do. You've taken my photograph before,* said the spirit, and then proceeded to give details of how, way out west, when Bright Eyes was a small girl, the gentleman had snapped a photo of her. When the man in the crowd returned home that night, he searched through all his photographs and negatives, and, lo and behold, he found the picture he'd taken: a young girl, about ten or twelve years old, of the Kickapoo Indian tribe, eyes as gorgeous as the Grand Canyon. Bewildered and now a believer, the man brought the photograph of Bright Eyes and gave it to Mary, who placed it in a locket and wore it around her neck for the rest of her years. It didn't take long for word of the breakthrough in Buffalo to spread like wildfire. Mary and Bright Eyes were now turning down hundreds of invitations and engagements all over the country.

But there was one invitation that the duo didn't turn down, and in the summer of 1902, Mary and Bright Eyes first stepped foot on the grounds of Camp Etna. It was the same year that Harrison D. Barrett was elected camp president. The two (or three?) were finally serving together at the same time in the same place, and Camp Etna was electric.

There is at a Spiritualist camp an atmosphere of more penetrating psychic appeal than can be found in any indoor temple of worship.

Many persons have observed the spiritual thrill which enwraps a visitor within some building long devoted to heartfelt religious service under any denominational head; this feeling may prevail alike in a dim lit, tumbledown shanty, or before the shining altar of a vast cathedral. Such is the vibration sweeting a great Spiritualistic encampment . . . The airy, open auditorium of a camp will permit larger numbers than could be accommodated in a city church or hall, to listen comfortably . . . therefore, a rare endowment is chronicled in a single statement when the fact is set down that at Camp Etna it was no uncommon thing, upon ascending the rostrum, for Mary Vanderbilt to face ten thousand people, drawn there in the hope and knowledge that she would act as interpreter to the angel world.

—*M. E. Cadwallader*

By now, Camp Etna was more than 300 acres long, with more than 130 cottages, good livery, spring water, and its own train station. The abandoned cottages of today were in tip-top shape, painted and primed prettily. Automobiles backed up for miles. Thousands of tents. Gardens. Swimming. Philosophy classes for campers spread out on blankets on the lawn. Mothers and their families, the old and young and in-between. Couples playing cricket. Boat rides on the pond. More and more groups within the association formed: the Young People's Improvement Club. A Junior League. There was the Sunflower Success Club. Saturday-morning circles. A lyceum. Gymnasium. Spiritualist Sunday school at the end of the week. According to the program notes I'd flipped through in Diane's museum, there'd been a lot of singing in those days. A lot of singing.

There was also a lot of healing. Underneath all the pomp and energy and socializing, healing seemed to have pervaded as Camp Etna's priority. Later in the day, I would return to Diane's museum and come across a document titled "A Bit of History of Camp Etna." The manuscript was old, cracked, and faded, compiled and composed on a typewriter by former camp president Clarence E. Stewart, in which he reports:

> Probably every phase of mediumship has been demonstrated here, among them, spiritual healing: there was the case of a young lady who was affected in every muscle of her body, and unable to walk or lift her hand. She was brought to the camp on a stretcher. Her case had been pronounced hopeless by the old school doctors, but after a course of Spiritual healing [at Camp Etna] she made a complete recovery and afterwards developed mediumship, lectured, and gave spirit greetings all over the United States and Dominion of Canada.

Following that all-star summer of 1902, Harrison Barrett returned to his native town of Canaan to reside for a bit. Two years later, upon accepting the nomination from the Democrats of Somerset County, Barrett ran for Maine State Senate and ran slightly ahead of his ticket in several precincts, though eventually lost to the Hon. W. G. Bailey of Harmony, Maine. Nonetheless, Harrison D. Barrett, a man who believed he could talk to the dead, attended the Democratic National Convention in St. Louis and sat with the Maine delegation as alternate for the Hon. F. O. Gould of Oldtown. This was not the first time, nor the last, that a Spiritualist played a role in American politics.

In response to Harrison's defeat, Maine's *Bangor Daily News* printed the following accolades of Mr. Barrett: "[He] takes a deep interest in political, educational and reformatory work of all kinds. He is an ardent admirer of Abraham Lincoln and the principles the great martyr represented," and went on to laud the Maine native (now present and permanent resident) as honorable, with the markings of eminence.

In a similar fashion, Mary returned to her home in Brooklyn, her reputation preceding her, and the demand for her services overwhelming. Wrote Elizabeth F. Kurth, then a recent president of the Women's Progressive Union of Brooklyn, of her encounter with Mary and the physical mediumship known as "billet reading" (one of Mary's specialties): "As to reading the sealed letters placed upon the platform, this type of mediumship must carry weight with even the most thick-skinned skeptic. In some cases, two or three envelopes enfold the communications. She gives full names, locations, and often the innermost thoughts of those to whom the guides take her—all of this with a feeling of surety. Ten years ago, Mary Pepper was considered a good platform medium; five years ago she was considered remarkable; today she stands as the peer of all demonstrators of spiritual phenomena."

But Mary needed more space. She needed a larger area to accommodate her followers, so she set up a meeting with a number of influential men of New York, and together they created the First Spiritualist Church of Brooklyn. The location: Bedford Avenue and Madison Street, inside the Aurora Grata Cathedral. There, throughout the year, Mary's ardent devotees and other Spiritualists could gather all in one place with weekly religious services comprised of spirit messages, readings from the scriptures, prayer, organ music, and a sermon. The pastor: Mary Ann Scannell Pepper.

"Tall, with the massive frame of women of mountain regions, but covered with the avoirdupois of the well-nourished woman, carried with the ease of one who has a fair comprehension of the laws of physical being," wrote a reporter from the *Australian Town and Country Journal* after one of Mary's church services in 1905:

"Mrs. Pepper's prayers are the most beautiful poetic supplications possible to hear or conceive," praised another parishioner. In another account, "Hundreds of people go to hear Mrs. Pepper out of curiosity. Hundreds go to ridicule. Meanwhile, she keeps right on with her work, and scores are compelled to embrace Spiritualism because of what they are told."

By 1906, Mary had risen to a level of prestige and leadership during a time when the nation's cultural acceptance of women in governing positions was still extremely limited and society still potently patriarchal. Her next stop: Russia.

She'd received a letter in the mail from the royal family. Or more accurately, Russia's royal family had sent her a test. Within the letter was an envelope, and within that envelope *another* envelope preserved in wax with the royal Russian seal. The tsar's request: for Mary to respond to the written question he'd enclosed within the wax-sealed envelope without opening it, and return both her answer to said question as well the letter within the sealed envelope, wax still untouched and unbroken. Mary obliged. Weeks passed, and then, she received another letter in the mail from the tsar congratulating her on passing his test and inviting her to Russia to be a guest of the royal family. She accepted, traveling to St. Petersburg where she'd remain for several weeks as personal psychic and medium to the tsar of Russia. At the end of Mary's stay, one of the women of the royal household brought her a tray of jewels and asked Mary to pick her favorite. Mary leaned in and pulled out a large diamond-and-ruby-encrusted golden cross.

After this first foray into Europe, Mary Scannell Pepper continued her travels abroad, all the while keeping her followers back in the United States abreast of her experiences. As a correspondent for *The Progressive Thinker*, Mary recounts her adventures:

> [In Germany] I was taken to the castle of the present Kaiser, through the gorgeous rooms where the "lady in white" is supposed to walk and give warning of impending danger to the royal household.

She went on to recount that many who would not believe in the phenomena of Spiritualism believed in *her*, in Mary, and as a consequence

> unconsciously believe in the communication and apparitions of spirits. . . . There are many organizations of investigators in Berlin, divided into lodges, which are secret societies on the principle of the Masonic orders in America, composed entirely of men. Women are not admitted members. They have their passwords,

emblems and regalia. The places of meeting are called chapels. The largest and most influential society is named "Psychic Lodge," whose master, on reading that I was in the city, sent a messenger inviting me to attend a meeting . . . The chapel was brilliantly lighted, decorated with flowers, and with tall candles burning at a crucifix in the center. The men in their black velvet and gold regalia were impressive . . . I felt in my soul the earnestness of these men and these sacred surroundings, investigating the most sacred thing that has touched the lives of humanity—the communication between the world material and the world spiritual—and I bowed my head in reverence to those unseen influences who had made me their message bearer. Bright Eyes's inability to speak the German language was much to be regretted; but the look of amazement on the faces of many present and their expressions of wonder fully attested to her good work.

Upon her return to Brooklyn, Mary met a man at church. His name was Edward Ward Vanderbilt, a zealous follower and recent widower who'd made a fortune selling wholesale lumber. The smitten Vanderbilt succeeded in wooing his pastor, and in 1907, the two got engaged—her most recent marriage had ended—then married, with Mary taking on Edward's last name, becoming Mary Ann Scannell Pepper Vanderbilt. The marriage was serene, with Edward, the devoted husband Spiritualist, and Mary Ann, "the sympathy and cooperation of her husband and the mental relaxation which the sanctuary of the home life afforded her."

Edward's children, however, believed none of it. On June 11, 1907, with the newlyweds still in their honeymoon period, Edward's twenty-one-year-old daughter, Minerva Vanderbilt, brought forth a request for an application to the Supreme Court of Brooklyn, New York, questioning the sanity of her sixty-six-year-old father in his relationship with Mary, as well as Mary's legitimacy and motives, claiming her new stepmother was "a woman of unscrupulous habits . . . a fraud upon the community, and nothing more nor less than an adventuress, seeking notoriety and profit." Minerva claimed Mary Ann was preying on the still-grieving widowed Edward. That, under the guise of a trance state, with Bright Eyes driving the bus, Mary was manipulating him to bankroll her.

On September 4, 1907, the *New York Times* ran an article of the trial, under the headline "SPIRITUALIST FAITH SIGN OF INSANITY: Alienist Says Vanderbilt's Belief in 'Bright Eyes' Shows Disordered Mind. IS SANE IN BUSINESS LIFE, Needs Treatment for Spiritualism, Says Dr. MacCoy. Defendant Weeps on Witness Stand."

When the trial reached a verdict, the judge ruled Edward Vanderbilt fit to think for himself, that he was competent and perfectly normal, "except for his belief in astrology, Spiritualism, and a few other things of metaphysical character." Minerva's attempt was throttled but not destroyed: the following year, Edward and Mary found themselves in a courtroom again, as well as the *New York Times,* this time positioned directly under an article covering President Roosevelt's plea for the chairman of the Republican state committee of New York to step down.

In its coverage, the *Times* reported that Mary, the "Spiritualist Bishop of Brooklyn," was being sought for charges of larceny, and that the husband of the "Spook Priestess" was being brought in for a second inquiry into whether he was lucid enough to handle his own affairs. Mary was arrested, and proceedings took place at the Brooklyn Supreme Court. The accuser: Minerva Vanderbilt, back for more. The court demanded that Mary bring forth Bright Eyes, too, but Mary wouldn't, explaining that she couldn't just make Bright Eyes appear whenever someone else requested—that spirits come of their own accord, not on demand. The trial against Mary pressed on, and she remained passive in her mannerisms and consistent in her stance: Mary was who she was, and she stood by her truth, and she didn't have to prove it to anyone. The verdict: guilty of the fire that destroyed the home at 587 St. Marks in Brooklyn, which went up in a blaze of glory just after Mary moved out and before Minerva moved in. Later that year, a sheriff's jury declared her husband to be incompetent, but that verdict was later set aside by a higher court of law.

"I like large audiences," said Mary of Camp Etna. "I like *light*." Less contentious than Brooklyn, in the woods with the Spiritualists of Maine Mary found respite; the atmosphere of at Camp Etna was open and airy, not cramped and contaminated. At camp, she didn't have to defend herself. At camp she was protected.

By 1910, Camp Etna had purchased the fifty-room Echo Farm and Hotel to accommodate more visitors, as people were pouring in in multitudes and from all over the world. They came in farmers' carts, wagons, by car, by locomotive, and by foot until they reached the rural mecca just sixteen miles west of Bangor. The camp was now selling up to two thousand tickets in a single day, with both Harrison D. Barrett and Mary Ann Pepper Scannell Vanderbilt serving at the helm.

On January 17, 1911, Harrison D. Barrett's obituary ran in the newspaper. He was forty-seven years old and had died of complications of a surgery months before. The obituary was a lyrical elegy, describing the Spiritualist as "a lecturer of no mean repute" and "orator of unusual ability with a fine poetic touch in language, and what is rare with this type of mind, he combined a keenness of analysis and profound philosophical grasp of those basic truths which the varied aspects of cosmic activity disclose."

Scores of tributes with similar sentiments trumpeted, and one particular anecdote told how he would walk the twenty-five miles from Canaan, Maine, to Camp Etna, barefoot, as Diane described, "with his shoes over his shoulders in order to present himself clean, polished and prepared for his appointment with Spirit," and for years after his death, Spiritualists throughout New England continued to celebrate the life and work of Harrison D. Barrett by marching on foot from Camp Etna to the Canaan Town Hall, where a stone commemorating his legacy still sits in a park that bears his name. It still happens on the third Sunday of November, but nowadays, Spiritualists make the trek by motorcade.

Then came Mary's time to go. In September of 1918, after her tenth summer serving as Camp Etna president and now fifty-one years old, Mary fell ill. She returned to her home in Brooklyn, where she was diagnosed with influenza and ordered to rest. As she continued to grow weak, the seventy-first anniversary celebration of Modern Spiritualism drew near, and perhaps sensing that "some day the silver cord shall break," and that death was right around the corner for her, Mary rallied.

Accompanied by her sister by birth, Harriet, and siblings-in-Spiritualism Mr. Luey Hill and Mrs. M. E. Cadwallader (author of Mary's biography), Mary traveled to Boston's Berkley Hall to deliver her valedictory. Amid unbounded enthusiasm from the audience, Mary rose to her feet, trembling with weakness and emotion, and scuffled onto the stage. Next, she began a roll call of close friends and Spiritualists who had recently passed, "as if a procession of spirit witnesses passed in a vision before her," reported Mrs. Cadwallader. "They have gone to their reward," declared Mary, speaking with deep feeling and gusto and then urging the crowd to be steadfast in their calling and cause of Spiritualism, "who will take their places?" The crowd roared. And then, in what would be her last public utterance, she declared, "My friends. I have found Spiritualism a good thing to live by; and I have come pretty close to finding it a good thing to die by."

Mary's final bout with illness passed quickly. On the Sunday morning of April 27, 1919, her "spirit emerged from earth conditions" and the human body known as Mary Ann Scannell Pepper Vanderbilt died.

In compliance with her request, the ashes of Mary's body were interred at Camp Etna, spread about and underneath a giant boulder in a gated garden, which Diane and our tour group now currently faced. The rock was thick and enormous, about seven feet long and four and a half feet high, and, even with my very limited retention of what science I had learned in school, I could come up with no idea how it could have naturally gotten there. There were no mountains or cliffs nearby, and as Diane wrapped up the account of the two Camp Etna legends and led us out of Barrett Square and onto the next stop along our tour, I stayed behind, gazing at Mary's grave, uncertain of what I was feeling.

It was mid-afternoon by now. A shudder of semis zipped down Route 2 and past the entrance to the camp, plowing ahead toward the interstate, a reminder of the living, breathing, eating, sleeping world that was still happening outside the quiet grounds of camp. I caught up with Diane.

"And that building just to the right of our entrance archway?" she said, pointing at a white clapboard A-frame with purple trim a few yards away. The building stood silent and unoccupied, and had a sunflower the size of a fully grown pig painted across its wall. "Depending on who you're talkin' to from camp, that's known as Clubhouse, or the Community Center, and up until the 1980s, it's the building that the nearby Harrison D. Barrett Church rented to hold its Sunday services."

It was also the building that caught Diane's attention and pulled her into Camp Etna. She hadn't ever planned to land here. It was July 2009, Red had been dead going on two years, and Diane was finally back in New England, working as a volunteer carpenter. Her tools in her truck bed, Diane was driving down Stage Road, unfamiliar territory, when the camp archway caught her eye. Diane hit the brakes, turned in, and parked her car so she could get a better look around. Scanning the place, Diane saw a dilapidated white building with a saggy roof and porch breaking off like an old scab. "I realized this place could use a volunteer carpenter," said Diane.

Our tour group passed the camp's Hot Spot Café and, approaching the corner of Pond Street and Bishop's Row, Diane perked up. "So I got back in to my truck and drove down to the corner of Pond Street and

Bishop's Row, where we stand now. Right here. In this spot. A woman was coming out of one of the cabins, so I got out of my truck and introduced myself."

The two women started talking, and soon they were both weeping; both were recent widows. "I told her it would get easier with time, and then turned around and looked around at the array of buildings in different states of disrepair," said Diane as our fleet passed a bushy garden with an assemblage of Buddha statues and one large angel holding a chalkboard with the word *vibration* written on it. We were now on Dover Street.

"So I told her," said Diane, "'It looks like you could use some help fixing this place up,' and she told me to go see the man in the purple house." So Diane drove down the street to go see the man in the purple house. His name was Don Skolfield, he was the camp's board president and one of the few men who existed on the grounds. "I said, 'Hi. My name is Diane and I am looking for carpentry work. I have my own tools and I will work for free.'"

Don accepted Diane's offer, and soon the two of them were up on a roof, working together to repair the old white building. Not long after that, Don and Diane got married.

"It seemed as though the late, great, Fiddlin' Red was leading me on a journey," said Diane, facing our group and smiling proudly at the story she told, her bright eyes beaming. "Now, who wants to go touch the Healing Rock?"

CHAPTER 3

Ghost Hunting 101

Barbara Williams occasionally uses tools like candles and crystals in her mediumship work. *Greta Rybus*

A few weeks later, I was perched on the edge of a lumpy, velvety armchair belonging to Dr. Barbara and Steve Williams, the husband-and-wife paranormal investigation duo of Camp Etna. The three of us were inside the living room of "Peacefull Solitude" (yes, two *l*'s), the couple's grape-colored clapboard seasonal cottage nicely perched on the fertile ground of 62 Pond Street, Camp Etna's main drag.

Up the steps and into their home (one of four), Barbara and Steve's little lodge felt solid and heavy and protective. Peacefull Solitude had a *vibe*. Perhaps it was the tenderness of the place—the darkness lit by a Victorian rose glow of carefully chosen Tiffany lamps and soy wax candles only to reveal a cavern of precious gemstones—selenium, rose quartz, black tourmaline—all within finger's reach from each nearby tabletop. I grabbed one and fiddled around with it.

"Tourmaline," said Barbara. "Blocks negative energies and psychic attacks." The living room, which smelled of lavender and spruce, was filled to the brim with homemade holistic medical remedies and tinctures. Peacefull Solitude *was* peaceful, but it also had a force. Or maybe it was just the natural expression of the matriarch of this nest.

"Spirit!" Barbara shouted, her voice curving up to the top of the staircase.

I jerked my head around, looking for an apparition. Barbara rolled her eyes and called again. "For heaven's sake, Spirit! Angel! Both of you, would you please pipe down!"

Her husband, Steve, saw how big my eyes had grown, and laughed, explaining that Spirit was their geriatric yet agile Brussels Griffon, and Angel their tater-tot-shaped, diaper-wearing pug.

Today was May 20: Mediums Day. The tail end of spring, with forsythias in bloom, birds hatched, and the mediums of Camp Etna officially unlocking their doors, and hanging their tin shingles. Or, if they didn't own a cabin or live on the grounds, they could make out a $30 check to the Camp Etna Spiritualist Association and put up their card tables, booths, tents, and set up shop. Hamburgers and hot dogs would be sold.

Soon, and sporadically, cars, trucks, vans, and motorcycles would arrive. They'd be looking for a go-between, a special person they believed (or at least hoped) had the ability to put them in touch with a particular dead person, answer a question, give them closure, offer some kind of peace. With today being Mediums Day, most sessions would last only fifteen minutes to a half hour and prices discounted, which meant the mediums of Camp Etna would be flooded, and at the end of the day, they'd donate their proceeds back to the camp.

Barbara looked out the window before pulling the shade halfway closed. Outside, her car was parked in the driveway, and a large magnet advertising Steve and Barbara's paranormal investigation company stuck to the passenger-side door. HAUNTED: ARE YOU LIVING WITH A GHOST? CALL (207) XXX-XXXX.

Even before I'd met Barbara in person, I was intimidated. Maybe it was because of her credentials—she had told me that she had a PhD in metaphysics and an ability to literally see beyond what most human eyes could, and when she'd answered my first phone call, her voice reverberated with power and confidence.

Now, inside Peacefull Solitude, we were together in person for the first time. The dogs had finally calmed down. Angel retreated into the kitchen, waddling toward the refrigerator then spreading herself out on the floor like an omelet. Little Spirit jumped into my lap, where he'd stay for the next two hours, snoring as I pet him.

"So, where were we?" asked Barbara. Her hair was the color of sterling, and streaked with natural blond and caramel that cascaded down her back, nearly reaching her bum. Upon her initial arrival at Camp Etna in 2006, a handful of the more gossipy mediums immediately called Barbara out on her mane, as if having long hair as a middle-aged woman made her a radical. "What I want you to know is this: I am a medium first. Being a medium is what led me to do, and being a medium is what led me to teach." I straightened in my chair, cleared my throat, stroking Spirit. Barbara lent me a calm smile. "Now, let me explain."

Before I understood the differences between them, I'd lumped the terms "clairvoyant," "psychic," "medium," and "Spiritualist" into one formless bundle—numerous terms for the same kind of thing. My mistake. There's an order to it all, Barbara explained, and whether or not you're a believer, breaking down the thicket of terms and battalion of categories is vital if you are going to learn anything about what Barbara and those in her community do. This is where Barbara had me start: basically, everyone is essentially a spiritual being, or an eternal soul temporarily functioning through a physical vehicle or shell or body. The physical body is never static and is always changing from birth to youth, middle age, old age, until whenever you die. After our bodies die, we (our souls, our spirit, our consciousness) still have the ability to communicate with those still living on Earth, and mediums are the humans (the hotels with souls in them), who act as the in-betweens of the living and those who have passed. Not all mediums are religious, or practicing Spiritualists. Some mediums can simply communicate with the dead and that's that.

Crucially, a psychic and a medium are not the same thing. Most mediums are psychics, but not all psychics are mediums. A psychic is a person who uses extrasensory perception (ESP) to identify information that is hidden from most people's normal senses by tuning into the energy of people, by sensing elements of their past, present, and future. Simply put, psychics use their intuition to read people and provide accurate predictions. Mediums are all this and more. A medium can read, convey, and relay information by the "living personalities" of the spirit world. The National Spiritualist Association defines a medium as "one whose organism is sensitive to vibrations from the spirit world, and through whose instrumentality, intelligences in that world are able to convey messages and produce the phenomena of Spiritualism."

Or, in Barbara's words, "I can see dead people. I am a medium, you understand? And being a medium is much more than reading tarot cards or predicting the future, although I can do that. Mediumship operates on a far deeper level. It helps us understand our genuine nature as an eternal spirit, which in turn brings about peace, and healing."

Within mediumship, there are two main categories of practice: mental mediumship, and physical mediumship. The rappings of the Fox sisters: physical mediumship. Table tipping: physical mediumship. Billet readings, Ouija boards, spirit photography, levitation, automatic writing: physical mediumship. This is the type of mediumship that was most common in Spiritualist practices, beginning with the Fox sisters and moving on up until the mid-1900s. You'd have to see it, hear it, touch it, taste it, or smell it to believe it.

Often, physical mediumship brings about an apparition, or "the dematerialization of physical objects by the spirit chemists, which are teleported to another physical location, where they are materialized to their original form." In his book, *Mediumship Mastery*, Spiritualist and medium Stephen A. Herman writes: "Physical is not dependent upon the spirituality, emotional or intellectual qualities of the medium, but instead is dependent on the chemistry of the physical medium or the group of individuals in producing the phenomena." He goes on to say that physical mediumship often involves the extraction of "ectoplasm" from the physical body of the medium, and possibly the sitters involved in the session. Ectoplasm, writes Herman, is utilized by the spirit personalities as a substance to produce physical manifestations that can be directly experienced by the five senses. Essentially, ectoplasm is just another tool dead people can use to communicate.

Nowadays, far from the era of the Fox sisters, and for many reasons which we'll get to later (two words: Harry Houdini), physical mediumship is much less common than mental mediumship. However, it's still being practiced, its varieties listed below:

- *Apportation:* the dematerialization of physical objects by the spirit chemists, which are teleported to another physical location where they are rematerialized to their original form
- *Automatic or Direct Independent Writing and Painting:* when an ectoplasmic arm of the controlling spirit may materialize over the arm of the medium
- *Etherealization:* when a partial or fully materialized spirit form is self-illuminated by an almost phosphorescent light
- *Fire and Cold Tests:* the handling of objects of extreme temperature by a medium while in an altered state and controlled by the spirit personalities
- *Independent and Direct Voice:* the creation of an ectoplasmic box to produce sounds by spirit personalities. Direct voice takes place with a spirit trumpet (a real tin trumpet-shaped device) that acts as a megaphone to amplify the communications
- *Levitation:* the movement of the medium or physical objects via spirit power
- *Lumination:* the production of light in a darkened room
- *Materialization:* the use of ectoplasm to create a partial or full form of a spirit personality
- *The Planchette or Ouija Board:* the use of such physical tools for communication by spirit personalities while controlling the medium
- *Raps:* percussive noises made by spirit personalities
- *Spiritual Healing Contact or Auric Treatment:* the use of spirit energies to impart physical cures through prayer and physical laying-on of hands within the energy fields of the recipient
- *Spirit Photography:* the use of photography to obtain images of spirit personalities
- *Table Tipping:* the use of table movements to convey information
- *Transfiguration:* the use of ectoplasm to create a mask over the face of the medium that is molded to resemble the features of the spirit personality
- *Writing on Skin:* the production of messages or images on the skin of the medium by spirit personalities

Then we have mental mediumship. This one is the trickier of the two, because mental mediumship involves the "inner intuitive experience" of the medium. Her craft is subjective in nature because the "viewer" or sitter can't see or hear or smell or taste or feel what the medium can during communication with the dead. "Mental mediumship," explains Herman, "is also dependent upon attunement of the medium with the spirit personalities." Each medium is at a different level with her or his craft. Some are self-taught and doing it wrong, while others are taught by a master and still doing it wrong. Every mental medium has their own specific skill set and ability, or a combination of the following:

- *Clairaliance:* clear smelling, psychically smelling
- *Clairaudience:* clear hearing, psychically hearing
- *Claircognizance:* clear knowing
- *Clairgustance:* clear tasting
- *Clairsentience:* clear sensing, psychically sensing or feeling
- *Clairvoyance:* psychically seeing
- *Interpretation of Tongues:* the ability to interpret the spirit message given in unknown languages through the gift of tongues
- *Psychic art:* art produced through the mental influence and control of spirit personalities
- *Psychometry:* the ability to read or discern information through the energy contained within a physical object about historical and present conditions of individuals or events associated with the object
- *Spiritual Healing Absent or Distant Treatments:* spiritual healing through prayer for recipients not physically present
- *Spiritual Healing Contact or Auric Treatment:* spiritual healing through prayer and the physical laying-on of hands within the energy fields of the recipient

I asked Barbara which one she was.

"All of them," she replied. "More or less. And I've also been able to do lumination, spiritual healing, photography, and transfiguration."

I asked her how it all worked.

"Other than the medium raising their energy to communicate with Spirit?" Barbara crossed one long leg over the other, then, with her almond-shaped fingernails, raked her hair off her shoulders.

"Everything in the universe," said Barbara, "everything is operating at a precise frequency of vibration, or energy. Mediums register higher frequencies of nonphysical energies—spirits—that cannot be detected through the use of our five senses."

I scratched Spirit's belly and furrowed my brow.

"Take dogs, for example," said continued. "Dogs are able to hear sounds no human could ever hear, sounds inaudible to our human ears. They can also smell things no human nose could ever smell. And just because we cannot smell certain smells or hear certain sounds does not mean they are not there."

She read my face to see if I was following, and I nodded for her to proceed.

"The rate of vibration in the spirit world is much quicker compared to the much denser atmosphere of the physical world, and in order for a medium to receive communications, she must raise her vibrations while the spirit simultaneously lowers theirs. They have to work together, and even if all of it does come naturally to the medium on this earthbound plane it doesn't mean that spirit doesn't have to work hard at communication, either. For me it just comes naturally. Always has. But we are all born with it, you know. The ability is innate. It's just that most people lose it when they're young. Adults just laugh and say their kid is talking to an imaginary friend. It gets discouraged or educated right out of them. But the tools still remain, it's just most people choose not to use them, or don't know how to do it or choose not to believe it."

"Then how does one turn it back on?" I asked her.

"It's about opening up and letting go."

I am a medium first.

Years before she even knew what mediumship was or where it came from or how to practice it safely, Barbara remembers saying goodbye

The recently renovated cottage belonging to Barbara and
Steve Williams. *Mira Pitacin*

to her mother. Or rather, she remembers that first day when she struck
out on her own. Barbara is from nowhere in particular, Pennsylvania.
Born in 1952 out of wedlock to a young and incapable mother, Barbara lived in her grandparents' house until, around age three, she was
adopted by an entirely different and quite affluent family.

"Pink sweater, white pearl buttons. I remember everything about
that day," she said, "I remember what I wore, and I remember I made
my mother wait in the car."

"Why were you adopted?" I asked.

"That's the question," she said. "I know now what I didn't know then: that I've always been able to pick up on energy. Let me explain: when people start out early in any point of their life and they have a loss, a big loss, a major shakeup, what happens is that they spiritually evolve. They have the option of spiritually evolving more and quicker. They have a choice to become a victor or a victim. When you become a victor at a young age, or at any point of your life," said Barbara, "then you look at life a little differently. Not temporarily. All of reality is a false illusion."

"After you were adopted, did you ever talk to your mother again?" I asked her.

"Not alive," she answered.

And so began Barbara's life as "the other": a young girl of Aryan descent, blond hair and steely green eyes freshly dropped into an Orthodox Jewish family of dark hair and dark eyes. Just as it went with her birth mother, there was never a bond between Barbara and her adoptive mother. Or father. And Barbara hated visiting her new relatives, too, because they were adamantly opposed to their family having adopted a non-Jewish child, and were not afraid to show it.

"I was raised not to talk to Gentiles. I had trouble identifying who to talk to, which was tricky, because I was also able to talk to the dead."

This brought a few perks. For instance, when Barbara and her family took road trips and visited historical sites, places like Gettysburg or St. Augustine, it was fun for Barbara because, she said, "I could see the ghosts killed in battle, those souls who still remained on Earth." It didn't frighten her. None of her spiritual abilities did. Being a young medium just made her life more stimulating, more expansive. As a young kid, talking to the dead came more naturally than talking with family. That is, until the moment where she was first able to do both at the same time.

It was the Ouija board. It's always the Ouija board. Barbara was twelve years old. She and a friend were messing around on a Ouija board, not knowing what they were doing, when all of a sudden Barbara went into a trance, and that's when the spirit of her birth mother came through.

A dark shadow appeared in front of the two girls, and while her friend was terrified, Barbara wasn't. She said she knew: *This one is for me*. She released her friend, telling her to go home for supper, while she stayed put to finish with this spirit.

"I'd never done this kind of work before," said Barbara, leaning forward with her face close to mine. Her eyes were feline-shaped with long, arching lashes, and her lids glistened with moonstone-colored makeup. High cheekbones, undoubtedly foxy. Her voice had a depth, was low and hypnotic. Measured. Unrushed. "I mean, I'd always been able to see and hear spirits, but I'd never been able to direct anything at them. But I had a life to live."

The spirit told Barbara that her name was Maria, and her appearance in front of Barbara was similar to what she'd looked like when she had been alive—tall, sad, young, and reckless, with long dark hair—and explained to Barbara that she'd given birth at too young of an age, was too irresponsible to have taken care of her daughter. It was all very powerful, and even though it was giving young Barbara some closure, she knew she wasn't ready to have that intimate of a communication with a spirit. Psychic powers, yes. Mediumship, no.

"I remember turning around and saying to my mother, 'Look. If you try to persist in contacting me now, I will not make it.'" Immediately after that, the spirit evaporated, never to appear again.

As a young woman, Barbara didn't hide her gifts from her family, nor were her practices discouraged. Her parents just thought it was a teenage phase, like Goth or being into photography, and paid it no mind because they were too busy focusing on setting Barbara up for their version of success—actively and vigorously training her to be someone along the lines of the next Miss America.

"I'm five foot ten," said Barbara. "And I was 118 pounds. A bowl of ice cream was one tablespoon."

By the time she was fifteen, Barbara was already a trained concert pianist. She spoke multiple languages ("Hebrew better than English"), attended Carnegie Mellon, and was at the top of every class and the best at every game.

"But then, once I came to realize that the expectation of my parents was that I was made to perform, I stopped whatever I was doing. I became dyslectic—started reading right to left, not left to right. I played tennis, and when I was getting ready to go to make state finals, I got tennis elbow. All of this: self-created!"

"What about Aikido?" said Steve, finally chiming in.

"That was later, Steve," Barbara replied, and gave him an eye roll.

"So there I was, pretending to be something that I wasn't. And on top of that, I would wake up at night—always—seeing spirits. I wasn't scared, but at night, it just got a little loud. It was hard to get to sleep because I could see and hear people in the corner of the room. They were talking and they were disruptive. I'd ask them to be quiet and they'd come over and look at me. They weren't nasty. But when you're tired, you're tired, and they were just so darn noisy."

While she talked, I pictured a miniature Barbara, hair in braids and turtleneck pajamas shushing a gaggle of luminous poltergeists, rolling her eyes, then flipping back under the covers. Because even back then, Barbara wasn't afraid. Instead, she trusted that her second sight (and sounds, and smells, and tastes, and feels) would prove helpful, and that her gifts were also tools to be mastered and would propel her forward in life, tools that could also keep her safe in the world of the living, and protect others too.

Take for example Henry Cooper the Third. "A non-Jewish boy," said Barbara. "We were going to walk down the road to the playground but the road was closed, so we decided to walk toward another park. On our way, we passed a little fence on the side of the road. My body stopped. I couldn't go any further. I became paralyzed—it was like I had a giant rubber band pulling me back. I couldn't explain it."

And so Henry Cooper III and Barbara turned around and went

home. The next day, the local news reported that a couple was assaulted—the gentleman killed and the woman raped—in the same park where Barbara and Henry had been headed and during the same moment of the day when Barbara's legs had refused her.

She straightened up in her seat. "Do I believe in my gods? You bet I do. I'm not going to ignore them, and I'm not going to be a victim, either. I'm going to be a victor."

Not long after that, and still young, Barbara left the home of her adoptive family. She was sixteen.

Steve, a man of few words, sneezed. We blessed him as he brushed the thighs of his denim jeans, stood up from his chair, and went into the kitchen. Angel yipped.

"After I left home, I knew my parents were looking for me, but I also knew how to hide in plain sight," said Barbara. "I taught myself how to do that. But what I didn't know then that I know now is that I can be *invisible* if I want to. It's literally just a matter of shrinking your energy down to where it wraps around you and cloaks you," said Barbara. "You become unnoticed."

"It works good goin' to the airports," Steve called from the kitchen. A glass clinked, the faucet turned on then off, and Barbara's husband returned to the parlor, handing me a cool glass of water. He sat down without saying a word, listening intently, eyes on his wife.

"Before I knew how to shrink my energy," said Barbara, "the minute I'd go into any airport I had people following me. And they would always have to do a strip search. My energy was very big, and if I don't tone it down, it's really, really big."

Steve chimed in. "I get heavy intuitive feelings."

"Oh yeah?" I said. "What does it feel like?"

"Oh, like, 'Oh, I'd better not speed through here today.' Or when you're looking for a parking spot . . ."

"Those are called your runners," said Barbara. "Talk to them. It's always worth it. Do it, and then wait a few seconds—you will always find a parking spot. But you gotta be specific with your wish, like,

'Within one minute of me getting here, I want a place right up front, where I can easily walk inside.' It pays to be specific."

"The universe will supply," Steve said, and then: "Angel, what the hell?"

The Velcro from the little pug's diaper had come undone, and Angel was scootching her butt across the kitchen floor, dragging herself by her front legs. We all watched, but no one got up.

"What's the difference between an angel and a spirit guide?" I asked. "Or for that matter, what's a spirit?"

Barbara gave me the breakdown: the afterlife or spirit world is not a static place, but one in which spirits continue to evolve. Spirit guides are people who have died, have gone into the spirit world, and, as part of their development (or karma), watch over you in this physical world. These are the spirits that are assigned even before your human conception—that is, when consciousness enters the womb of the mother—to protect you on the Earth plane. More often than not they're your ancestors, but not necessarily always. They're attracted to you spiritually and vibrationally, as you are to them.

Angels, on the other hand, are of an entirely differently plane. They're nonhuman spirit and have never been incarnated into a different form. Like spirit guides, they're there to protect, and, unless it's a life-threatening situation, angels must wait until you ask their help.

"And spirit, in general?" I asked.

Barbara looked away from me, pausing for a couple of breaths before saying anything. "Say you lost a sibling at a young age. He had fulfilled his commitments. The lesson was not for him, but for those who remained. As awful as that is, it teaches us that life is not a permanent thing. Our *spirit* is a permanent thing. Our physical life is not permanent. Experiencing life with him, appreciating the moments of life, not questioning whether it has meaning, except for love. That's what matters. No matter how long or short, it's about the quality, not the quantity," she said. "It's the *intensity* with which you love that heightens the spirit."

"And what about God?" I asked. "How would you define God?"

"God," said Barbara, "is everything."

I was doing my best to wrap my head around everything I was learn-ing, but there was a question burning inside me, growing hotter by the moment, that I was afraid to ask. I thought it might be a selfish one, and I wasn't sure what the proper etiquette was in bringing it up, because it was the type of question that people paid Barbara money to answer. I didn't want to be one of those people who, for example, approached my father, a family doctor, when we were at the dairy sec-tion of the grocery store on a Sunday afternoon, rolled up a sleeve, and asked him if he could real quick examine the particular wart that had been bothering them for the last two months. But here I was, sitting in front of a person who might possibly be able to see someone I loved who had died. It was possible she was capable of doing the impossible. I had to know, so at the risk of imposing, I asked.

"Is there anyone here for me?" I exhaled. "Do I have a spirit guide?"

"Yes, I can tell you," said Barbara. She was hesitant. "If you want."

I could've begged her to tell me but managed to restrain myself, reply-ing, "Yes, please," instead. Barbara's eyes quickly blinked up and glanced behind me, blinked again and she was back looking into my face.

"There is a man. Elderly. Button-up top, shirtsleeves rolled up. He's wearing spectacles, and I believe he's from your father's side." I furrowed my brow, trying to think. I had no idea who Barbara could've been talk-ing about. I didn't know the history of Dad's side of the family terribly well, or much about my ancestors. I felt intrigued rather than disap-pointed, intrigued by this new possibility rather than weighed down with grief over the relatives I had known and lost. "He watches over you," said Barbara, "plus he keeps you out of trouble." And that was that.

A few days later, I found myself in the middle of a workday afternoon pussyfooting about the indoor perimeter of my own home, smudg-ing tangerine-scented oil across every window frame, door hinge, and crevice while chanting in unison with a CD of the Buddhist Om. I was with Barbara and Steve, and we were trying to rid my place of any accumulated negativity or "residual energy" that might be left over from an angry deceased alcoholic recluse I'll call, for privacy reasons, Lucille, from whom we'd purchased our home four years earlier. It was Barbara's idea. After I'd responded the other day that *No, Barbara, my children do not sleep through the night,* she'd offered to come check out my house and look for ghosts, free of charge.

It was our first house, and my husband and I had bought it cheap, with all of Lucille's furniture and a good deal of her belongings still in it. Neighborhood legend had it that Lucille's son and husband had died long before her, and that after they'd passed, she took up drinking as if it were a competitive sport. She'd gradually morphed into a grouch, pickled and reclusive, eventually passing away in a nursing home, completely alone.

When we moved in, the house was set up just like she'd left it—popcorn plaster ceilings, mustard-yellow linoleum floors, vinyl soffits, Masonite paneling, crusting lead paint on the beams, and sad musty couches with a faint odor of cat pee. One day soon after moving in, while I was exploring the dank and dusty basement of our new nest, I raked away a ball of cobwebs and discovered a bunch of old gardening tools. They seemed pretty prized. Soon after, I noticed in our yard that despite it being neglected and overgrown and covered in weeds, evidence of Lucille's love of landscaping existed; her superb green thumb still peeked out throughout the yard.

Since then, in her honor and as a personal-growth challenge, I'd been teaching myself to garden and had been working hard to revive what Lucille had planted there, years and years ago. But often, as my bare hands were digging in the soil, I'd find shards of glass, broken alcohol bottles that I suspect she'd thrown into the yard in fits of anger, rage, or depression.

I'd spent a lot of time wondering about Lucille, and I could swear that sometimes, actually, more and more often, I could feel something heavy surrounding our house. Something thick and contagious, almost like a tangible bad mood. The atmosphere of our new home, our first home as a brand-new family, felt gray, no matter how hard we tried to hype it up with positive energy and new life. I imagined what I felt was Lucille, or what might have been her last moments in her home before she was taken away—angry, sorrowful, unhinged, and still lingering around our house, enduring. So when Barbara suggested she and Steve come investigate, I said yes immediately.

It was about noon when the ferry to our island would arrive, bringing Steve and Barbara for the cleansing. As I walked out my door and got in my car to pick them from the terminal, I was overcome with anxiety. It wasn't a fear of Lucille. It was a fear of my own self, of what I might reveal—I assumed that as a psychic and medium, Barbara would read my mind, and I'd never seen a ghost and worried she'd be able to sense my skepticism. In addition, whenever someone is telling me something they believe to be a fact or their truth, my first personal inclination is to agree with whatever that person is telling me; I have a bad habit of wanting to be seen as courteous and pleasant. But when it came to ghosts? I didn't think I was a cynic, but I wasn't a believer yet, and I didn't want Barbara to sense my doubt. When we'd met for the very first time at Peacefull Solitude, it seemed like she'd figured me out in less than the amount of time it took to use hand sanitizer. And now, as I started the engine and backed out of my driveway, I feared that in no time I would blow any further opportunity at field research with Barbara.

As I approached the ferry terminal, I pictured how it might go: once the three of us got to my home, Barbara would have already read my every thought. This would be a disaster, because whenever I try to control my inner monologue—in this case, trying to veer it away from my skepticism of ghosts, or of Barbara and Steve's claims—I respond by automatically conjuring up my least desirable thoughts and images: butts, poop, racism, blood, guts, my parents having sex. It's a weird response. Perhaps this is the gift with which I was blessed.

Passengers were walking off the bridge, and I spotted them: Barbara, tall and radiant, her mermaid hair swaying like a willow tree. Steve stood behind her, as he often did. Gnome-bearded and wearing acid-washed blue jeans and a bright tie-dyed tee, Steve was carrying all their supplies. He was sweet to his wife, so sweet and supportive, and, you could almost say, resigned.

This was a common theme I'd noticed about the Spiritualists at Camp Etna: pivoted on the axis of novelty and healing, the camp was a place where women were the major players. The majority of the members of the camp were women, and women occupied the majority of the leadership positions. They were respected and trusted to make decisions based on their own individual intuitions. In fact, the camp and its inhabitants had no allegiance to the tradition of patriarchy. Instead, they operated on a faith placed in the deceased, and a faith placed in women.

Barbara met Steve on December 13, 1998, after a few failed marriages; it was a blind date. She'd already had two children—Nadia and Nyles—from a previous marriage; it was their bus driver who gave Steve Barbara's number and told him to call her. "I think he was attracted to my Harley." Barbara laughed.

"I'm not gonna lie," said Steve as he climbed into the backseat behind me. "It did influence me a little bit."

On their first date, Barbara told him about her clairvoyance. Steve told her he was an atheist. "I looked at him and said, 'No, no, you're not.' He was just sick and tired of all the dogma and all the crap people shove down your throat. He believed in something, but he didn't have a name for it."

In time, Barbara showed him the light of Spiritualism: that you could believe what you wanted, that you didn't need to prove it to anyone, and that you could live according to your instincts. Most important, you live by the Golden Rule, treat others as you'd like to be treated. Also: ghosts really do exist. By February 14, 1999, they were married. Barbara's fourth. Steve's fourth. And fifth. Let me explain.

When she was about nineteen years old, Barbara saw a psychic who told her she'd be married five times. "Steve always remembered that story. Somehow this always stayed in his mind, so Steve went ahead and married me twice."

On our way to my street, Barbara suggested a detour—a brief lap around the island (which is only one square mile). I drove, with Barbara in the front, Steve in the back. We passed by the island's brick elementary school, a basketball court, a chicken coop, the Methodist Church, and several island summer cottages.

"Stop! Here," Barbara called out. "This place." I idled the car in front of an old cedar shake house that looked like a small barn. It was painted red, it was pretty, and I knew it was very, very old. "Oh yes, that one," she said, pointing right at it.

"See that person in the window?" Steve asked Barbara and not me, looking in the same direction as his wife. I saw no one.

"Yep," Barbara replied.

"In the rocking chair, looking right at us," Steve continued.

"Which window?" I asked. "Where?" I was frustrated; I couldn't see what they said they saw. I wanted to see it too. I wanted to believe. "Why am I not seeing it?"

"Barbara can literally see ghosts," Steve finally answered. His wife had always been able to, clear as day, alongside people, leaning on buildings like it's no big deal, like they weren't out of place, and this was one major difference between Steve and Barbara. Her sight of ghosts was literal; his was not. "I just see them in my head," Steve explained. "I close my eyes, and that's how I see it."

"It's called your mind's eye," Barbara said, still looking at the house as we slowly drove on. "Yes, that one for sure. Definitely." Days later, during a family bike ride, I heard my four-year-old son Theo say the same thing—that place was definitely haunted. A few days after that, my dog walker, James, now a college student who'd grown up and lived on the island his entire life, said he'd grown up hearing the same thing—that that place was haunted.

Our haunted house island safari came to an end and we pulled into the driveway of my home. I welcomed the duo into my living room, and immediately Barbara told me she could definitely sense residual energy.

"The woman who lived here—her son committed suicide, didn't he?"

I'd been told by neighbors that he had.

"And the woman died all alone, yes?"

Yes, that was true too.

"If your kids aren't sleeping in their beds, there's probably a reason for it," Barbara said again, and suggested we stop gabbing and proceed with the cleansing.

We were to cleanse the home of anything that could bring negativity or darkness into our life. The three of us would begin outside in my backyard, then come back inside and work our way up, starting in the basement until we got to the last room on the second floor of the house.

Steve opened the box they'd brought along, which contained all the items we needed for today's ceremony: one compass, one bag of black tourmaline, one bag of tobacco. Cornmeal, sage, one container holy water, a container of banishing oil, one of house-blessing oil, and one of protection oil. One large seashell, one large feather for smudging, a bottle of four-thieves vinegar, a blessings script, a medicine-wheel script, white sea salt, black sea salt, one lighter, one Om CD, a pad of paper, and a pen.

Both Steve and Barbara took what they needed, closed the box, and the three of us stepped outside and into my backyard. "Watch out for dog shit," I warned. We stood on the grass behind my kids' swing set in the corner of the yard, the region my husband and I referred to as the "poop cemetery." I apologized, and put my hands behind my back, waiting for instructions. Steve lit a large gray-green bunch of dried sage, Barbara pulled out a piece of paper and began to read, commencing the cleanse:

"*Bless the element of the earth, all my relatives, it is indeed so.*" Above us, dark clouds were gathering. "*Bless the element of the earth, the power of the physical, we call in Archangel Uriel. Bless the element of the earth and the power of the physical. Turn to the East, bless the element of the air, the power of the mind, we call in the Archangel Raphael."*

Steve fanned the sage and Barbara continued reciting until she hit all the elements and all directions, north, south, east, west. The sky dimmed a shade darker and it started to sprinkle. We held hands, trampled the tourmaline rocks into the soil below our feet, let go of hands. Instantly, a tremendous thunderstorm began to pour down as we hurried indoors.

"I am a medium first. Being a medium is what led me to do. And being a medium is what led me to teach." In the mid-1980s Barbara was working as a pediatric nurse in Boston. She'd made friends with a respiratory therapist who also happened to be a Jesuit priest who had also worked with the famous paranormal researcher Hans Holzer. The priest asked Barbara if she'd like to join him and his team in investigating cemeteries, and she obliged. "That's why I have a soft spot for these yahoos who go on paranormal investigations. I was one of them. But I had an edge over what they were doing because I could see Spirit and they couldn't."

Since she was raised in an Orthodox Jewish household, Barbara was never baptized, so each time they met at the cemetery, the priest would douse her in holy water. "I didn't understand what all the hubbub was about—I'd only talked to people who were dead, and they certainly were not harmful."

Barbara continued to learn how to investigate at cemeteries until she witnessed a series of unfortunate events unfold, involving a shaman and a refusal to sacrifice an animal, which led to the inability to coax out a dark spirit, leading to the death of a loved one. It had been a friend's child who had been sick for years, battling an illness, and as a last resort to cure the child, the mother had called a shaman, but no one had known what they were doing, and it didn't work. I asked her to tell me more, but Barbara refused and quickly shut down my probing; it was all too painful for her to talk about. "All I can say is that Spirit had gone into the weakest link of the family. The whole thing blew me right out of the water."

In the aftermath of that awful episode, Barbara knew she didn't have enough information about the paranormal, so she dedicated herself to learning more before she practiced. It would be twelve years.

"My study wasn't about *how* to see Spirit; my study was how to protect people and keep people safe. I had firsthand experience of something that shouldn't have happened. What you can't see can hurt you."

From physics to metaphysics, three to four courses at a time, Barbara steadily learned how to use her gifts to protect people, how to keep them safe from what they couldn't see. She spent twelve years honing her craft and sharpening her sword, pushing past the path of naturopathic medicine (in which she's certified) and obtaining a PhD in metaphysics while she was at it. Soon she found a Spiritualist church, met Steve, married him, and while the couple was vacationing in North Conway, Maine, some friends suggested they check out a place called Camp Etna. Not long after that, they purchased their cabin, in 2007, for $1,700.

"But there were no mediums up there at the time. Camp Etna was a Spiritualist camp with no mediums, just shut-ins: mediums that never left her house, mediums who were no longer doing any readings, mediums who stopped practicing."

By 2009, Barbara had taken over the programming of the camp and Steve began fixing up the old buildings. Since then, Barbara, now fully educated in the paranormal, has led Ghost Hunting 101 and Beyond; Divination and Scrying; Orb Photography; Pranic Healing; Hypnotherapy; and Candle Manifestation.

We were now in the basement of my house. Upstairs, my dogs were barking nervously, and the Om CD was chanting out of my laptop, which I held stiffly in my hands. Steve lit more sage and let it burn in a conch shell while I trailed Barbara around the basement, rubbing oil on all the exit points of the structure, as per her orders, then followed her up the narrow and ragged basement staircase.

"*White magic, entity attachment points, entity energy reproduction pro-grams, eggs, cocoons, sperms, placenta, entity slag, entity trail, diseases, mini-entity, entity halters, and all voodoo. Clear all European black magic, India black magic, Kahuna, Aztec, Inca, Mayan, Egyptian, Druid, Atlan-tean, Lemurian, Alien, Satanic, and Wicca black magic,*" she recited as she headed up to the second floor of our home, which contained our master bedroom, our children's bedroom, and our one bathroom.

Barbara was meditative and composed while I hustled to keep up, trying to be as intentional as possible while smudging the oil along the windowpanes and simultaneously apologizing for the unmade beds, the piles of laundry, the balls of dog hair in the corners of the room.

"You cover everything," said Barbara. "And if you don't, it's a problem."

During a thin sliver of silence, Steve touched my shoulder and leaned toward me, whispering, "It sounds like hocus-pocus, but it really does matter." I agreed, then asked, why the sage?

"Sage is positive ionization," Barbara answered without looking back. "It's indigenous to the area too. In the true spirit of cleansing, you must use things that you resonate with and that are from this area that you have bonded with."

We forged ahead.

"*White magic, entity attachment points, entity energy reproduction pro-grams, eggs, cocoons, sperms, placenta, entity slag, entity trail, diseases, mini-entity, entity halters, and all voodoo. Clear all European black magic, India black magic, Kahuna, Aztec, Inca, Mayan, Egyptian, Druid, Atlan-tean, Lemurian, Alien, Satanic, and Wicca black magic.*"

With the smoke, the strangers in the house, the storm outdoors and the changes in air pressure it brought, my dogs were tense. Then the fire alarm went off, which set the dogs straight into panic mode.

"Oh Lord," I sighed, running downstairs to take out the fire alarm battery, or really, batter it with a broomstick.

"Bless this home and all who live here," Barbara prayed, unwaver-ingly, above me. "May the joy, happiness, love, kindness, abundance, and prosperity of God exist here. May this place be a place of love and harmony. So be it."

Soon the rain stopped. Barbara instructed Steve and me to go outside to wrap things up by pouring white sea salt onto the ground, outlining the perimeter of the house. "Salt has, for thousands of years, been the go-to cleanser," explained Barbara. "Salt is a physical and spiritual cleanser. People have gone to the shores, to the ocean for healing. Bathing and breathing in salt. We as human beings are made mostly of water and salt."

Once Steve and I finished with the salt, we waited on the front porch for Barbara. By now, the skies above had cleared, but a thick ocean fog still seeped around our neighborhood. "I did some pranic healing on your dog's legs," said Barbara as she walked out the front door, then closed it behind her. She reported that my home was now clear—that there had been plenty of residual energy but we'd cleared it—but when she'd stepped outside and onto the front porch, she could immediately see that there were a lot of people in the surrounding areas who needed to be crossed, aka dead people taken from the Earth plane who hadn't yet crossed over into the white light, and that with Barbara's guidance, we could help them. They called it "soul rescue."

"It is a process where prayer and reasoning come together to try to explain to an intelligent haunting that they have died and need to move on to be with their loved ones," said Barbara. All Steve and I had to do is join hands with her and focus on guiding these lost souls into the white light that beamed up and out from within our three-person triangle.

"Now," said Barbara, "shall we release some spirits?"

We stood out on my front porch in the middle of the afternoon and released some spirits. I have to admit, it felt pretty good, like volunteer work. Ghost hunting was one of Barbara and Steve's specialties. In fact, they'd be chaperoning a group of rookie paranormal investigators soon.

"Ever been to ParSem?" asked Steve, and invited me to join the duo at Parsonsfield Seminary. Barbara was their resident paranormal docent and raised money to restore the building by leading groups of paranormal enthusiasts who paid her to chaperone their ghost hunts. I accepted the invitation immediately.

After the cleanse, Barbara, Steve, and I sat somewhat awkwardly around the dinner table making small talk about my dogs, particularly the dog on whom Barbara had done her pranic healing. After dinner, the pair packed up their belongings, I drove them back to the ferry, and we hugged and said our goodbyes.

At home, nothing appeared to be all that different. I had about forty-five minutes to myself before my family would be home, so I decided to do a little gardening in the backyard. As I was walking to the porch door, a sharp recognition passed through me. Levity. A feeling of grace and dexterity. Kind of like a white light.

So maybe the cleansing did work. Perhaps we actually had cleared the place of all gargoyles and dark spirits or any lingering voodoo or witches or sorcerers. Maybe, in the act of the cleanse, we'd produced a new feeling, a new point of connection between me and my home. A new memory, perched on top of the other layers of memories that existed within these walls. Whatever it was, I couldn't see it. But I could feel it.

"I got my first scratch here!" someone said. We were waiting for nightfall. We were indoors, lingering around what appeared to be one of Parsonsfield Seminary's old classrooms. Large chalkboards hung from the walls. On one, and in cursive, was the name of today's group, a society of New England paranormal sleuths.

They were young, most of them in their late twenties, most of them dressed in black and fiddling around with loads of fancy equipment, recording gear, night-vision goggles, and infrared cameras they'd brought with them. They were giddy and hyper as though at the beginning of a sleepover, which, technically, I suppose this was, and which would make Barbara and Steve the evening's parents.

Years back, Barbara had been given the keys to the Parsonsfield Seminary as a docent, and tonight she and Steve would be chaperoning the investigation, as they had done countless times before for countless paranormal enthusiasts and meet-up groups, making sure no one did anything stupid or stole anything from ParSem or made a mess or let a spirit use their body. Barbara knew how it all worked, and she also knew all the hot spots, where the ghosts preferred to hang and how to talk to them, how not to. If groups wanted to get more bang for their buck, they'd listen to Barbara. Steve had brought some new piece of equipment that he wanted to try out, too, and he was pretty excited. Something called a Knix, a special kind of recording device that could also be adapted for ghost hunting.

Located in Parsonsfield, Maine, just off State Route 160 and close to the New Hampshire border, The North Parsonsfield Seminary, or ParSem, is a pristinely preserved campus of four buildings and former Free Will Baptist Seminary. Founded in 1832 by a group of Free Will Baptists, the school was the first of its kind in the nation, beginning as a high school with 140 students, both boys and girls, in its first year. The school and its practitioners would come to be deeply involved with the abolitionist movement, eventually operating as a stop on the Underground Railroad in the 1840s, ministering to fugitive slaves from the South heading to Canada. One of the school's earliest principals would go on to establish Bates College, and three other founding fathers became senators and politicians. But what ParSem was most famous (or infamous) for, especially among groups like tonight's, was its hauntings.

In 1853 and at precisely midnight, ParSem went up in flames, the school burning mysteriously, and tremendously, to the ground. "The bell tower flickered in flames while the children ran from its pillar-brick walls," stated one account of the tragedy, and the fire was said to have killed at least three schoolchildren and two fugitive slaves. After the fire, the seminary would be rebuilt and classes would resume until it eventually closed down in 1949. But even after the school shut down, rumors would continue to circulate that the place was haunted—that the headmasters of the school had been abusive, rigid, torturous. That there was child abuse, and the worst kind. And that all that bad energy still remained, and the ghost children still roamed the halls and classrooms of ParSem with their demonic headmasters keeping watch over them, keeping them stuck.

"Are you all protected? Have you protected yourselves?" Barbara asked the group, which was still unpacking their gear and gabbing away excitedly and not responding to her inquiry. She rolled her eyes, unamused.

"Protected themselves from what?" I asked, and followed Barbara back to a table where Steve had been unpacking their duffel bag.

"From attachments and lower energy forms," said Barbara. "All you have to do is say the White Light Prayer."

Barbara stood over the belongings Steve had scattered over a folding table and scanned the pile, then plucked out two large dummies. Old-fashioned, big eyed, shiny-faced grinning ventriloquist dummies.

"Pretty creepy, right?" said Barbara, holding one up then setting it down in a chair. "This is what you'd call a trigger object. Trigger objects could be anything—a bear, dolls, lights, jewelry, anything, depending on the ghost's preference, and can be used to help a ghost be more interactive." The dolls were a recent acquisition that Barbara had picked up from an antique shop in Maine, and they were from the time period of the ParSem ghosts whom Barbara was especially here to help: the kids.

"There was much abuse that went on in this school," she said. When Barbara brought this up with the board of ParSem—that the place was haunted by the small children who had attended the school—the board thought it was pretty cute, or at least that it would draw in visitors. But then people at ParSem started hearing things, seeing things, and they started bringing things forward to Barbara, things like running sounds on the top floor of one of the buildings in the campus. So again, Barbara had to explain it to them. Ghosts.

"But what they didn't understand was that a place doesn't get haunted with intelligent hauntings because it was a wonderful place, or that kids want to come back after they die. We really had to educate the board," Barbara explained. In their paranormal investigations, she and Steve started receiving the names of the children and of situations that they would then have to validate. "I didn't know the place from Adam. The people in that area, a lot of the families still live there and so a lot of cover-up is done. They did not want to air their dirty laundry. Steve and I have evidence of a child who was obviously in distress and we have a long audiotape of that."

There are three kinds of hauntings. The first: intelligent hauntings, in which the ghost may appear visually and can be responsive to external conditions. These are the ghosts we (or some people) can see. These are the ghosts who seem to frequent certain sites and can at times be photographed as orbs or distortions in photographs. "We can get voices and at times communicate with them via ghost box or on tape," said Barbara. They're the ones she and Steve try to target, because they can communicate with them and resolve the issue, and help them cross. Sometimes they need a little help, and the help is basically light. Light, or energy, or prayer.

The second kind of haunting is one that seems to replay a scene or incident. It's like a tape on repeat. "It may be vocal as well, and we refer to these as 'residual' hauntings," said Barbara. "It's like they're in a time warp. They are not aware of any present-day observers. They're not there. Ghosts are not present. Instead, it's the energy pattern that is present. It's an energy pattern on loop. If I walk on a carpet around a circle for ten years, what you would have is a worn pattern in the carpet at that time. And it's very similar with energy."

There are hauntings, and there is the releasing of ghosts, which is what Barbara and Steve do. It's what we had done on the porch of my house, and it's what makes Barbara and Steve stand out from other ghost hunters, like the ones they are chaperoning tonight. While the members of the New England Ghost Club were out and about, Barbara and Steve would be babysitting them, but they'd simultaneously be releasing trapped spirits into, well, heaven.

By now, it was dark outside and time to turn off the lights inside the seminary. The ghost hunters had already formed into two groups—one cluster had lined up at the door and would head over to the former dorms of the school. The other group—the one led by Steve and Barbara— would stay in this main building.

"The third type of haunting," said Barbara, "is very rare and often debated." She slipped the ventriloquist dummies under her arms, their bulging eyes still peering out from behind her sleeve. "The third kind of haunting is the demonic, or inhuman. These may never have been human at all to begin with. I feel that these could be mostly inter-dimensional beings—their main goal is to break down the human spirit or free will. And usually these ones have to be invited in, which, many times, they will by accident, like when people are experimenting with ceremonies without proper protection."

"Which would we be doing today?" I asked, hoping for please-not-the-third.

"The first one," said Barbara, and flipped off the lights.

Our groups split up and ventured off. I made sure to stick close by (translation: cling to) Barbara and Steve. We'd take the stairs to the second floor, investigate the auditorium, and perhaps after that, the attic above it. On went the walkie-talkies. Off went some flashlights. I gripped the staircase banister and stood in line behind Steve.

"Don't forget to cut the ties when you leave," Barbara reminded the other group as they took off and out the door. "And do *not* go into trance in there."

Barbara turned to me. "Trance," she said, "is a very deep level, or really, deeper level of meditation." She glanced back at the group, which was now out of sight, and motioned in their direction. "But they didn't seem like the type that even knew how, right? Still, you can get an attachment this way." Barbara growled a little. "Do you think I say that because I have nothing better in the world to say? Why else would I be telling people to protect themselves all the time? It's because I don't want people to get hurt. I want them to have a good experience when they validate the continuation of life after death."

Cautiously, Barbara led us up the darkened stairwell. Of course the stairs creaked. Of course we tiptoed. Blindly, we rubbed the walls beside us with our hands, feeling our way up the stairs with our fingers until we reached the second floor. Barbara swung left and guided us into what was the auditorium, but with the lights out, it was a vast and airy obscurity, like we'd entered a black hole.

The group dispersed into the black room immediately, but Barbara and Steve hung back. They leaned on a big wooden table, and while our eyes slowly adjusted to the darkness, we listened as everyone else cased the joint like exterminators.

They were there for the thrill of the chase, to play with their equipment and to catch the ghosts in their act. They were there to hunt. And while they bungled around the dark room, poking and prodding with their gear and gadgets, eager to catch some ghouls, all Barbara had to do was look and listen. She didn't need the heat cam or laser grids or infrared motion sensor. Tonight she was chaperoning a group whose money, which they'd handed her at the beginning of the night, she would immediately donate to ParSem's restoration fund, but she didn't do this kind of thing generally for the cash. Beyond that, ultimately it seemed the sincerest motive that Barbara and Steve had in mind when mingling with the departed was more along the lines of an act of community service to the deceased: they were there to release trapped souls.

"Do not go to the attic alone, please," Barbara called out into the darkness.

"Sorry about that!" a voice apologized.

"There is an older gentleman up there and he will attach to you," Barbara explained. "He is disruptive, and he has pushed many people." Then she turned to me and said, "The younger spirits usually don't come out when he's out and about."

About ten, twelve minutes passed. Then fifteen. By now, my eyes had adjusted to the darkness a bit. I stood up and walked toward the

center of the room, toward the sounds of shuffling feet and little clicks
of plastic shutters. Suddenly, there was a loud noise. A voice.

"Business. Solo. Human."

The voice was piercing, monotone and sharp, and came from the
head of the room—the auditorium stage, maybe?—and it clearly did
not belong to a human.

"What the heck was that?" I barked, and reflexively gripped an arm
next to me, which happened to be Steve's.

"Business. Solo. Human," said the voice again. It sounded terrifying
and disgusting, like a demonic robot.

"That's the Ovilus," said Steve. "It just picked up on something." The
Ovilus, I'd learn just moments too late to prevent a near stroke, was a
piece of paranormal investigation equipment. Pocket-sized and pow-
ered by batteries, the gizmo was said to "convert environmental readings into words." A voice box for ghosts.

Rapidly, one of the lady hunters jumped onto the stage. She wore a
sexy babydoll dress, which was cut very high and showed off her legs,
which had striped stockings hiked to the middle of her thighs. Her top
was cut low and exposed her bosom, which had been hoisted up and
covered in red and silver glitter. I watched as the woman paced about,
waving around the gadget in her hand. Then she dropped to the floor,
kneeling down center stage, and with the seriousness of MacGyver she
took off her backpack, unzipped it, and pulled out a teddy bear. Unlike
everything else that was happening at the moment, the bear looked
typical, basic brown, and fuzzy. The woman set it down on the stage,
scooched herself back a foot or two behind the stuffed animal, and sat
cross-legged. She looked at the bear.

"Did you make it warm in here?" the woman asked.

Silence.

"I brought you a toy," she called out. "Would you like to play with my
bear?" But it wasn't just a bear, and it wasn't just a toy. It was a trigger
object.

Next, a barrage of questions. "Do you like my bear? What is your favorite color? Will you come talk with me? I'm a nice person. Don't be so shy. Won't you come play with me and my teddy bear?"

"Too much activity," Barbara mumbled under her breath. She was now standing next to Steve and me. "She's being too aggressive," she said, and then called out to the lady on the stage. "Just give it time. Don't force it."

But no one wanted to listen to Barbara's advice. All around the room the hunters were moving about zealously, pressing buttons and adjusting controls on their equipment, positing question after question, speaking in baby voices, a tone that only thinly veiled their desire, which was starting to skirt feverishness and impatience.

"They were just kids," Barbara said gently. "So they're going to be shy. We must be patient because they're afraid." She was getting frustrated, protective. "Any child who is a ghost will be like that. They don't know that we aren't ghosts. And they don't know why we're here, or who we are. So why should they trust you?"

Finally Barbara walked toward the stage, where, by now, all of the investigators had gathered and were interrogating the teddy bear. Calmly, Barbara suggested that the group climb down and try a different approach. Something softer. "One way to get through to the children," she explained, "is to tell stories, play games, sing songs. Those are things children resonate with. Something like 'Ring Around the Rosie.'" So that's what all of us did next—Steve, Barbara, me, the hunters, all of us holding hands and singing and skipping for a couple of rounds while the teddy bear remained silent.

After that, we checked out the attic. It was spooky, but no ghosts appeared. Too shy, said Barbara. And maybe the headmaster was nearby and lurking, guarding the ghost children.

Steve led us out of the auditorium, back downstairs and through the front doorway, where we spilled into the night. Next, we'd be cutting across the lawn and heading into the girls' dorm. Someone from the other team had radioed that they may have possibly picked up on something. It was approaching ten p.m.

As our group made its way across the dewy grass toward the old dormitories, Barbara slowed her speed until she, Steve, and I fell behind. It was intentional.

"You should go," she said, stopping in front of the shadow of a trunk of a wide tree in the middle of a vast lawn. Barbara placed her hand on my shoulder. "Home. You should go home. You're not going to see anything tonight except more of this kind of thing."

"What do you mean?" I asked.

"These spirits were Free Will Baptists," said Barbara. "They were a very religious sect. Do you think they're going to like seeing people walking around like that, practically naked?"

Barbara explained: the ladies of tonight's hunt were too scantily clad, the men too gruff. They were all too loud and pushy, their equipment intimidating. "The Free Will Baptists," she continued, "they were conservative. And this," she motioned to the group ahead, which had just reached the dorms, "this isn't what it was all about. So they're afraid to come out." To the other investigators, tonight was about thrills, about having goofy fun. The realness, explained Barbara, the important stuff could be found in the healing work, in the crossings that she and Steve did. Soul crossings. That was their true talent, their mission.

She lifted her hand off my shoulder and then placed it on the thick, knotty bark of the ancient tree. There the three of us stood in the open field, halfway between the dorm and the parking lot. Above us, the moon was round and brightened the sky. "We do more than just look for ghosts," said Barbara. "We are the way-showers. We are the keepers of the light."

CHAPTER 4

Rosabelle, Believe

At its peak in the early 1900s, there were more than
130 cottages for the summer community.

Barbara and Steve have a certain defensiveness around those who pay them to "hunt ghosts," as have many Spiritualists throughout history—a well-earned posture from a group that has come under attack for decades. "There will always be bad apples," was how Barbara put it. In the early 1900s, more and more people claimed to be connected to the spirit world; anyone could be a medium, and many people were.

By the start of the twentieth century, the role of mediums had shifted and morphed into a whole other spectacle—they weren't just leading séances at family dining tables, nor were they considered valiant women articulating their own personal truth on a public platform. Now when they stood on stages, it wasn't with the intention of defending their sex, nor was it so much an attempt at reforming or freeing the repressed. Spiritualists and their sitters were now focusing on the materializations of spirit rather than some secret wisdom of women.

"Initially, regular mediumship (like clairvoyance and clairaudience) was enough, but as adherents began demanding more and more proof, the pressure to produce phenomena for financial gain became a worrisome trend for Spiritualism as a religion," writes Rev. Todd Jay Leonard, PhD, a medium, Spiritualist, and Camp Etna alum, in his book *Talking to the Other Side*. Mediums were going headfirst into darker places: trance states, or literally stepping into closets. It was the beginning of sensational mediumship, where trumpets floated around a darkened séance room while candle flames danced and music played out of nowhere.

"Sitters in a séance who paid good money to see a deceased parent, aunt, uncle or grandparents appear to give a message became the norm; people not only wanted a message from the medium, they wanted to see, touch, and talk to the apparition." It was now all about sensationalism, with value placed more on seeing the mediums and less on believing them, which, in turn, ended up emphasizing women's passivity.

Some of the new Spiritualist practices (or acts, really) were downright humiliating—mediums being "gagged and blindfolded, or tied into a sack and nailed to the floor," just so audiences could be assured that whatever spirits did appear were not a hoax, and that the medium wasn't a magician or a fraud. Persecution followed, as did claims of witchcraft and charlatanism, sullying Spiritualism's legitimacy and deteriorating the safety of its practitioners.

Scores of researchers and teams of scientists followed, and independent gumshoes took to the parlor rooms, hoping to drain the swamp, as it were. In particular, one anti-Spiritualist crusader brought his investigations to our nation's capital and the Ninety-Sixth Congress in his quest to make mediums, and their religion, disappear.

The year was 1926. It was the year that brought the births of Harper Lee, John Coltrane, and Hugh Hefner and marked the passing of Annie Oakley and Robert Todd Lincoln. The first liquid-fuel rocket had been launched, out of Auburn, Massachusetts, and up into the air, and Henry Ford announced the forty-hour workweek. It was a time in history that brought about social naissances and electric creations: the invention of the first color television. The jukebox. The electric razor. The packaging of frozen foods.

It was the age of miracles, and there would be no going back. Instead, forward movement: the African American Great Migration and the thunderbolt of artistic, social, and intellectual black creativity that followed. The Harlem Renaissance. Miss Zora Neale Hurston. The great Alain LeRoy Locke. Duke Ellington. Langston Hughes and his "Weary Blues."

But still there were lynchings. Membership in the Ku Klux Klan had peaked at nearly 5 million members. Americans who could distracted themselves, as they always had and always would, now with the silver screen. Movie actors were elevated to a whole new level: celebrities. The year 1926 also introduced new kind of superhero: the athlete. There was Babe Ruth. Lou Gehrig. There was Frederick "Fritz" Pollard, one of the first African American players in the NFL (and the very first African American head coach). There was DeHart Hubbard, the first

African American to win a gold medal two years prior at the 1924 Paris Olympics. The long jump.

There was Prohibition and zoot suits. Al Capone and bootleg liquor. The ruling of the US Parcel Service (which, at that time, must have somehow made sense) that prohibited adults to send children via parcel post. There was the shipment of Hemingway, Zelda, and F. Scott Fitzgerald to Paris to roost beneath Gertrude's wing. It was all painful and terrible and beautiful and thunderous and you could call it modernity, but most refer to it as the Roaring Twenties. Among this swirling storm of energy and pursuit emerged a new way for women of the nation to be, a new type of feminism. It was the age of the flapper.

Hair: bobbed with bangs, perhaps a Marcel wave. Out went the constricting corset. Up went the hemlines. Makeup was painted on with abandon, elegant necks exposed, perhaps draped with a long thread of pearls or a feather boa, like snakes in the Garden of Eden. Boyish, sophisticated, and self-aware, the flappers of the 1920s utilized their bodies to redefine acceptable women's behavior. They danced, mimicking Josephine Baker. Arms flailing, hips grinding, kicking and dropping to the floor. They drank publicly. They were engaging in premarital sex. The new feminists of this era possessed different goals and methods from feminists of the late nineteenth and earlier twentieth century— they were less concerned with political parity and instead desired social equality, and they carved out for themselves the right to thoroughly *enjoy* themselves as much as the men did.

In the wake of the Great War, the dissolution of the women's movement and the suffragists had weakened women's influence on society. Now, women of this era faced fewer political choices and were being presented with social ones instead, perplexing alternatives over whether (and how) to present themselves as equal to men or as different from them—either deserving of special privileges and treatment as women, or entitled to the same rights, therefore the same treatment.

But still, in nearly all spheres of their lives—sexual, social, political, familial—the majority of American women held very few positions of power. "In the wake of the war and the disorder that came with it, much of American society now clung even more tightly to conservative nationalism and hierarchical gender norms—in particular, the white middle-class idea of a sexually discreet, monogamous marriage, with a passive female homemaker supporting a dominant male breadwinner— hoping to heal the wounds of the war and make the world they'd been used to feel stable again." The progressive social ideals of the flappers had not sunk in with most of mainstream America. These new feminists were considered by much of the country to be rebellious radicals, entertainment to watch not emulate, or were even considered a threat.

In Spiritualism, where at least 50 percent and up to 80 percent of practicing mediums were women, the opposite remained true. Like the flappers, Spiritualists of the Roaring Twenties had a platform centered less on political activism and more on the upheaval of restrictive gender norms. Refusing to settle for male domination remaining a way of life, the Spiritualists infiltrated the patriarchy, albeit a bit more discreetly than the flappers: during readings, and claiming spiritual inspiration, female mediums of the 1920s often urged their mostly female clients to avoid loveless marriages and divorce their abusive husbands, or stay in them but pursue extramarital relationships. By the end of the decade, in the United States and abroad, the religion of Spiritualism had reached its zenith: 14 million in faith.

And then, right around the time Margaret Sanger (birth control advocate and sex educator, an activist who would establish what eventually became Planned Parenthood) was giving a lecture on birth control to the women's auxiliary of the Ku Klux Klan in Silver Lake, New Jersey (which she referred to as "the weirdest experience" of her life), a small man with a large head and tiny hands was serving up a platter to the courts in Washington, DC, in an attempt to not only put an end to the advancement of Spiritualists but to silence them completely. The man: Harry Houdini.

Born in Budapest in 1874, Erik Weisz grew up to become a magician, escapologist, stuntman, aviator, actor, film producer, and superstar who traveled the world performing acts of trickery. He was ambitious and successful, and one of the highest-paid performers of the century. He was often recognized for his tag line *Will the wonders never cease?*—the cue that Houdini had reached the end of his magic trick. Born fourth of seven, Harry had always had a profound bond with his mother, Cecilia. It's been said that as an infant, whenever baby Erik would bellow, the instant Cecilia pressed him to her chest, her son would be immediately soothed into a silent calm. As Harry grew up (and grew more and more famous) he sent his mother letters without fail—*Greetings from Appleton, Wisconsin. Flying High at Digger's Rest, Australia. Safely escaped the belly of a whale carcass in Boston*—with Cecilia penning her son letters of encouragement in return. In his writings, Houdini referred to Cecilia as his "angel upon earth" and the "guiding beacon" of his life.

Houdini did marry. On June 22, 1894, and age twenty, Harry wed Wilhelmina "Bess" Beatrice Rhaner, a showgirl from one of his acts whom he privately called Rosabelle, plucked from the lyrics of a romantic waltz:

Rosabelle, sweet Rosabelle,
I love you more than I can tell,
O'er me you cast a spell,
I love you, my Rosabelle!

Nonetheless, Cecilia remained his number one. He bought her a home in Harlem and lavished her with gifts: on one occasion, he purchased a dress that had been made for the queen of England, had it tailored, and gifted it to his mother. Even into his adulthood, Cecilia dressed him, and it's been said that, every now and then, when he was an adult and needed to be calmed, Harry would sit in his mother's lap.

And then she died. It was 1913 and Houdini was thirty years old, giving a press conference in Copenhagen, Denmark, when he was handed a telegram. It was urgent: Cecilia had suffered a stroke. Instantly, he broke all of his contracts and upcoming performances in order to return to America as quickly as possible. Unfortunately that meant two weeks of transoceanic ship travel until his ship docked in the States. But it was too late, Harry's mother was already dead, and no magic trick could bring her back.

The magician was never the same. With a broken heart, Harry Houdini turned his grief into fuel. In some ways, it was good: Houdini became a proselytizer for a new holiday—Mother's Day—which was, in great thanks to him, formally established in 1914. At the same time, his acts grew increasingly wild and weird and seemed to have an undercurrent of sinister recklessness. Here was Houdini hanging upside down from skyscrapers in straightjackets. There he was nearly drowning himself in his "Chinese water torture" box, or burying himself alive. As time went by, Houdini grew increasingly dark, more taciturn, maybe a bit wicked, and it was during these years that he first began focusing his energy on studying psychics and mediums, to prove them to be frauds and expose their tricks. However, Houdini also made a pact with his wife, Bess, that when he died, he would try to make contact with her, if at all possible, from the other side. The two of them devised a secret code so that if he went before her, it would be Bess and Bess alone who could validate the legitimacy of whatever message might come through from the other side.

It was in 1920 that Houdini first met Sir Arthur Conan Doyle, most famous for stories of Sherlock Holmes. The two were an unlikely pair, two of the biggest celebrities of the time, both curious about each other's passions. In the wake of the death of his son Kingsley during the Great War, Doyle had become a pious believer in life after death and a zealous missionary of Spiritualism. While Houdini had sent Doyle some of his work—the results of his investigation, which included a debunking of several mediums that Doyle greatly admired—Doyle initially supported Houdini's sifting out the corrupt mediums; his new companion was just getting rid of those bad apples so that the sweetness of the true fruits could be realized.

In 1920, Houdini penned the book *Miracle Mongers and Their Methods: A Complete Exposé of the Modus Operandi of Fire Eaters, Heat Resisters, Poison Eaters, Venomous Reptile Defiers, Sword Swallowers, Human Ostriches, Strong Men, Etc.*, which contained his first printed declarations on the occult (which he referred to as "spiritism"):

> The great day of the Fire-eater—or, should I say, the day of the great Fire-eater—has passed. No longer does fashion flock to his doors, nor science study his wonders, and he must now seek a following in the gaping loiterers of the circus side-show, the pumpkin-and-prize-pig country fair, or the tawdry booth at Coney Island. The credulous, wonder-loving scientist, wringing from Nature her jealously guarded secrets, the knowledge of which benefits all mankind, he gravely follows that perennial Will-of-the-wisp, spiritism, and lays the flattering unction to his soul that the is investigating 'psychic phenomena' when in reality he is merely gazing with unseen eyes on the flimsy juggling of pseudo-mediums.

The next year, Doyle suggested that his friend Houdini join him in trying to contact his mother, Cecilia. One Sunday afternoon in June, while on a lecture tour throughout the United States, Doyle officially extended the offer and invited Houdini to join him and his wife, Jean, a self-proclaimed medium, in their room at the Ambassador hotel in Atlantic City. Houdini accepted.

"I was willing to believe, even wanted to believe," said Houdini later of the séance. "With a beating heart, I waited, hoping that I might feel once more the presence of my beloved mother," and that communicating with her would have "meant to me an easing of all pain that I had in my heart."

The séance commenced and Jean, who would attempt to deliver the message from the spirit world in the form of automatic writing, closed her eyes and went into trance, with her hand and the pen she held rapidly moving across the paper underneath them. *Thank God, thank God!*

At last I'm through, the message revealed. But as much as he wanted to, Houdini wasn't buying it. Houdini didn't just want evidence—he wanted facts. "My sainted mother could not write English and spoke broken English," declared Houdini. Her first language was Hungarian; Jean's writing was in completely formed English sentences, and this marked the beginning of the end of the notorious friendship between Doyle and Houdini. Soon after, and as if his life depended on it, Houdini fully plunged into a staunch crusade to bring an end to the practices of mediums and Spiritualism. "Vultures who prey on the bereaved," he called them. "Human leeches."

In the years that followed, Houdini's moments were a succession of campaigns—during tours, shows, and personal appearances to promote his films, the magician projected slides, photos, graphs, and elucidations breaking down how he believed the mediums were using trickery disguised as supernatural gifts. He'd attend séances, but undercover, and once he gathered what he felt was sufficient evidence of fraud, he would leap up, dramatically flinging off his disguise.

In April 1923, the book *A Magician Among Spirits* was published by Harper Brothers. Its authors: Harry Houdini and American writer C. M. Eddy Jr. (who, incidentally, was not credited for his part). The book's objective: a chronicling of Houdini's exploits during his campaign to discredit Spiritualist mediums. The manuscript topped off at 324 pages, with sixteen chapters, including "Slate Writing and Other Methods" and "Why Ectoplasm?" and "Spirit Photography," among others. Within the first few pages and just following a photograph of the towering Doyle and petite Houdini side by side and smiling, the book's dedication appears:

IN WORSHIPFUL HOMAGE I DEDICATE THIS BOOK TO THE MEMORY OF MY SAINTED MOTHER. IF GOD IN HIS INFINITE WISDOM EVER SENT AN ANGEL UPON EARTH IN HUMAN FORM IT WAS MY MOTHER.

On July 23, 1924, roughly two years and two months after the publication of the book, Houdini caught wind that an entourage of scientific investigators (that he himself had created, years ago, to catch fraudulent mediums) was preparing to endorse a medium, a woman dubbed "The Blonde Witch of Lime Street," and award her with $2,500 for being the real deal.

This so-called witch's name was Mina "Margery" Crandon. A charming flapper, mid-thirties, attractive and wealthy, Margery was one of the most well known and credible mediums in the country at the time, right up there with Mary Ann Scannell and Bright Eyes. After witnessing Margery during a séance in his London home, Sir Arthur Conan Doyle extended the invitation to Houdini's medium-debunking crew, which consisted of *Scientific American's* J. Malcolm Bird, psychologist William McDougall of Harvard, former MIT physicist Daniel Comstock, and two members of the Society of Psychical Research, Hereward Carrington and Walter Prince, to witness for themselves Margery's credibility. Upon extensive and countless examinations, the Boston team was just about ready to give Margery the money and the clout for verifiably demonstrating a "visual psychic manifestation," but once Houdini heard of this, he dropped his ropes and straightjacket and headed straight for Margery's séance to expose what he felt was trickery.

Traipsing up to the fourth-floor walkup in the sweltering heat and into the séance room at Boston's 10 Lime Street (Margery's residence), Houdini and his scientific panel took a seat. Margery did the same, on one side of a three-sided Chinese screen, and the demonstration began.

In no time, Houdini had jumped out of his chair, shouting, "I've got her!" breaking up the séance. "All fraud," he declared. "Every bit of it. One more sitting and I will be ready to expose *everything*."

Margery's defense came through the voice of the channeled spirit of her deceased brother, Walter. In a gruff man's voice, Margery lambasted Houdini right back: "Houdini, you goddamned son of a bitch," said Walter through Margery, "I put a curse on you now that will follow you for the rest of your short life."

Afterward, the committee remained hopelessly divided. Houdini held another séance. And another. And another. But the committee continued to remain conflicted. Even the *New York Times* was impartial about the whole thing: "Margery Passes All Psychic Tests, Scientists Find No Trickery in Scores of Séances with Boston Medium." But the resentful Houdini in his antipathy pressed on, his own magic quite familiar to the mediums he so despised, and on October 19, 1924, the day after a spirit lecture at the Ku Klux Klan Auditorium in Fort Worth, Texas, he published the pamphlet "Houdini Exposes the Tricks Used by Boston Medium Margery," hoping once and for all to expose this vexing woman.

Houdini declared that these séances were a form of legalized fraud (although he himself in his American manhood was now rich from performing magic tricks). He derided the sexual liberties of the mediums, calling the ladies immoral and "as low as one can imagine in a human being," and shunned sexual desire in them while simultaneously criticizing the way they looked. Houdini's antipathy toward the Spiritualist women of the Roaring Twenties was astounding, despite the fact that his own ways were uncomfortably like theirs.

Margery soldiered on as well. Her husband began inviting more and more disbelievers to their house to witness his wife's skill for themselves. But it all exhausted her. She reached the point—perhaps it happened not long after she was accused of emitting butchers' offal (which she said was ectoplasm) from her vagina—where Margery hit the bottle and began drinking excessively. But her supporters remained steadfast. Some offered to beat Houdini to a bloody pulp. Some took the more peaceful route of offering him prize money: $10,000 to a charity of his choice if he would only just see the light of the truth of Spiritualism. Houdini never would, and he was far from finished with his smear campaign. Then, in February 1926, with chaos in tow, Mr. Houdini took to Washington.

"I am an author; I am a psychic investigator for the scientific magazines of the world; and then I am a mysterious entertainer," Houdini professed as he identified himself to the Ninety-Sixth US Congress, which had gathered that day to discuss H.R. 8989, the cumbrously

Fifteen faces of dedicated Spiritualists from Camp Etna's past.

titled bill amending "Subchapter 5 of the Code of Law of the District of Columbia, as Amended to June 7, 1924, relating to Offences against Public Policy," authored by politician Sol Bloom, a former entertainment impresario and sheet-music publisher. Simply put: Houdini was there to testify for a bill that sought to make it a crime to be a psychic medium, and sought to make fortune-telling illegal and punishable by six months' incarceration and financial penalties.

While Spiritualism's female mediums and ministers had always claimed their religion was far-removed from magic tricks, Houdini insisted they were all the same, livid that the same people whose faith was a "curse . . . leaving in its wake a crowd of victims whose plight is frequently pathetic, sometimes ludicrous, oftener miserable and unfortunate, and who are always deluded," were now profiting off the nation's decision-makers who employed them for their own spiritual counsel.

The trial was a goat show. It lasted four days and was speckled with antics from the very beginning. For his first act, Houdini presented a telegram with a message written inside, demanding that one of the mediums in the audience read through the paper envelope and reveal what it said. The mediums remained unresponsive, and Houdini grew outraged. He declared that these mediums were stripping men of their masculinity, that the women posed a danger to the nation, and that Spiritualism encouraged sexual transgression.

"Do you know how many crimes have been committed in a dark room where a medium has one of the opposite sex in the room for hours?" Houdini vented, and then went on to add a racist component to his argument: "[If the medium] is a colored man, and he gets white women in there . . ."

But the mediums had done their own homework and came to the trial prepared. They'd been given a warning: prior to the hearing, Houdini had sent a woman named Rose Mackenberg (who was the chief of his team of undercover investigators) to rake through DC and find fraudulent mediums and psychics. Sympathizers—politicians, especially—had warned the mediums about Rose, so when it was time for the Spiritualist minister and medium Jane B. Coates and astrologer, tarot-card reader Madame Marcia Champney (who had been medium to the former First Lady Florence Harding and many DC politicians) to testify, they were more than ready.

When Coates took the stand, she did so with confidence and defended her practices as a matter of faith, as "prophecy, spiritual guidance, and advice are the very foundation of our religion," and appealed for protection under the First Amendment. She took on a pious attitude, charging that Houdini's attacks on her and her fellow mediums were disrespectful and unchivalrous and insisted that no fortune-telling had ever occurred in the White House or with any senators, making sure to compliment President Coolidge as a "great soul and a good Christian." She suggested that Houdini and his assistant were the only ones accusing the president of séances, and that "with his foul language and insinuations," Houdini was spreading rumors and undermining the nation's chief executive, and had put assistant Mackenberg in danger, practicing "black magic" on the woman and hypnotizing her. "She obeys him as in a trance," Coates declared, and suggested that her fellow woman Mackenberg switch teams and expose Houdini as the fraud. "He is in your power and you can ruin him," Coates told Mackenberg. She went on to end her statement: "This man Houdini, who speaks evil, sees evil, hears nothing but evil; who stands here in the midst of lawmakers and utters evils words against scientists . . . has been practicing trickery and fraud for so long that men are tricksters to him."

Next came Madame Marcia's defense, which was itself impressive with emotion, as "the talented political operative played to perfection the role of the simple, aggrieved woman." She suggested she was a simple, middle-class, traditionally conservative matron whose merit Houdini had attacked, a hardworking American woman. "I have never gone to school . . . I am too ill to be here . . . after being deserted by a husband with two little babies I had to earn a livelihood . . . I am earning bread and butter for a mother ninety-eight years old, and I have all I can do in my physical state." She reprimanded Houdini for calling the former First Lady, the late Florence Harding, a "degenerate or weak-minded imbecile" for consulting mediums, which reverberated with a committee that was already sensing that Houdini was liable to make intemperate attacks on honorable women. She pointed out the magician's Jewish identity, and how he had lied earlier in the trial when he claimed Wisconsin as his birthplace, which undermined his self-portrayal as a defender of American values. Now it was Houdini's character that was in question and on trial, not the Spiritualists'.

As the proceedings lumbered on, more emotional monologues sprung forth from congressmen, mediums, senators and their wives, detectives, and crystal-ball readers. Variations on themes of divorce intervention, sexual identity, gender norms, misogyny, ghosts, black-magic consultations, solipsism and enlightenment, evil, motherhood, family values, power, and religion—essentially all of the anxieties of the nation seemed to work their way into this trial. The switch had been flipped, and Houdini eventually had been put so thoroughly on the defensive that he brought in his own wife as a witness "in an effort to reestablish his masculine authority by demonstrating the gender hierarchy of his marriage." He presented Bess to testify as a docile and submissive woman, as if this would win over those sitting at the head of the courts. While the gallery by now was quite entertained by Houdini's fracas, and in an attempt to appease his masculine pride, Houdini pressed on, "asking his 'girl' to affirm monosyllabically that he was 'not brutal to [her] or vile,' or 'crazy, unless it was about [her],' and awkwardly, that he was 'a good boy' and then summarily dismissed her from the witness stand."

At one point, Houdini was punched in the face. One politician became so dizzied by the rumpus that he fainted. Police were called. National newspapers covered the story. Eventually, in the last frigid days of February 1926, the four-day trial came to an end. The bill had collapsed.

Months later, August of that same year, as Margery Crandon continued her practice and channeled the spirit of her dead brother Walter, she declared grimly and confidently: Houdini had "but one more year to live" and would be gone by Halloween.

Come October 22 of that year, Houdini traveled to Montreal, Canada. Reposing on a couch before one of his acts, he chatted with three fans—students from McGill University.

"Would you mind if I delivered a few blows to your abdomen?" asked one of the students, who had heard that Houdini had boasted of rock-hard abs. So yes, of course, Houdini accepted the young man's challenge—a punch to the gut.

Later that evening, after his performance, Houdini was unable to dress himself. He was experiencing severe stomach pains, but even with a temperature of 104, he continued on to the next show—this time in Detroit, Michigan. After finishing act one, Houdini collapsed. He was revived and insisted on performing the rest of the show, but collapsed again. On October 25, Houdini finally agreed to be taken to Grace

Hospital, where he was found to have a ruptured appendix and peritonitis. But it was too late—the sepsis had taken over his system. Up until his very end, Houdini battled it out, but on Sunday, October 31, 1926, the great magician finally let go. "I can't fight anymore," Houdini told his brother by his bedside, and died at 1:26 p.m. Halloween.

Bess didn't break her promise. Soon after Houdini's death, his widow started holding "Houdini Séances" to see if he really could come back. She consulted with mediums, offering $10,000 to anyone who could help her make contact with her late husband. Many tried to bring him forward, but with no true success. On October 31, 1936, ten years after Houdini's death and before giving up her attempts for good, Bess decided to give it one last try. Her location of choice: Hollywood, California.

"This is a Houdini night," announced Edward Saint, the man who would be leading the evening's séance, at the beginning of the spectacle. Saint was also Bess's business partner, manager, significant other—or said-to-be secret husband—and a former carnival barker. He was not a certified medium. "With the spotlight of the public on Houdini; with the whole world paused to see or hear Houdini step on this side of the curtain."

The evening's performance was to be broadcast around the world—a mega-séance, if you will. Two more widows of two other famous dead magicians (the late Howard Thurston and the late Charles Joseph Carter) would also participate, and the event was to be held on the rooftop of the Hollywood Knickerbocker Hotel on Ivar Street, just off Hollywood Boulevard.

"Now that Houdini, Carter, and Thurston have joined forces on the other side of the grave," announced Bess, "I am going to make, here in Hollywood, the one supreme effort to contact these great magicians and maybe together one of them may 'come through.'" There were more than three hundred people in attendance that night, sitting in bleachers and facing the séance table, upon which a few items were placed: a bell, a spirit trumpet, and Houdini's famous Mirror Hand-cuffs interlocked with another pair of cuffs. This was the "Houdini Shrine," and above it hung a glowing red lightbulb as well as a portrait of the late great magician. The ceremony began at eight thirty at night, and was described in *Goldston's Magical Quarterly* as such:

> A majestic march emanating from the concealed speakers of a powerful public address system broke the silence—all lights on the roof were extinguished except the ruby light over the shrine—the members of the inner circle rise to their feet—the assemblage does likewise—all standing at attention while the little widow, Mrs. Beatrice Houdini was ushered to her place and seated by her manager, Edward Saint, a life-long friend, who then took his place, the music died down and all reseated themselves and then—silence—hushed almost oppressive hopeful silence.

Time stretched like rubber as Saint desperately tried to entice the great Harry Houdini to step forward, to emerge, give some kind of sign, make some kind of contact, but to no avail.

"Dr. Saint spoke, his voice rising to a mad, sobbing pitch. Sobs could be heard too from some of the friends in the audience." Another news-paper reported that the sound of a saxophone could be heard "sobbing" from the street below. Eventually, the night would come to a close, with the following dialogue broadcasting around the world:

Saint: Mrs. Houdini. The zero hour has passed. The ten years are up. Have you reached a decision?

Bess: Yes. Houdini did not come through. My last hope is gone. I do not believe that Houdini can come back to me, or to anyone. After faithfully following through the Houdini ten-year compact, after using every type of medium and séance, it is now my personal and positive belief that spirit communication in any form is impossible.

I do not believe that ghosts or spirits exist. The Houdini shrine has burned for ten years. I now reverently turn out the light. It is finished. Good night, Harry.

In the end, Bess Houdini closed the doors of the Houdini shrine, shut off the red light above it, and left the rooftop with Edward Saint. Seconds later, the temperature cooled and what had been, minutes prior, a very clear sky suddenly erupted with a torrential downpour, inundating the dedicated spectators still left lingering on the bleachers.

In the eyes of his widow, Houdini had not come through. Their pact had been taken to the grave but had not been fulfilled, and this spectacular séance marked the end of Bess's decade of attempts at contacting her deceased husband. It was time for her to move on. "Ten years is long enough to wait for a man," Bess declared at the end of the night.

But what was the secret code from the great beyond that Bess had been waiting all those years to hear? The puzzle of ten words for his sweetheart that Harry created, and that, once decoded, spelled out what Harry never did: *Rosabelle, believe.*

CHAPTER 5

Loyalty Lodge

Kelly Dawn Purington, a psychic medium, practices
table tipping—an old method of channeling spirits—
inside the Gladys Laliberte Temple. *Greta Rybus*

Deep in the dusky hollows, a tree root was rotting, providing nutrients and shelter for the ground beetles beneath it. The soil was clammy and soft as I faced Arlene Grant, and she, me. It was June and unusually hot outside; the muggy air felt like a warm, wet blanket draped over the shoulders of anyone who dared venture outdoors, but it was safe in the shade.

The property of Arlene Grant and her cottage, "Loyalty Lodge," was planted in a spectral spot on the southwest side of Camp Etna, just behind the temple, covered in an awning of grand oak leaves, black ash, and balsam, and tucked into Packard Square like a secret.

"Houdini was good for Spiritualism," cracked Ms. Grant, and she gritted her teeth while holding open the aluminum porch door of her home, not yet inviting me in. "What happened in the 1920s is that they cut out a lot of fucking bullshit."

Gone but not forgotten, Houdini and his highly publicized pursuits had left a mark on Spiritualism and tarnished the reputation of mediums. But it hadn't killed the religion, nor had the summer retreats been wiped out either. Rather than fold, Spiritualist churches and summer camps changed their operations almost entirely.

"As the twentieth century unfolded, American Spiritualism . . . emphasized stasis, issuing formal creedal statements of belief and eclipsing its own eccentric and theologically innovative past," writes Dr. Darryl V. Caterine in his book *Haunted Ground*. "As I continue to peruse the brochures [of sister Spiritualist camp Lily Dale] I see a clear transformation in the 1930s: the camp becomes more 'serious.' Gone are the advertisements for the old bowling alley and Ferris wheel and promises to visitors of the health-restoring properties of its well waters."

Come 1940, the National Spiritualist Association went ahead and banned the practice of physical mediumship, and Spiritualism got to taking herself much, much more seriously.

In the wake of Houdini, the Spiritualist movement had been knocked off its feet, and anything that could render the religion duplicitous was, for the most part, set aside. Table tipping: gone. Floating trumpets: gone. Spirit photography and planchette: removed, or at least removed from the main frame of the picture. Mediums moved away from automatic writing, automatic painting, ectoplasmic proof, writing on the skin, and levitation as spirit communication went from external to internal. Major damage had been done, marking the end of a time that would come to be known as the Era of Great Mediums.

A low breeze brushed my cheek then swept Arlene's short silver hair over her left eyebrow. The wind had a familiar yet distant scent: campfires, marsh water, burnt Folgers, damp socks. I had just walked over to Loyalty Lodge after a serene and air-conditioned visit with Barbara, Steve, Angel, and Spirit at Peacefull Solitude. Barbara had given me a personal lecture about soul protection, emphasizing a simple practice that was vital for mediums, and all humans for that matter (but that many tended to forget or skip) of keeping away negative energies, not letting one's self absorb them unaware. She stressed the importance of prayer that must accompany power, of psychic self-protection, of meditation and grounding and centering. That kind of thing. Just as our chat had ended and I was feeling fresh and light and sparkling heading out the door, Barbara austerely instructed me to never forget to say my White Light Prayer—to envision myself surrounded by the brightest light and the best and highest of energies—and to always be generous with my tree-touching when on campus. *Just press your palms against a tree*, she'd said. *It'll absorb all your negative energy and zoom it into the ground, rendering it harmless.* Barbara explained that one had to keep their ego in check, especially here on the grounds of Camp Etna, where there was such a strong current of power running through. *Psychic self-protection*, Barbara called it. She'd even written a book on it. Before I stepped out her door, Barbara had also told me that I was a bit of an empath myself. Being an open soul like that made a person vulnerable, she'd said, which made it even more vital that she protect herself.

"Well, shit. Come in if you want," said Arlene, sounding both vexed and coy. She was a medium-sized woman, both in height and in width, about seventy years old, modest, wearing no makeup, her hair chopped off. Her face was quite pretty, her eyes hesitant. She wore a housedress that swayed a little as she strode ahead. Right before her porch door slammed shut, I caught it and followed Arlene into the house as she lowered herself slowly into a leather recliner then muted the television. *Judge Judy.*

Arlene Grant was a bit of a Camp Etna national treasure because she was one of the last of the living "old-school" mediums there, one of the few who had been trained by the last of the living from the Era of Great Mediums of the 1920s and one of the few who conserved their wisdom and teachings. Arlene Grant was priceless—a relic of the past, of a bygone era of Spiritualism, a particular time period of teachers, a particular generation. Arlene was one of maybe two or three of the Spiritualists who had arrived at camp in the 1960s and stayed (the other being Cathymac, who now resided in Massachusetts), and she was one of just two mediums who still lived at camp year-round, the other being Katie Dobbins, who I'd been told was another talented medium, living legend, and shut-in, and was suffering from late-stage cancer. Unlike Katie, who worked from her couch for a psychic hotline, Arlene hadn't been practicing her mediumship for quite some time—decades, even. Like Katie, Arlene had become a bit of a shut-in, closed off entirely from the hubbub of the community and the summer activities at the camp. Within a year's time, Katie would die and Arlene Grant would be the very last living and breathing year-round elder of Camp Etna. Whether she'd preserve the wisdom of her foremothers—pass it down to a new generation of mediums to keep alive—was yet to be decided, but it wasn't looking good.

"Sit down," said Arlene, squinting at me, kneecaps exposed from under her dress. I sat down as instructed, looked up, and scanned the room. Photographs of Arlene's past hung proudly on the brown wall, vertical wooden panels the color of a deer's thigh. Once, Arlene had been a redhead, skin like a nectarine, exceptionally gorgeous. From the family pictures, I could also see that she was a mother, possibly a grandmother. In one photo, I recognized the younger version of one particular man: the tall, mysterious person from the Camp Etna board meeting way back in the winter. Dwight Grant, the lanky, taciturn drum maker better known as Duey. Underneath the carpeted stairs going up to the second floor of Loyalty Lodge, two framed certifications. One appeared to be perhaps a Reiki accreditation. The other I couldn't quite make out, other than the two words that ran across the top of the paper: *Morris Pratt.*

"What the hell do you want to know about this place?" asked Arlene, and I answered her with my first question: how had she ended up here to begin with?

"Oh God." Arlene cackled. "Good Lord almighty. How did I end up here? I married a fucking Indian, that's how."

Arlene Grant was born in Brooklyn, New York, and spent a good part of her youth living on Knickerbocker Avenue and Decatur in a four-bedroom railroad flat, not far from where I had lived ten years ago as a broke young artist during my own stint in the city. I told Arlene that I found it interesting how that part of Brooklyn had changed significantly in the past ten years. How a place white people once pretended didn't exist had now made it impossibly expensive for the people who had lived there all along to remain.

"Two windows in the front and two windows in the back, a railroad tenement," she sneered. "Now, you tell me, how the hell do you gentrify those things?" Arlene's father grew up on the same corner in Brooklyn, and her mother was from Williamsburg. She was their only child.

"Then one day, this Indian gets off the bus in Manhattan." Arlene laughed, scratching both elbows. "I didn't know he was an Indian. I had no idea what the hell he was." Arlene bent down and picked up a plastic bottle of Poland Spring from the floor, pressed it to her lips, and took a swig. "So the Indian asks me a question, and one thing led to another . . . but that's neither here nor there. Anywho, I figured I'd never see him again—he went to Vietnam."

Outside, an engine roared then sputtered. A hammer clanked, followed by a pause. Then, a mass of bluish-black exhaust appeared from behind an oak tree.

"That's him," said Arlene, motioning to the cloud of smoke outdoors. "The fucking Indian."

Outside, Duey was fixing up a motor home or camper of some sort for their next road trip. I couldn't get a straight answer on whether they were still married or had divorced—they lived in separate cottages now but spend plenty of time together, just the two of them plus their two dogs. Plenty of motorcycle trips, long and short—to Florida, to church, to powwows across the nation, to the bank. It was vital to get off the twenty-seven acres whenever they could, especially after being here for so many years, particularly as the few hardy souls who braved the solitude, the unforgiving low temps, and the wilderness-like atmosphere that a winter in Maine brings.

Arlene folded one knee up into her reclining chair and leaned onto it. I sat back onto the couch, too, and then, out of nowhere, a tiny black dog jumped into my lap, something that seemed to happen in nearly every cottage that I visited at camp. He was a squirt of a dog—a mutt; something like a mix of a Chihuahua and possibly vampire bat. Black, silky, and a little crooked. Old, with failing eyesight—his pupils were a cloudy, hazy white, like a lychee fruit.

"That's Macklemore." Arlene smiled big. "The Terror of Tiny Town."

Macklemore purred and licked my hand, snuggling into my lap like I was no stranger.

"Careful though," said Arlene. "He can be a little fuck." She said she'd rescued him from a puppy mill in Florida, and as I stroked Macklemore's corn-chip-shaped ear, I pictured Arlene and Duey driving down the highway on their Harleys, zooming out of a biker bar in Tallahassee or Miami or Destin with little Macklemore in a sidecar down below, wearing a little chin-strapped helmet fashioned out of a coconut shell.

A loud pop from outside—perhaps the engine backfiring—shocked me back to the present, but Arlene was unmoved. With her left hand, she pointed to the window without breaking eye contact with me. "And then this asshole turns up again." Beyond the windowpane and among the chestnuts, there was no sight of her partner. "You see," said Arlene, "Duey's like a bad penny—he always turns up. Back and forth and back and forth."

Just then, the front door opened and the bad penny lumbered in. His body was long and lengthily proportioned, as if he'd been stretched out to tower above the pines. He wore steel-toe boots and burlap pants, had a wiry beard and long hair, gray, white, and bristled like steel wool, and underneath it all, a face that was the spitting image of an older Fred Gwynne (*The Munsters*; *Pet Sematary*; *Car 54, Where Are You?*).

"What'd I tell ya?" Arlene sneezed. "A motherfucking bad penny!"

In long strides, Duey walked past us, saying nothing, and stepped into the dining room, where he hovered over a rat's nest of envelopes on the table.

"Don't forget to cash those checks, ya hear?" said Arlene, to which he responded with a simple "Ayup." After a few seconds, Duey turned and walked back toward the porch door, and just before opening the door and leaving the cottage entirely, he pivoted, poked his head out, and looked at me. "Arlene left me at a gas station once, she did. Down in Florida. For no good reason, she just drove away and left me stranded theyah." His tone was completely unbothered, unrushed.

Arlene shot back. "Because he was taking too long! Listen, honey," she said to me, "we'd been driving halfway through the country. Duey is seventy-four years old and slower than shit going uphill. He was driving me fuckin' crazy, because I move faster than him. So, I left him theyah." And with that, Duey went back outside while Arlene looped right back into the story of her introduction to Camp Etna.

Arlene was sixteen when she first met Duey, and it was quick. Not long afterward, she got pregnant (not Duey's) and had her first child. Unlike her Irish Catholic parents, Arlene was unmarried and a self-proclaimed flower child, an active protester against the Vietnam War. "So I moved to Greenwich Village with my kid," she said, "and was

working at the [antinuclear organization] Clamshell and getting pro-
testers into Canada. We wandered. Me and my kid migrated from commune to commune. I marched in the civil rights protest with MLK. I
marched in Mississippi and the March on Washington." Arlene sighed
as if it were insignificant. "I was in all of that shit, too. But that's neither
here nor there."

But Arlene was wrong—it wasn't neither here nor there; it was
precisely right. What the young Arlene had left her home to take
part in was an awakening—a movement of young people that shook
up the country and cracked it wide open to a new era of spirituality,
and it was just what brought Arlene to where she sat today, in addition to "marrying a fucking Indian." After two world wars, Vietnam
had become the accidental architect for an overwhelming need for
change in the United States, and a new movement was birthed—the
counterculture; the hippies. Their goal: peace, love, freedom, and
an evolution of consciousness. Arlene had caught onto that longing and was searching too. Like her comrades, Arlene looked away
from Western values, the capitalist politics and the conservative
churches they'd been raised in and instead, looked to the East for
other options and practices. This resulted in a plethora of transcen-
dent programs for the counterculture movement to dabble in: Hin-
duism. Buddhism. Native American Mysticism. With these belief
systems newly added to the menu came sides of gurus, new leaders to teach these imported practices, ranging from meditation to
yoga to energy work. On top of that, many hippies sought to expand
their pilgrimage through the use of psychedelic drugs, which they
believed would transcend what their eyes could see and help them
discover the truth of life itself. And this is where Arlene differed.
While she believed in many of the thought processes of Eastern philosophy, she'd already grown up seeing beyond what met the human
eye. She didn't need LSD to take her to a new level; none of this was
new to her. Arlene wasn't looking for a new leader—in Spiritualism,
the medium was the messenger. Arlene didn't need a guru just like

Despite the changing of hands and ownership,
Loyalty Lodge has always kept its name. *Mira Ptacin*

she hadn't needed a priest. She was just looking to find her people,
a timeless group rather than a new-fangled experiment. So when
the enormous influx of hippies flocked to new counterculture communes dabbling in esoteric and free-love practices, Arlene ended up
splitting from that path and took a road back to the old-school. This
map led her to Camp Etna.

"So, finally," said Arlene, "the Indian comes back after two tours of
the Vietnam War." Duey lived on an Indian reservation in Maine, so on

a lark, Arlene and her offspring moved up there with him. Soon after this, she found Temple Heights, a Spiritualist church. It was a friend at Temple Heights who told her about the nearby Camp Etna, and in no time Arlene, with her young family in tow, joined the camp community.

I pictured a younger Arlene, her magnificent flock of ginger hair, cloistered with a gaggle of half-hippie, half-pioneer women, and their community, how it must've looked a bit like Woodstock and a bit like *Little House on the Prairie*—something more bustling but less modern than the empty cottages and barren grounds of today. I thought about how the Camp Etna of Arlene's earlier years must have been a good fit for the appealing things she had been looking for in new movements of the 1960s—women's lib, world peace, experimentations with free love and self-direction. An era that encouraged self-guidance, communal living, meditation, a close relationship with nature and the environment, and feminism. Plus, women could finally wear jeans.

When Arlene arrived, the community at Camp Etna was prosperous, and had been running smoothly for decades. Unlike the new hippie communes, the Spiritualist camps like Etna, Lily Dale, Camp Chesterfield, Wonewoc, and Cassadaga, to name a few, had an order to them. Elders were in abundance, herding in their families, passing along antique secrets and ancient lore, bringing in new members. In response to Houdini and other investigators, as well as any fraudulence that surfaced, Spiritualism had toned down her majesty and performance in general, and the community was now focusing on its core values rather than the spectacle and entertainment that had taken over its identity. By the time Arlene arrived at camp, the practice of mental mediumship, the more subjective of the two forms of mediumship, was now the preferred skill set for mediums to master, both at Camp Etna and nationally. At the camps, and within the religion, the central focus of mediumship was on healing the heart and the community, and communication with spirits. It was less about experimentation and more about nurturing what was timeless and had always been a part of their Spiritualist practices. Drugs were not allowed. Talking to the dead took precedence.

"It was a good place for me. A place to live. It was a good place for Duey too."

When she said this, Arlene immediately brought me back to Diane's historical tour, to her earnest lecture and the Crayola marker–outlined chart of important dates, and how Diane had stressed, strongly and emphatically, that Spiritualism began with the Native Americans, that they were the original mystics.

"We had several Native Americans here then," said Arlene, reminiscing. "George Paul—he lived up on Bishop's Row," she continued, motioning to the wall behind me. "George Paul was a Micmac. We had Al Dana. Al Dana was a Penobscot."

Arlene stretched out her arms in front of her then pressed them down into the arms of her chair, "This place started before the Spiritualist movement way back, because these were Indian hunting and fishing grounds. The tribes would migrate, stay here in the winter, and then they'd migrate someplace else in the summer. Depending where the deer is, the huntin' is, the turkey is. They're still nomads, the ones that are still around. At one point, the whole East Coast was Algonquians, but they don't exist anymore."

Arlene said this: the land had always belonged to the natives, and then the white man came and screwed it all up. Ages ago, she explained, there was a banding together of five Algonquian language–speaking tribes, which was called the Wabanaki Confederacy—a name that translated to "People of the First Light" or "Dawnland" because they were the first to meet the sun's rays when it hit the East Coast in the morning, and were said to be the first to have encountered the Europeans when they arrived in Maine in the sixteenth century.

The tribes: the Mi'kmaq, Maliseet, Passamaquoddy, Penobscot and Abenaki. Their territory: present-day Maine, New Hampshire, Vermont, and Massachusetts, as well as mainland Nova Scotia, Prince Edward Island, New Brunswick, Cape Breton Island, and parts of Quebec south of the St. Lawrence River. The Wabanaki Confederacy was disbanded in 1862, yet the five Wabanaki nations still exist and remain closely aligned. All but the Abenaki now reside in Maine.

"Now," said Arlene, "we got four tribes in Maine but we got five reservations. The Passamaquoddy got two reservations. One is on Route 1: Pleasant Point Reservation. The other is Baileyville." She went on to state her point that since the colonizers arrived in Maine, Native Americans have been treated as second-class citizens, if not less.

"Indians were always here," I said, restating her point.

"Yeah, that's what I'm sayin'," said Arlene. "The Indians were always here. This land was one of their places. It was Penobscot before and during Buswell's Farm. They stayed down by the pond, by Etna Pond. They camped down there. This was their place! This is their land! This land is very magic, and it's very sacred," she said, and Barbara's words popped into my head again—the residual energy, the power of this place, her emphasis on psychic self-protection—as did all the similar words the mediums of camp had said before: that these grounds were special—there was something electric about it. Coming to Camp Etna took you to a place like The Twilight Zone, a place where time stood still. "This is a magical place, but it is also a dangerous place," I'd been told, and that if you didn't protect yourself—your energy or your ego—it could destroy you.

"There are times you can hear them, even now," said Arlene. "You can hear the drumming. You can hear the singing. They're still here. They're very obvious. And they're sacred. Their spirits are still here."

"What about Duey?" I asked.

"He's sober now."

"No, what I meant was, as a Native American, what does Duey think of Spiritualism?" I asked.

"Well," said Arlene, "for one, the Indians do not believe in funeral parlors. If you don't love your people then you take them there, because you have so many hours for viewing and then the body is all alone. It shouldn't be alone! The Indians believe there are three days for when the spirit is leaving the body to go to the spirit world. You've got those three days. From the time the body comes home, they're laid out at home, they start the ceremonial fire and cannot go out until the body goes to the cemetery, and that sacred fire stays lit and maintained by fire keepers for twenty-four hours and cannot go out until it goes to the cemetery!" Arlene coughed and wrung her hands. She seemed slightly bothered. "But that's neither here nor there. *My point is,* the Indians were here long before me, and it was an Indian who brought me to Camp Etna."

In the 1960s, long before she knew this place inside and out, when she was a young woman with a head full of fiery hair and limitless ideas, Arlene Grant (and company) walked through the gate of Camp Etna for the very first time. This is what she may have seen: a sunny, fresh, dancing colony full of people like her, women like her who saw things as she did, who had come from all over to this place that finally felt like home, a place where they'd finally be able to live their new lives as simply and deeply as a haiku. The convivial atmosphere of Spiritualist camp had been dismantled, and in its place was a calmer, more utopian environment. When Arlene arrived, the community at Camp Etna was prosperous.

"Here's how things used to be," Arlene said, speaking fondly. She held up her index finger. "First of all, unlike *now,* where we're open the entire summer, we were only open during the month of August every year." She shifted in her seat and shook her finger toward me. "We had a medium of the week, OK? And we had four weeks, OK? So we had four mediums of the week. You got that?"

I did.

Arlene continued. In addition to the church services, Spiritualist camps and communities had (and still have) "lyceums" (Greek for "place of conversation"), which are the educational wings of their communities. Within the lyceum at Camp Etna, the community would engage in classes on Spiritualist history or the meaning of the Spiritualist principles; they'd listen to lectures from guest speakers and visiting mediums. Campers would practice their mediumship in regular meetings of "development circles" and engage in meditation and energy work, to connect with the dead, with one another, and with their spirit guides. In a nutshell, the main focus of campers was on energy and vibration, with the camp's teachings centered on intuition, in all the shapes and forms that she took.

Arlene's arms were lean and her hands were strong, but they were also a bit nodular and twisted, gnarled and a little cupped, as if she were holding an invisible handgun. I looked at them, and the instant Arlene noticed me noticing her swollen knuckles and tensed fingers, she looked into my eyes then quickly looked away, turning her body away with her.

"We had a class here one night, I'll never forget it," she said, crossing her arms over her chest and sliding her hands under her armpits. "We were over on Dover Street, and the medium of the week said, 'We are going to do an experiment.' She had two folding tables, and you get two chairs. You cover the table with a black cloth. The medium would have a person sit on either side. You put the lights out. Then we started using energy, working with our energy, putting our hands on the table, the other person would do the same, and you'd be a certain distance apart, you concentrate your energy, you draw your energy, and all of a sudden you see the sparks going back and forth . . ."

Arlene laughed. "As it turns out, Duey was walking around outside at this very same time too. He was up near the restaurant and went down to sit on an Adirondack chair facing the temple. And the temple was all dark, but he could hear the bell tower with the ding-dong upstairs . . . *Ding-dong! Ding-dong!* Back and forth back and forth. And when we came out of the temple, Duey was just sitting there and he says to us, '*What the hell are you doing in there?! I'm sitting out here and the damn bell tower is going up and down up and down over the building!*' It wasn't just dinging. It was *levitating.* We were literally moving the whole bell tower! Moving it! The entire thing! There was so much energy being generated inside the building that the bell tower was going up and down, up and down. *Ding-dong! Ding-dong!*"

Arlene laughed again, this time a little wildly. Then she steadied her breath again. "That's why they have classes. We didn't know what we were doing. And you gotta train your mind to pull it in, draw in that energy."

"You gotta train your mind," I repeated.

"Back in the 1960s," said Arlene, motioning with her eyebrows to the barren patch of gravel beyond her window, "there'd be three hundred cars in the parking lot. They came from all over, honey. The place was *packed*. We had cottages all the way to the pond, hundreds. Everybody— all the great old-time mediums, all of them—everybody served there."

Arlene quieted and smiled for several beats, seemingly lost in a memory. "And *then*," Arlene cried, "on Saturday night the restaurant was closed because they had Saturday-night supper put on by the Ladies' Auxiliary instead. And I tell you, it was jam-fucking-packed! Everyone! From all over! Was invited! Truckers! Town folk, you name it! We served boiled dinners—turkey. Pot roast! We used to have two to three settings, maybe more! It used to be five bucks and we made *moneyyyy*."

Arlene rubbed her fingers together, then placed them on her stomach. "I mean, you know, what the fuck," she said. "Loretta used to run the restaurant—Loretta Fairjohn. She was the kitchen cook and a fantastic medium. Her parents lived in Little Enchanted Cottage. Loretta's mother was a fantastic healer—she'd just put your hand on an open wound and it would go away. But yeah, Loretta. She baked the best goddamn homemade pies. She was the best goddamn trance medium who baked the best goddamn pies."

A trance medium is an example of mental mediumship, the kind that wasn't banned by the NSAC, and that was being practiced at camp in the 1960s. A trance medium is one who goes into a meditative state, which would then enable the spirit (the dead person) to regulate the medium's mind and body to speak through her; the spirit of the dead person would "blend with the medium's aura and subconscious mind and speak through the human . . . the medium must speed up their frequency, and the spirit communicator must slow theirs down, in order for them to be able to link and develop a mutual platform for communication."

Take, for example, the well-known, still-living trance medium Elaine Thorpe, a soft-faced British woman, perhaps fifty years of age, with a gentle voice and cantaloupe-colored hair in the shape of a lion's mane, a calming face, pâté-toned with two pink cheeks and thinly drawn chestnut eyebrows, completely nonthreatening. In once particular You-Tube video—an interview—just before Elaine did a live trance demonstration, she explained what happened and how it felt when her spirit guide, Jonathan, "blended" with her as they went into trance together:

> You start relaxing, you see pictures in your mind. I start off and ask for protection, and then I ask for the spirit or the guide to come to me. When you start to relax, you feel him stepping in from the back, a slight chill down the back. You can feel the blending, you can feel his face blending in over yours, you can feel all his stature coming in, all his energy. And he'll say to my mind, "Are you ready?" and I'll say through my mind, "Yes, I am."

Elaine's regular voice was what could be identified as a woman's voice—not exactly high-pitched, but feathery, dainty, soothing. When she explained herself and how trance works for her, she did so straightforwardly, without much emotion. Elaine explained that she has some "regulars"—spirits who come through her during trace—sometimes it was her twin sister, who had passed away, sometimes it'd be a spirit named Gray Wolf. But most often, she worked closely with a spirit guide named Jonathan James Hunter, born in Britain in 1845 (whom she'd gone on to research, track down, and apparently—or supposedly—verify).

> So he waits until I'm ready, he asks, and then we'll go ahead and he'll start to speak. It [feels] sort of like I'm sitting in my own body and he's sitting in it as well. You're in the background and you're

listening to his conversations, like I've gone drowsy and his head is up here and I'm down here. It feels rather strange because you feel very drowsy but you can still listen to his voice, but it's above your head.

About fifty minutes into the interview, Elaine closed her eyes, relaxed, took a deep breath, and within several minutes, her face became a bit animated, yet her eyes remain closed, and then, she spoke to the interviewer: *"Good evening my dear, and how might you be, dear lady? How might you be?"* And just like that, Jonathan James Hunter had arrived. He spoke in a low voice, a deeper tone, instantly. *"I have looked forward to this, and I have been waiting in the wings . . ."* As I was watching the fair Elaine's face on my screen, her body's movements and mannerisms had absolutely changed into something more animated, and she'd assumed the role of what seemed to be a confident, amused man. But what was most remarkable was how instantly, how seamlessly and apparently effortlessly her voice had dropped into a deep, utterly baritone voice. *"I gradually learned to blend with the vocal cords* [of Elaine]," he said, *"and we got used to each other."* Whatever was happening, I stopped seeing Elaine and instead was picturing some guy sitting down on a couch smoking a cigar, jovially carrying on a conversation. I found more videos. In one in particular, Jonathan, in his low, smoker's voice, spoke of heaven: *"You don't have a physical mind but you are still able to think. When you first get in the spirit world, you think of something and it is there. You have to learn to control yourself . . . you have complete love and understanding and compassion."*

"The mediums we had here at Etna back then were the real deal, let me tell you something, honey," said Arlene, now standing up to go turn off *Judge Judy*. "And Gladys Laliberte. Gladys was the camp medium, an unbelievable medium—a real, true Spiritualist medium. They were the real deal back then. I never met anyone back then that wasn't." Arlene remained ensconced in these memories, far back in a place that

I couldn't join, and she stayed for a few moments more. "I mean, what the fuck."

She continued. "On Monday night we had Angels. In another class, we did crystal healing. We had a table where the person would lie on it, the medium would place the crystals on all the chakra points, and we would all do energy work from the feet all the way up. Man, oh man, the healings were great," she said. "And then on Wednesday the medium would have a message service—gallery readings. Everyone would pay two dollars and everyone would get a reading. And all of this was by donation. *Donation.* Passed. Around. The. Basket. 'Love Offerings,' we called them. But now? Now it's all about the money. Now no one comes!" Arlene pounded her fist on the small folding table in front of her and did not regain her composure.

"You know about the time this place almost burned into oblivion?" Arlene asked excitedly, changing directions but only slightly. I recalled the landmark event from Diane's timeline hanging in the inn—how in 1922 a fire destroyed more than half of the camp buildings and its original temple. In her diary entry, camp secretary of the time Mary Drake Jenne had reported it: "On April 5, the temple, the store, the boarding house and 83 cottages east of Pond Street were destroyed by fire. 48 cottages and 7 other buildings were saved. When the fire was out, Mr. Packard [a devoted Camp Etna member] stood atop a picnic table and declared fervently the summer season would go on as planned."

"That fire was fucking huge," said Arlene, eyeballs bulging. "The train's metal wheels at Camp Etna's railroad stop gave off sparks, and it was a very dry summer season. We didn't have a whole lot of fire equipment—we still don't in this goddamn town. It was devastating. But they rebuilt the place. Rebuilt the temple too."

"Yes," I said, agreeing, "and that shortly after the fire, a new temple was erected in its place but collapsed several decades later due to heavy snow load on the roof, and that's when they built a third one, named after Gladys, which stands there today." I recited this back to Arlene with some allegiance, hoping to gain her trust or maybe just to cheer her up in her yearning for the way things were. "I learned about it during Diane's historical tour," I said.

"Diane told you that?" roared Arlene, and her voice boiled. "That fucking broad isn't even a medium!" She punched her palm with her other fist. "The fire happened in 1923, but that broad is saying it was '22 or '24! That broad doesn't know diddly shit."

A bitter mood took over the room and Arlene wrung her hands like she was applying lotion or ointment. She looked uncomfortable. I was uncomfortable too.

"George Paul," said Arlene, "George Paul the Indian built *that* one back in 1972." She pointed in the direction of the nearby temple. "But he wound up in the hospital because someone beat the shit out of him and went to prison. They were Indians! Al Dana got drunk, came over, tapped George, they got into it real bad. We tried to break it up, but by the time the police came, George Paul got seventy-two stitches in his face and Al Dana went to prison for attempted manslaughter. He was hardcore. But that's neither here nor there," said Arlene. "My point is: you got all these new people coming in changing this place. It's not the same anymore. This place has changed."

Compared to the more glorious and lively years of her past, Camp Etna did seem to have faded. Rather than being overcrowded, there were only a few cars in the parking lot. But the bones of the grounds still remained, the landscaping was nice (Diane's labor—she'd been resurrecting all the perennials that had been planted here during the camp's early beginnings), and this week's programming was vibrant and enticing: Past Life Regression. Manifestation Made Simple. Dowsing for Answers. The Self-Hypnosis Journey. Even so, classes remained low in attendance. In general, people just didn't gather like they used to. Outside of Camp Etna, the concept of community was becoming a lost practice, a ghost that even I could see clearly. I think Arlene and I both knew that. We both blamed progress and modernity; it's just that we were blaming different sources.

"I don't know any of these new Spiritualists coming this summer, these visiting lecturers and their bullshit, and I'll be damned if I'm going to spend any money to take one of their classes." Arlene's voice then quieted a little. "And anyways, I can't afford to go to anything." Arlene took a swig of water and sighed. "Nowadays, it's all about the money."

I pulled out this summer's brochure from my bag. It was well designed, orderly, and professional-looking, with canary-yellow type perched on top of reddish-brown glossy paper. *Celebrating our 141st Season,* it declared proudly on the cover. Classes were open to the public and went from $15 or $20 to $40 to $350. Duey's Native American drum-making course was listed in there too (one of the more expensive rates of $230). Then there was the end-of-season campfire, the luau, and the camp talent show: all free.

"And now we have all this metaphysical shit too," said Arlene. "Ghost hunting, paranormal crap. Tarot cards and angel painting and all that bullshit, when this place used to be just straight-up Spiritualism. The thing is, honey," she continued, "if you're a medium, all you have to do is look around this fucking campground, because they're here. You don't need any equipment, cameras or tables or trumpets, to do that." Of this, she was fully opinionated.

To an outsider like me, most of the mystical activities didn't seem all that different from the kinds of things happening at this place years ago. A lot of practices from the '40s and '50s still remained—the lectures, platform readings, message circles; even the chakra readings and Reiki from the 1960s had stuck around. But still, I was a neophyte to Spiritualism, so maybe I was calling classical music jazz, or jazz music classical. Was it really all that different? I pressed, thus detonating Arlene.

"Back in my day, you had to jump through hoops to prove that you were the real deal. You couldn't just say you were a medium—you had to prove it. You had to be *certified.*"

Arlene looked at the sleeping television and then back at me. Without breaking eye contact, she lifted one arm into the air and pointed a bent finger in the direction of a framed certificate on the wall. "The Morris Pratt Institute," said Arlene. "Haven't you ever heard of Morris Pratt?"

Morris Pratt was a person (rest in peace). Morris Pratt is also a building. But more than anything, Morris Pratt is an institute, a school that trains mediums and is the organization through which Arlene Grant became certified. Following the advent of Spiritualism in the United States, a perfervid believer by the name of Morris Pratt had promised that if he ever became rich enough, he would use his fortune to invest in the teaching and training of Spiritualism and fund a school for the scientific teaching of spiritual truth. As luck would have it, Morris Pratt did become a successful business farmer, and, true to his word, he built his "Temple of Science" in Whitewater, Wisconsin. The Morris Pratt Institute explains its founder's history this way:

> Just four years after the organizing of modern Spiritualism, it became apparent that the "grand and fearless lecturers of the day were passing on to the world of spirit." This weighed heavily on the mind of Moses Hull [a Seventh-day Adventist minister, who'd later become a Spiritualist lecturer and author and would eventually team up with Morris Pratt to create and establish the Spiritualist training school]. While serving at Maple Dell Park, Mantua, Ohio, he openly projected his feelings. The officers there were very sympathetic to his idea. Thus, plans were drawn up and an announcement made that "The Training School was to be organized." In 1888, Morris Pratt [now wealthy enough] bought property and constructed the most expensive home in Whitewater. The building was assessed at $30,000 and was some 48' wide and 85' long. It contained two large auditorium halls, one of which seated nearly 400 people. Pratt designed the building as a temple and a school for Spiritualism.

The subjects to be taught at the school were Science, Mathematics, and Language. Special courses were Oratory, Voice and Physical Culture, English and Rhetoric, Bible Exegetics, Higher Criticism, Logic and Parliamentary Law, Comparative Theology and Psychic Culture. The principles of the school were:

a. Maintenance of the individuality of each student,
b. perfect freedom of thought and expression so long as unkind personalities were avoided, highest authority,
c. reason and experience accepted as the highest authority,
d. no discrimination because of one's ideas,
e. all narrow and sectarian ruts carefully avoided, and
f. the desired aim to make all students original thinkers.

However, Morris Pratt himself passed to spirit on December 2, 1902, before his dream became an operational reality. Thus, Moses Hull followed Pratt's plans and opened the school on September 29, 1903. The result was "The General Course," consisting of twenty-six lessons in the "History, Philosophy and Religion of Modern Spiritualism" and later the "Advanced Course" consisting of thirty lessons dealing with "Spiritualism, Philosophy, Mediumship and Comparative Religion . . ."

The original school was open to both men and women, and its general education courses could be taken by anyone in the community. Overall, the school claimed to seek "nothing because it is new and unpopular; it accepts nothing because it is old and popular. It seeks only truth." By the time Arlene enrolled, the Morris Pratt Institute had shifted its curriculum to a strictly Spiritualist one; it's where mediums were trained, tested, and, if they passed, verified.

"You would have to take so many lessons and classes to become a healer," said Arlene. "Learning to be a healer came first." Then, Arlene explained, a Morris Pratt student would have to go on to higher classes to become a medium, and before a student could become certified as a medium, she had to have documentation from six people that stated what happened during the medium's reading and certify that the medium was accurate in her messages.

"And then if you want to become an ordained minister, you had to become a *licentiate* minister for two years," she said, holding two fingers in the air, "and then you could take your test to become ordained. *That* was a process that took two years, and out of that process you had to do a *pastorial* skill class for two weeks! And it was *intense*. For two weeks you went to funeral parlors, you went to nursing homes, we went to hospitals, we ministered to the sick, we ministered to the grief-stricken, this was *intense*."

Her tone began to grow louder and louder, to the point where she was nearly yelling. "After you attend Morris Pratt," Arlene said dutifully of her alma mater, "you *are* a medium, you *are* a healer, you *are* a minister. Because those ministers can *do* counseling, they can *do* the marriage counseling, they can *do* the grief counseling. Back then, you went to Morris Pratt for higher learning, and that learning took years."

Arlene's face crumpled again. "But when you become a minister and a medium in ninety days, like they do nowadays, you're not qualified for shit!"

"Even those who grew up seeing ghosts?" I asked.

"Yes. *Verify and clarify!*" Arlene's tone was fierce and vehement. "Loretta Fairjohn would always say, *Verify and clarify.* Otherwise it's just generic bullshit. And if you didn't abide by the rules back then, you didn't pass, or you didn't have certifications. But now, everybody's psychic! Everyone's a medium!"

Duey reappeared, grabbed a set of keys off a coffee table, and, on his way back out, whistled to Macklemore, who faithfully jumped off my lap and followed him out the door. Right before the door slammed behind them, Arlene called out, "And Duey, don't forget to go to the pharmacy!"

She turned back to me. "You ever hear of John Edwards? Famous medium. He's on TV, he does sold-out shows, the guy is rich, all of that.

Well," she said. "He's an *asshole*. John Edwards does what I call 'fishing.' I wouldn't pay two cents to see this dude. He fishes!"

Arlene lowered her voice and demonstrated the technique. "I have a Michael or a Mark or an M . . . someone has come here to speak to a person whose name starts with the letter M, and it belongs to someone over here . . . Marie, Mary . . ." And she kept going with it. She was pretty convincing.

"For Christ's sake!" cried Arlene. "The medium should *know* if it's a male or a female coming through, you asshole, because a medium can *hear* them! A medium can *see* them!" She spat on the ground, on the carpet of her own home, and I loved her for it. "You've got to be verified! When you came out of Morris Pratt, you were the real deal. *Clarified and verified!*"

I was starting to get a little woozy and light-headed, as if a flu were approaching, and asked to use Arlene's toilet. She led me to her kitchen, and directed me to back into a tiny bathroom and closed the door, which was not a door but a thin wooden shade that didn't provide much privacy or room for personal care, but neither one of us paid any mind.

"You know," she said from the other side of the shade, possibly addressing me, possibly herself, "Duey planted Loretta Fairjohn over there, after she died. She had to have a blood transfusion and they gave her the wrong type of blood. . . ." Arlene's stories were tremendous and delicious, like goodie bites—all the most flavorful parts, the best and tastiest bites set aside for one potent delivery. And she was Grinch-like, a jackknife of a woman, and I was under her spell. Several people at camp had told me that I should always bring a baby when visiting Arlene, because babies make Arlene melt. If I didn't bring a baby, then I should at least say a prayer before I arrived, and they told me that time stood still inside Arlene's cottage, so if I ever wanted to leave, I should also set a timer. I hadn't done any of these things and was starting to think I should have. Through the gaps in the bathroom door's wooden panels, I could see Arlene looking out the window, scanning the grounds.

"And *this* house, *my* house?" she continued. "Before I bought this place, well, Clyde Wood had lived here. He was Camp Etna's secretary treasurer and he had one leg. He lived here with his cat, Sugarfoot."

I flushed the toilet and stepped out of the bathroom, stood next to Arlene, and looked out the window with her. From her perch, Arlene had a pretty good view of the community, a panoramic view; Loyalty Lodge was placed a good deal farther from the main hub of Etna, nearly retreating into the woods of camp and a little isolated. Perhaps in this darkly shaded spot at camp, Arlene was perfectly situated; her location gave her the opportunity to be one of those neighbors who was able to avoid her own story by tending to the narrative of others.

"You talk to Karlene yet?"

I shook my head no. "Not yet," I said.

"Karlene Tanner. She's Gladys Laliberte's granddaughter. Just moved back to Etna, lives in her grandmother's cottage. You talk to her yet?"

Arlene continued to scan the grounds. "That cottage over there?" She pointed. "That belongs to Kelly Dawn Purington. Table tipper. She's here because of me."

I couldn't see the cottage itself, but I knew the general direction. Plus, I'd met Kelly recently, by way of Barbara. We had table-tipped on her porch. Kelly was sweet. She had black hair, and her eyes sparkled like a Christmas ornament. I remembered Kelly to be soft-spoken and serene, how she'd told me what kind of mediums to avoid, and how to spot a fraud. Like the fortune-tellers sitting on the streets, or the ones who tell you you're cursed, and that you have to buy candles—their candles—to lift the curse. After we talked for a little bit, Kelly rubbed her hands together and we table-tipped. The spirit of Gonzo, my childhood dog—the one who had belonged to my little brother before he himself died—came through. Kelly said that when the table had rubbed up against me, it was because Gonzo was probably trying to lick me. I had never imagined my dog would return to me, or that a table could carry the spirit of a dog, but I went with it, and regardless of the absurdity, it made me feel a little better. This was something I'd been noticing by then—when I just went with it and didn't think too much about it, when I accepted the medium's message, a small, hidden, hurt part inside me let itself feel a little better.

"Kelly was in the middle of getting a divorce," said Arlene. "And she was looking for a house. I was the one that brought her down here. Thanks to me, she bought her cottage for a dollar."

Kelly had mentioned this too. That she was fairly new to camp—one of the newer generation of mediums on the grounds. That it was hard for her sometimes because she was so sensitive. *"I can't do this all day long. I can't go around picking up on everyone's energy,"* she'd said. *"Because when I leave my mind during a reading, I go into the stratosphere."* She echoed the chorus: that it is very, very hard to be a medium, and as a new medium, she was learning that sometimes she had to shut herself down. She was also teaching this in her development classes to other new mediums: that if you don't want to wind up being depressed or an alcoholic or entirely rigid, mediumship required protection. You had to keep your ego in check; it wasn't a competition. Mediumship was about being a channel, and there was enough room for everyone. The key to being a good medium, Kelly stressed, was that you must protect yourself from your own ego and all the darkness it brought, that you must love one another. Also, if you decided to be a *professional* medium, that you should run your mediumship as you would a business, because if you didn't run it like a business, it would fold.

"And then there's Kelly's boyfriend, Chris," Arlene continued. "Chris does the 'Primal Empowerment' class." She raised her cuffed hands up and made air quotes. "What the hell is that all about, 'Primal Empowerment'? Who knows? Probably something to do with Africa. Because he's black. He's a good guy. He works at Planet Fitness or some shit.

"Anyway, Kelly decided, after all of this shit, the divorce and all, to be here. One day she's a runner for Mediums Day. The following year, she's a medium. Between two summers, I don't know what happened, but now all of a sudden she's a medium doing mediumship? How did that happen so fast? It takes *years* to get certified. Next thing I know, she quits her job and is doing psychic readings over the phone, doing parties and readings and all that shit. One day, all of a sudden she's a medium, because you don't need to be certified to be a medium here!"

"It is well noted," states the Morris Pratt Institute's website, "that the Morris Pratt Institute and the NSA[C] were closely affiliated, therefore it was natural that the Morris Pratt Institute became the Educational Bureau of the National Spiritualist Association of Churches." And that is what happened: through the NSAC, Morris Pratt was the institute of choice that trained and verified up-and-coming mediums. But then, in 1986, after a series of unfortunate events, Camp Etna split off from the NSAC and went independent. And when Camp Etna went independent, they invested in their own rules and didn't have to answer to any higher-ups anymore. What this independence brought with it was the freedom for mediums to join without being certified anymore.

By the 1980s, all Spiritualists camps and churches were part of the NSAC. Every year, the association would have its convention, and that year, the convention was on Mackinaw Island, in Michigan's Upper Peninsula. At the convention, someone asked the NSAC president, a man named Joe Merrill, about something called the Stowe Fund, and, according to Arlene, it was the beginning of the end of Camp Etna's relationship with the NSAC.

"The Stowe Fund was something that we *all* owned, all camps and churches as part of the NSAC, and it had over a million dollars in it. For church and repairs and shit. And Joe Merrill responded bluntly, 'None of your damn business.' I mean, what the fuck!" On top of that, the NSAC wanted all the churches and camps to turn their deeds over to them. "So then, three of the reverends from Camp Etna told National go fuck yourself, in plain English. And that's when our guys— Rev. Irene Miller, Rev. Charles Harding, and Larry Hilton—started the American Federation."

After Mackinaw Island, Camp Etna had gone and done her own thing as the American Federation of Spiritualist Churches. According to Arlene, when Etna broke off from the NSAC, it was a bloodbath. But after the dust settled, camp was up and running again, and established their own new set of guidelines and rules for training, certification, and practices.

"I was the first president," said Arlene as she led us back into the parlor of Loyalty Lodge and we both sat down. "And I was president up until the end."

Two years after forming the federation, Camp Etna broke off from it and went independent, and this is where stories conflict from member to member. According to others, not long after forming the federation, too many egos took over and began poisoning Camp Etna. "In 1989, we found out you gotta have all this tax crap, exemptions, et cetera. No one knew that. When you're under the NSAC umbrella, that's taken care of." What people can agree on is that things got messy, Rev. Irene Harding left, Camp Etna broke from the federation and became independent, and has remained independent, and this is where Arlene finds her beef—the rules aren't the same as what they used to be.

Churches at the camp have come and gone too. They've changed. To be a member of Camp Etna and live on the grounds, you have to be a member of a Spiritualist church. In the off-season, a new church called Healing Light began renting the Gladys Laliberte Temple in the winter. It's a Spiritualist church, but it's independent as well, a separate entity from Camp Etna, and abides by its own rules, although many who attend it, and who lead it, are members of camp. In fact, Arlene was just one of the few who does not, and will not, attend. With the mention of Healing Light, Arlene took off and got going again, unrelenting.

"And that new church? The Healing Light? It has got to go. Their pastor, Janet, ordained their new pastor, Washian, in ninety days! And she does past-life-regression shit, which is very dangerous, and hypnotism—I wouldn't have her hypnotize a flea. How did she get ordained? Through the mail! In six years, that church has not produced one medium. And up until the year 2000, there was a church service every night! Now? I wouldn't go in the damn church if you paid me! I'd go see Barbara, but that's it. Barbara's good. But I've been around, and I've done my deeds. But the Healing Light Church, their rental contract is up in June, and we are voting their asses *out*. The board is hemorrhaging money out to keep that church warm in the winter."

Arlene went on to say that sometime when she turned seventy, she decided she was done paying her dues. No more church for her, and she couldn't remember the last time she set foot in a Spiritualist church. Now, at age seventy-four, and having been a medium all her life and at Camp Etna close to half a century, Arlene hardly practices what she had so believed in.

"The thing with Spiritualism today," said Arlene, making a point to both herself and me, "Spiritualism has had its ups and its downs. And ups. And downs. And now, most of your old mediums, the teachers, the old Spiritualists, they have passed on. My mentors? Gone. My teachers: gone. The old-timers: gone. And now you have this whole new realm of people coming up that are, well, they haven't been in it all these years. And they come up here and the next thing you know . . ." She swallowed and pressed on. "They dance for gods and goddesses and bullshit. And we pay them. Something is very wrong here. Something is very wrong here. This is not right. This needs to stop. Someone must put an end to it."

I stretched out my legs and twisted my back around, which was beginning to throb a little and go stiff. I was absorbed, if pretty confused.

"All the stuff we used to do here at Camp Etna," said Arlene, "it's not what is being taught to them today. None of it. Because there's no teachers. No qualified teachers."

"If what you say is true, then what about you?" I said finally. "Shouldn't you? Why don't you train them? Why not teach the new generation, then? Why not step up, Arlene?"

"Why don't I?" she said wearily. "Because I'm sick! I'm sick! I don't practice on the others, and I don't teach others because I have to save all my energy for myself." Arlene stood up and walked away to her dining room and picked up some medicine bottles and returned to her lounge chair. "I got a disease," she said, sifting through her handful of prescriptions and unscrewing a lid. "I got scleroderma. You ever heard of scleroderma?"

Scleroderma is a hardening of the body. It is an autoimmune rheumatic disease, a systematic sclerosis. A chronic connective-tissue disease; the word "scleroderma" coming from two Greek ones—"*sclero*" meaning hard, and "*derma*" meaning skin. The tissues of involved organs—internal and external—become rigid, inflexible, unbending, and fibrous, causing them to function less efficiently and eventually fail. Some call it the Medusa disease. In essence, Arlene's body was turning to stone.

"No doctors around here know a goddamn thing about it," she said. "And no one can do anything about it." To much of the medical community, scleroderma remains a mystery, and no one has discovered the cause of it. "I don't practice because I need to save all my energy to keep myself alive," said Arlene, and my heart cracked a little.

I took a deep breath. I missed my kids at home, and I had no idea what time it was or when I'd last eaten. The heat and humidity made my body feel torrid, achy, and dizzy, and all I wanted to do was be drenched by a cold glass of water.

The phone rang, snapping me back to attention. Arlene had been expecting a call from the cable company, she explained. She was livid and planning on sticking it right up the butts of the cable company, as they'd been wronging her—overcharging her, as she was supposed to be getting the Hallmark Channel for *free*. As Arlene leaned over to answer the call, I walked over to the medium, bent down, and gave her a kiss on her cheek. The phone rang again, and she looked at me in surprise.

"I'll call you soon, and thank you," I said, and gave her one more kiss on the cheek. Ambivalent, Arlene smiled, looked at the caller ID, and then picked up the telephone. "About fucking time," I heard her say as I walked to the front door.

†·†·†

CHAPTER 6

Water Witching, or Dowsing for Answers

Crystals and other "high vibrational stones" are part
of a daily practice for the women at camp. *Greta Rybus*

W e were letting the metal tell us where to go.

Two copper sticks as thick as inchworms on a mulberry bush, both bent into perfectly angled L-shapes—one rod in each hand. Our wrists limp, our eyes facing downward, not watching the uneven ground on which we trekked but staring longingly at the rods in our hands. Today, we would be giving permission to the sticks. Today we would tell our minds to be passive, to just be the conduits and let go while we'd tiptoe around the breathing lawn, searching for something we couldn't directly see. Something vital. A life-sustaining source. Today, we would be looking for water.

Maine is a righteous state of fewer than 2 million people living on more than 4,000 mostly tiny islands and one large wing positioned north and a little east of New Hampshire, south of Canada, and flecked along the Atlantic coast. Deeply greened by the sun, Maine's mainland is just about the size of Ireland, a country where similar predilections prevail: stoic vulnerability, aloof independence, and ferocious modesty. The number-one supplier of blueberries, lobsters, and genetically pure-bred mice, Maine also has more moose per square mile than any other state. It is the grayest state in our nation: with the median age at 42.7 years and rising, Maine tends to attract retirees and retain its older residents while the younger ones flock to snazzier places for work or to avoid their own boredom, even though Maine's state motto is "The Way Life Should Be."

Maine is nearly 320 miles long and 210 miles wide, with a total area of 33,215 square miles. This makes her the thirty-ninth largest state, but she is home to 17 million acres of forested land. The Pine Tree State also holds nearly 6,000 ponds and lakes, 32,000 miles of rivers and streams, as well as 3,478 miles of coastline. All of this glorious land is divided into 16 counties, which contain 488 incorporated municipalities consisting of cities, towns, and plantations. All phone numbers in Maine begin with the area code 207, and if talking to an inquisitive tourist, as we have many—it's a major source of our income—one would explain that the state is sectioned into the following regions: Casco Bay and Greater Portland; Acadia (yes, like the tourist-riddled national park); Kennebec Valley, The Lakes and Mountains; Mid-Coast; the Maine Beaches; the Maine Highlands; and Aroostook County. However, if you're asking a true Mainer—which, in Maine, is defined not just as someone who was born here but a person whose parents (or is it grand-parents *and* parents?) were also born here—the answer you'd receive if you asked, "What are the parts of Maine?" would be this: Southern Maine (or even more specifically just Portland); Central Maine; North-ern Maine; and Downeast. Between Southern and Central in Penob-scot County is the little town of Etna, taken from its natives and settled in 1807 by six white men from the nearby settlements. At first, the town was named Crosbytown, after the Crosby family of Hampden. Then in 1820, Benjamin and Phineas Friend, brothers and two of the first colonizers of the place, incorporated and named the settlement Etna, after the famed Mount Etna in Italy, home to one of the world's most active volcanoes. Why after a volcano in Italy? The only explana-tion I could find was that the early settler Benjamin extended his index finger and when it landed it on a page of an old Webster's spelling book, it landed on the word "Etna."

Before the first white settlers drew their own borders and laid claim to the earth below them, the area was a lush and fertile land occupied by the Penobscot Indians. Since the retreat of the glaciers some 12,000 years ago, the indigenous inhabitants, ancestors of the Wabanaki, lived a life in tune with the pulse of nature—hunting and fishing in the heav-ily forested lands of what would be known as Maine, with an economy and spirituality connected to the state's woods and waters. At one time there were more than twenty Wabanaki tribes, but after the white inva-sion of their lands, the natives faced a near extinction, as did their way of life. Bounties were placed on Wabanaki scalps, tribes were pushed off their lands, children were taken from their families, and Christi-anity replaced their holistic and earth-centered spirituality. In 1808, the first white child was born in Etna. More and more families came from nearby areas, erecting log houses and barns made from yellow ash trees and split cedar. The pursuits of the white settlers were chiefly agricultural. They established farms on the prosperous soil, made the land work for them, and grew bountiful crops of corn, beans, wheat, and rye. They raised chickens and cows, and collected whatever they could from these creatures to eat or use or sell. At one point, Mr. Benjamin Friend, town-namer, began harvesting and manufacturing something called potash—an alkaline potassium compound found in the ground—which could be used as a fertilizer to boost crop yields and crop quality (and a key ingredient in industrial products, like soap or soda).

In a brief account of the town, author George J. Varney writes of Etna's earth: "The surface is quite broken, but the soil is, for the most part, a good, light loam, producing fine crops of potatoes and hay. Pine, spruce and hemlock are the principal forest trees. The town is drained by several small streams—Kinsley and Soadabscook Streams being the largest. Kinsley Stream furnishes some waterpowers, two of which have been occupied by a sawmill and a shinglemill." Soon after the two mills were erected, both of them, and three more built after, all eventually caught fire and burned down, burning down with them the attempt at powering the town with water.

The first recorded death in the town of Etna was unnamed but identified as the child of a Mr. John Jackson. The second death—a Mr. Calvin Sylvester—was in October of 1813, when he died of consumption, and the first marriage solemnized was of Sylvester's widow. By the year 1835, the townsfolk bragged about having not one doctor or lawyer among its citizens, but instead having preachers. By 1840 there was a Baptist church and a class of Methodists and a post office; mail was carried on horseback once a week. By 1850, the town of Etna had a population of approximately 802 humans.

Nearly two hundred years later, the number hadn't quite doubled. As of June 25, 2017, approximately 1,222 humans are bound by gravity to Etna's 24.97 square miles. Compared to New York's 27,000 people per square mile or even Portland's ever-rising population density (950 people per square mile and climbing, *fast*), the people of today's Etna are spread out like butter at just 49 humans per square mile, which makes for a pretty good place to go unseen (or on the contrary, to stand out).

The towns of Stetson and Levant bound Etna to the north, Dixmont to the south, Carmel to the east, and Plymouth to the west. On the northeast part of town, there is one long iron stretch of tracks that belong to the Maine Central Railroad, which was constructed in 1854, and which some called "The Little Etna." The train invited many men to work and live in shanties on Henry C. Friend's pasture near a clump of cedars, and its whistle is said to have sounded like a terrible, shrieking, savage animal. Its construction was finished in 1855, and went as far as the Etna Bog until it stopped and let out the last of its passengers. This is also the train that once carried up to 2,000 Spiritualist passengers in one day to Camp Etna. Back then, passengers would step off the train at Pond Street and head up the dirt road, suitcases in hand, through the woods and in the direction of the temple of Camp Etna, causing the population of the town of Etna to skyrocket. Today the railroad makes no more stops in Etna or the camp. The town itself has compressed, has made itself small once again.

Presently, the town of Etna has one post office; one general store (Etna Village Variety); one gas station (also Etna Village Variety); and one school (the Etna Dixmont school). As of 2016, the median income for a family was $37,750, with men bringing in approximately $30,057 versus $21,250 for women. Like many towns in Maine, people did what they had to do to get by, and it was pretty common for folks to have two, three different jobs—high school principals moonlighting at the L.L.Bean flagship store, cleaning women working weekends at Target. According to Rita, the part-time administrator at Etna's town office, of the three people who work with her—Debbie the town tax collector, another separate Debbie the town clerk, plus Rita herself—only one of them lives in the town of Etna.

I live two hours south of Etna, in the Casco Bay/Portland region of Maine. It's my second time living there, but my first as a married person and mother. Portland is the city I moved to after graduating from college in Michigan. I attended a documentary school—just a semester-long program—where I first tried my hand at writing about other people as a narrative journalist. I wrote about a funeral-home parlor—the topic of death was my first beat as a writer. It's clear to me now why I'd chosen this topic, but back then I thought it was entirely random. Subconsciously, I was fascinated and bewildered by the way American culture embraced death—particularly after the loss of my brother. I was seventeen when he passed—he was fourteen, driving with my father to help my mother close down her restaurant one Saturday night when their car was hit—T-boned—by a drunk driver. His death was sudden, and the funeral and designated mourning period that followed seemed just as sudden, just as absurd, just as confusing. Looking back at it now, I wrote about funeral homes so I could better make sense of them. Shortly after I began taking my writing seriously, I left Maine for New York City to advance my career as a writer. It worked, and I never thought I'd return to Vacationland, but I did. In search of a slower pace, I eventually left the Big Apple and returned to Maine, this time bringing with me a husband, two dogs, a first book, and a mental cyst of anxiety and stress. There has always been something magical about this state—the combination of isolation, fresh air, pine trees, modesty. It's a good place to hide, a great place to disappear.

Usually I take 295 North to get to Etna from my home—it's a straight shot. The drive is fine—it's a highway—and it's also gorgeous. Today, however, my route was different. I wanted to see more, feel more of the area surrounding camp, so I took Route 2.

I passed sagging barbershops and rainbow-colored trees, hand-painted campaign signs sharing yards with baying hounds and so many For Sale signs that I wondered if they're for sale because everyone here is old and dying. I passed a public supper, a potato patch, a rutabaga patch, a pumpkin field. I dipped into the whispering towns of Pittsfield,

Carmel, Stetson, Hermon, Dixmont. Before getting onto State Road, I slipped into East Newport to see the home of a woman I know. She didn't live there anymore—she's in prison, and she's in there for thirty-seven years. On Tuesdays, I teach memoir to her and a group of about nine other women. Some were in for drug charges. Several of them killed their husbands. All of them had been battered—sexually, physically, psychologically. She had too. She and I were close in age and I adored her. We clicked the instant we met—we loved the same books, the same stories, the same movies—and it wasn't until about two months into class that I found out, from someone else, why the young woman from East Newport was in prison: she had killed her daughter, a toddler. She'd been abused by her partner, everything of the worst kind, and he had threatened to get custody of her young child. So, to escape a life of hell, and, I suppose, the same for her daughter, she had given her kid too many Benadryl and then suffocated her until she slept forever. And then the woman swallowed as many pills as she could get her hands on, then went to a graveyard and went to sleep forever, too. But she woke up. That hadn't been part of the plan. When I learned all this, I was pregnant with my own daughter. It broke my heart entirely. I didn't know how to accept all of this, all of what had happened to my student, my friend, but I knew she wasn't evil. I could bet that she was so shaken from the abuse, and on top of that she must've had postpartum depression that remained for some time, and with all the fear and hormones, her wiring must have been whacked out of place, spinning her out of her mind, alone in her grief and anxiety, and perhaps she thought that this was the only way out. All I had for her was compassion, so I went to go see her home. She told me where it was, and about the horses she'd had as a kid that were still roaming in the pasture, the trees she climbed as a kid, the brook nearby. I drove there, and I saw all the things she'd written about in class, and it crushed me. There were toys still in the yard. After I drove away and before I pulled into the gates of Camp Etna, I had to turn off the engine and sit in my car for a few minutes, just breathing.

———

"Just keep your eyes on the pendulum," said James as the weight dangled from his hand. I'd taken a seat at James Kidder's four-hour tutorial, Dowsing for Answers, and I was forty-five minutes late but there was plenty left. I leaned over the purple-painted tabletop until my chin touched the surface, then I looked up at my instructor, who steadied his hand, which steadied a line, which held a purple rock—amethyst, perhaps—that was the shape of a diamond.

I'm lucky they hadn't left on me. A few minutes prior, Ernie VanDenBossche and James Kidder, two of the few men at camp, were just standing up from two white rocking chairs and were on their way to sit on one of their porches, maybe crack open a beer and relax when I skidded down the outdoor deck and nearly slid into them, panting, "Am I too late? Am I too late?"

Basically I was, but James accepted my money anyway—$30—and agreed to run the class for one very tardy student and give her a lesson in Water Witching 101. This was a crash course in dowsing (searching for water), not to be confused with a crash course in dousing (drenching in water). We would be using metal rods to find something hidden in more ways than one.

Ernie decided to hang around, too, not entirely as student, but not an instructor either. Ernie was a long-standing Camp Etna member. He was a medium, and a board-certified hypnotherapist and certified instructor with the National Guild of Hypnotists. He was on the camp's board of directors—had given the benediction of the winter meeting I'd attended. He was the life partner of another member of camp, Bonnie Lee Gibson. She was a pretty lady with poufy dark hair and a white chunk of bangs, like a skunk. Like her husband, Bonnie was a hypnotist and a medium. Ernie was a good guy, and I assumed he was sticking around for his friend James's sake.

Unlike Ernie, James was not a medium. Again: it's important to understand that not all Spiritualists are mediums and not all mediums are Spiritualists. There's a big distinction between the two, like the difference between a noun and a verb—a Spiritualist is a member of the Spiritualist religion, while a medium is a person who is said to facilitate communication between the land of the living and the spirit world. Nearly all of the mediums I'd spoken with say that everyone is born with the capability to communicate with the spirit world, that it's as innate as laughter and reflexive as a doe licking her fawn, but not everyone has figured out how to flex that muscle, or believes that they can, or wants to. While the small group of mediums at Camp Etna consider themselves Spiritualists—most were seasonal residents, sticking around for the summertime—one does not have to be a Spiritualist to be a medium. At the same time, not all Spiritualists see dead people, nor is this a requirement should a person want to join the congregation at Camp Etna. In fact, skeptics are more than welcome.

James rocked the pendulum and said nothing. He was a dowser, but he could not see dead people. His partner was another camp Spiritualist named Laurie Xanthos, a medium. And then there was me, the only neophyte here, and for the first time at camp, the only woman too. Ernie sat back down in his rocking chair as I stared at the pendulum hanging from James's hand above the purple picnic table, and we both waited with bated breath for further instructions.

James set down the pendulum. "I ran a water department," he said in a broad Mainer accent, which came out more like *I ran a watah depahtment*. "I ran a water department, so that's how I used to find old water lines." He scratched his mustache.

James "Jim" Kidder must've been about sixty-five years old, and he had a nonthreatening face, a face you could trust. Blue jeans, belt, beige button-up short-sleeve Hawaiian shirt with olive-colored palm trees. He was a man of measured words, of shy demeanor and a full head of white hair.

It was hard not to notice men on the campgrounds, but not because they're loud, or have a superior or silencing presence. In fact, the presence of men on the campgrounds felt, to me, quite the opposite of what I was used to outside, in the "real world." The men here were more passive than aggressive. They were agreeable, supportive. The men (or husbands) I'd met at camp were something I'd categorize as a "best male supporting actor." It's like no one even noticed that there were so few men, it was just what was normal, what they were used to. It was a steady balance between what some refer to as the energy of both the male and female divine. Witnessing it felt wonderful.

"So," James continued, "the old records would say 'Mr. Smith's old front porch.' Well, Mr. Smith died back in 1880."

"So really you're not finding water," said Ernie, interjecting and polishing James's statement for accuracy, which also shifted the purpose of his friend's anecdote, and startled James a bit. "You're finding metal." This made James a little flustered, but he continued. I went ahead and assumed he was also just a little bit bashful.

"I used to find pipes in the ground," said James. "I used to drill wells. We knew there was hardly any water, and when people wanted to build, they needed to find water." He pushed the pendulum and its chain to the side of the table, then, just as unceremoniously, slid over in its place two bent metal rods. Once the dowsing rods were in the middle of the table, equally between him and me, James put his hands back in his lap.

"People used to use sticks," he continued. "I worked with this guy. He was an old man. He used to use a sapling, six to eight feet. He'd go out and cut it fresh. He'd walk the property and when it got to water, the stick would bend down to the ground." James set his right hand on the end of one the metal rods on the table and kind of picked at it, rubbed it; I don't think he was doing it consciously.

"The old man would dowse," said James, as solemn as a lemon. "He'd find a spot, get on his knees." He took a breath and cleared his throat. "He'd tell you it was thirty feet to the ledge and then the stick would start bouncing again. Then it'd stop, and he'd tell you it's a hundred and twenty feet to water through the ledge. Then he'd ask it, 'How many gallons per minute?' and it'd start bouncing again."

James was talking about a water witch.

Or at least, that's how some people refer to them, which makes them sound spooky and mysterious and beyond human, but mostly they're known as dowsers, if dowsers are even heard of or known by younger generations, or city folk or urbanites or people who just generally don't think for long about where we get our water.

Before you had your tap water, assuming you have easy access to tap water or any drinkable water, someone had to find that water source. It's never been easy to find water. Nowadays, if you want to determine the depths and extent of the different water-bearing strata underneath you, you can have hydrologic, geologic, and geophysical insight and understanding. Today, if a person in the town of Etna wanted to find their source of underground water and drill a well, they would pick up their phone and call a hydrologist or a well digger. But even with today's drilling technology and knowledge, the special equipment and complex machinery, locating and drilling for a good water supply can be difficult. Even professional well drillers understand this and will never give you a 100 percent guarantee of success. The results aren't always what you might expect, and drilling can be tricky, especially when the areas in which they're exploring are underlain by igneous rocks like basalt, limestone, or granite, because basalt, limestone, and granite don't contain porous spaces through which water can flow. In underground areas like that, the water must move through very narrow breaks in the rock, and to get this water, the well has got to intersect through enough of these tiny fractures in order for it to produce useful amounts of water. A lot of the time, well drillers, when they're setting up on the surface of the ground, go ahead and guess before they start to dig. The cost of hiring a well driller nowadays? Somewhere between $6,000 to $8,000.

Back in the day, before all this drilling technology (and still sometimes today), people would call upon someone else: the water witch. Before there was drilling, there was dowsing. Divining. Doodlebugging. Dowsers—people who came to your home, walked around your land, pulled out their pocketknife, and, after cutting off a fresh sapling from a tree, found for you the life-sustaining element of water.

"The first thing we want to do is . . . here are some rods," said James, pronouncing it more like rahds, and handed Ernie and me two rods apiece, which looked like coat-hanger wires bent into a right angle a third of the way down their length. "These are made of brass."

"Why brass?" I asked.

"Some people use copper," said James. "These just work well for me. What you want to do is hold one in each hand," he instructed. We followed James's lead and quickly began playing with our rods like kids given their very first slingshots.

There are all types of dowsers. Some dowsers search for wells, whereas others advertise their services to find lost pets, or determine which vitamin to take. Some dowse for the paranormal while others dowse for disease. People dowse their cows to see which ones are pregnant or which watermelon is the best to buy. Dowsing is a lie detector and a weather forecaster. You can dowse with anything from a pendulum to a pencil. Some dowsers still use wooden sticks. Some have adorned rods with handcrafted handlebars and carrying cases. Some dowsers use gloves. Some scoff at this. The other day, I came across an article called "How I Dowse as a Middle School Teacher." And beneath that another article entitled, "Adding Dowsing to Your Workout." Some dowsers charge a rate of $100 per dowse (pretty much the average) while others ask for nothing at all—it's just a favor for a friend or neighbor. If you're ever looking for a dowser meet-up in Las Vegas or Little Rock, you wouldn't need to use a rod to find your people—dowsers aren't hard to find; dowsing is practically ubiquitous. Or, as the American Society of Dowsers (ASD) puts it on their home page: dowsing is a way of life.

"Now," said James, "one of the things about dowsing is that you always have skeptics." He tightened his grip on the copper rods. "It's like a pendulum—it doesn't take much of a muscle movement that you don't see to get it to move, and it can be same with dowsing. A lot of folks are skeptical with dowsing."

"There are a lot of people skeptical about *all* of this," I said.

"Well, there are," James replied calmly. "That's why you need to be real specific on how you ask your questions."

"Specific on how you ask the rods?" I asked. "Or are we asking spirits?"

"Your rods," said James bluntly. "Now, let's say you want to buy a new car. You ask, 'Will I buy a new car in 2017?' and it's going to say yes or no. And then you ask, 'Will I buy a new car in the next six months?' And it's going to tell you yes or no. And then you ask it three months."

Ernie and I nodded in agreement. "You want to have your answer to come to a certain point," he said, and made the shape of a triangle with both his hands, "so you need to think about how you are going to word your questions. You can't be too general."

I looked down at my rods, which I had gripped fiercely in my hands. I didn't think I was ready to free them yet, let them take over or whatever I assumed they were going to eventually do. I felt like I was holding the plant from *Little Shop of Horrors*.

James demonstrated the hold, which seemed fairly simple: from the starting position, let your wrists sag a bit rather than try to keep the rods facing straight. Don't grip tightly, but don't let the sticks swing wildly, either. In the hands of an expert dowser, the rods should be parallel and steady and aiming in the direction you're to head. My rods and I weren't sure who was in charge; we weren't natural dance partners, to say the least. How much was I supposed to lean or lead or support or let go? Why was just one swinging? What did it mean? Why were they crossing now? The delicate balance of holding these two sticks the correct way before even beginning the dowse was much easier said than done.

"Everyone got their rods? So before you go looking for water, let's establish your yes and your no," James continued. "But before that," he said, and looked at me and not Ernie, "the first thing we're going to want you to do is relax."

I tried, but my composure tensed and just went awkward instead.

I furrowed my brow and exhaled, impossibly pushing myself to relax. "OK," I sighed.

"Hold them out in front of you," said James, and Ernie and I held our rods out in front of us, chest-level.

I wanted to be doing it right. I was very focused on whether I was doing it right or not. "How much of a grip do I want in it?" I asked. "Is it resting like a bow? Like this? Or less? Or more?"

"We used to use willows, applewood," said James, answering indirectly, or maybe not at all. "Some dowsers would hold it so tight it can take the bark right off." Ernie whistled. "But with these," James went on, "you just hold the rods level so they don't move. Then you first ask it, 'Show me yes.' Think of a question in which you know the answer already," said James. "How about how many kids do you have?"

"Two," I told James, and smiled.

"Ask it if you have two children," he said, and I did, and in an extremely measured and slow pace, the rod in my right hand turned to the right.

"There," said James. "Now you have your yes."

Depending on whom you ask, dowsing has either been around since the dawn of humanity, or it made its debut sometime around the fifteenth or sixteenth century, but there seems to be no formal conclusion. The American Society of Dowsers begins its own historical account of the timeline of dowsing starting with the discovery of cave paintings in the Atlas Mountains of North Africa that contained an image of a person holding a forked branch in his hands, surrounded by a group of tribesmen. From there, the ASD timeline alludes to passages in the Bible ("both Moses and his son Aaron used a dowsing device referred to as 'the rod' to locate and bring forth water . . ."); then on to Chinese emperors 2,500 years ago; and to 400 BCE on the Greek Island of Crete, in the blind Greek poet Homer's *The Odyssey*, where the dowsing rod is given the Caduceus, which was passed from Apollo to Asclepios, the ancient Greek god of healing. Some say dowsing gained prominence in the fifteenth century among

German miners when deep mining was in hot demand. Other sources cite the year 1638, when Queen Elizabeth's royal mines in Wales were being excavated for calamine and silver. Some considered dowsing a sin: in the early 1500s Martin Luther declared dowsing for metals was an act that broke the law of God's first commandment. In 1662 dowsing was declared satanic by a Jesuit scientist by the name of Gaspar Schott.

Some say it was the early German and English immigrants brought the practice of water witching with them to the United States, but really, the origins are vast and foggy. What is clear is that the practice of dowsing has more or less survived, even following the development of well and drilling technology. During the Vietnam War, the US Marines turned to dowsing as an attempt to locate weapons and enemy tunnels. Even today in remote and rural places not much different from Etna, Maine, the homegrown homeopathic experts still flourish. In her research on dowsers in New England, journalist Kate Daloz discovered that more than half the domestic wells drilled in Vermont *each year* are located by dowsers. Recently, as a last-ditch effort to find the source of the massive population of carpenter ants living within her walls, my therapist finally found success after she dialed up a New England dowser. And my friend Gretchen told me recently that when she built her first house in Maine a decade or so ago, she worked with the local dowser because it's just what you did. Suffice it to say, one could spend years rounding up, lining up, and pinning down all the historical accounts of the use of dowsing and even then, the massive tome would be an impossibility, because the very definition of the verb "dowse" itself means "to search for," and when haven't we been doing just that?

Ernie laughed.

"What, Ernie?" I asked, rolling the handles of my rods between my fingers. "What's so funny?"

"I asked it a thought in my head and it answered for me," said Ernie cleverly, holding his rods in front of him. If I hadn't known it was Ernie speaking and standing at my side, I would have sworn that it was Mr.

Fred Rogers—uplifted, steady, positive; the unrushed G-rated tone and tempo of their voices were identical.

"Well, what did you ask it?" asked James.

Ernie smiled big and proud, cupped his hand to the side of his mouth and leaned toward me. "She loves me, she loves me not," he whispered. "My wife."

I turned to James, who was pushing in his chair now. "Dowsing isn't for sissies, is it?" I asked. "But is it considered Spiritualist?"

"That's the thousand-dollar question," James replied.

It was fine for him to leave it at that, because it was no one's place to answer it. Spiritualism has always been resistant to being defined. I thought of dowsing as a kind of cross-training for non-mediums, or mediums, or psychics, or really anyone. Dowsing was more or less a practice for the subconscious, a meditation, an exercise in intuition.

Once, a medium told me that nothing is said in the higher spirit world; the language is intuition. He went on to explain that when you meditate and you're good at it, you go to the same place that you go to when you're asleep, as far as brain waves are concerned. He stressed that when you educate yourself in different forms of meditation, you become what is known as "intuitively literate." He explained that you produce alpha and beta waves—the same wavelengths that go hand-in-hand with activating a child's imagination. But the more we grow up, this medium warned, the more we get serious and responsible and involved in life, the more we lose that level of relaxation and that level of creativity and intuition. "You have the child's imagination inside of you," he said, encouraging me, "and being intuitive is part of your genius. That's why Albert Einstein said, 'The intuitive mind is a sacred gift, the rational mind is a faithful servant.'" It was a misattribution, as Einstein had never said this, but nonetheless I dug what the medium had said, and excitedly.

"Well, then. Let's all go give it a try now," said James, as he stood up and extended his arm to face the direction I'd begun to refer to as the Great Green Lawn in front of the Gladys Laliberte Temple.

Camp Etna's church and holy meeting grounds,
the Gladys Laliberte Temple. *Greta Rybus.*

"Into the wild!" cheered Ernie, and we dowsed.

We were told to find a source of water. Specifically, James instructed us to locate the old Camp Etna water pump. Ernie and I split up and took to different regions of the area. Bowing my head toward the rods and the ground, I scanned the dappled shadows of the camp. Chopped sunlight came through the treetop canopies with the bleached energetic light of the sun peeking through. Forehead facing my feet, I stepped through blades of green grass, milk thistle, sand. I heard some wind chimes in the distance. My rods tilted this way and that. We searched. This was not an unusual day at camp. I lifted my head to peek and looked around; I could see Diane, plowing with her hands in a pile of soil next to the Ladies' Auxiliary, pulling out the weeds and chanting, *"Om mani padme hum"* (I am an eternal soul). She waved at me as a woman in a long dress strode by, breaking the space between us. Dark purple, full of grace—it was Barbara leading a ghost-hunting class; her students trailed behind her like ducklings as they passed Loyalty Lodge, where I'm sure Arlene sat, flipping through channels, thinking about the world outside, which included a nearby Duey chopping wood. Janice's minivan kicked up some dust before it parked in front of the Hot Spot Café. A screen door opened and slammed shut. The camp was alive with activity, like a log in a forest full of potato bugs.

James hollered in my direction. "Go ahead and just walk now," he encouraged. "And try to keep the rods at about mid-level."

Before lowering my head again, I told myself to resist the urge to rubberneck, to look to see what direction Ernie had taken to or where he'd drift to from there. I had to do this at my own pace, not get so distracted by whether I was doing it fast enough. I figured Ernie had to have some idea where the wellhead was; he'd been coming here since slim broke the mule, and probably knew where every waterline, sink, shower, hose, Internet cable, telephone wire, bathroom, and birdbath stood. Plus, he was a psychic and a medium. If I were going to learn anything, it'd be best not to compare myself to anyone else here. I tried my best not to peek up at him during the hunt. I didn't want to cheat. Instead, I looked back at James, gave him a closed-mouthed smile, gripped my rods, and took a step.

I dowsed. I toddled along, repeating the phrases James had instructed: *Relax your body. Relax your expectations. Hold your rods in the position of two hand guns and point them straight in front of you. Walk along, concentrating on what you're looking for. Quiet your mind. Your mind is an instrument—don't let it play you. Instead, just watch the rods. Once you're picking up on something, your rods will alert you. Once you've found your line, walk towards it, walk along it, again holding the rods straight ahead. If the rods stay pointed ahead, you're on the right track. If you lose your way, the rods will steer you back.* It all sounded pretty straightforward and simple, and therefore, had to be easy.

"You want to just walk," James called once more, noticing that my rods, despite being brass, were practically limp. I took another slow and steady step, and one of my rods started to turn a little, so I followed it.

In a position statement, the National Ground Water Association asserts it "strongly opposes the use of water witches to locate groundwater on the grounds that controlled experimental evidence clearly indicates that the technique is totally without scientific merit." The United States Geological Survey (USGS) has a similar stance—our land is so water-rich that you can get wet drilling just about anywhere, if you drill deep enough. But the practice of dowsing, particularly dowsing for water, has not evaporated. The American Society of Dowsers has nearly 5,000 active members and rising, and each year, countless dowsing conferences, classes, and workshops are held for dowsing enthusiasts to gather, in the United States and abroad. A recent study financed by the German government and published in Stanford University's *Journal of Scientific Exploration* analyzed the successes and failures of dowsers searching for groundwater at more than 2,000 sites in dry, arid regions of Third World countries (Yemen, Sri Lanka, Zaire, Kenya, Namibia). When they evaluated the results of the ten-year period of study, they found dowser success rates to be incredibly impressive—for example, out of the 691 holes drilled in Sri Lanka upon the dowser's instructions, there was an overall success rate of 96 percent. In addition, these dowsers were able to predict the depth of the water and yield of the well to within 10 or 20 percent. Now, one might argue that dowsers are only reading the subtle clues of the landscape, like how a bad psychic might read the facial expressions and body language of a grieving client, or employ the tactic that Arlene described as "fishing." But the study further noted that the underground water sources found by these particular dowsers were often more than 100 feet deep and were so incredibly narrow that placing the drill just a few feet to the left or right of the dowser's location would mean missing the water completely.

I looked up from my rods again to get a sense of where I'd wandered, not to cheat but to note my progress. I had led myself to a row of recycling bins and garbage cans and landed in a whole other direction from James and Ernie. *What am I doing wrong? Why aren't my rods working?* Maybe I wasn't concentrating hard enough. I squeezed the rods a little harder, then released. Looking down at the metal sticks, I wondered how they'd been made, and pictured someone with wire cutters, clipping then reshaping a metal hanger, which made me think about the tools used in back-alley illegal abortions, which made me feel awful. I was even more distracted now, and the sounds of my streaming thoughts and judgments continued to flood my head and drown me in a lake of my own absurd mental chatter. *My sticks are broken. My sticks are on strike. They don't want to work with me because they can see how awful I really am. They know I'm a journalist. Which stick is the boy, and which one is the girl? Are they brother-sister, friends, are these rods married? Why am I so weird? Are people watching me right now? Why am I so far from everyone? What's wrong with me? Will there be a snack break?*

I stepped through a small patch of violets when a man's voice declared loudly, "I've located the wellhead!" It was Ernie. Lowering my rods, I peered over in his direction. Ernie was leaning up against the base of a fat oak tree and waved me over cheerily. From where we were, both James and I walked over toward the oak, the shade, the pump, and Ernie. When we arrived, Ernie grinned widely. In front of him, stark and blatant, hidden by nothing at all, was the old red water pump, which, having been too busy forcefully wanting my dowsing rods to work, I had failed to see.

We were back on the purple porch, sitting in the shade in rocking chairs, and more people had joined us. Two women, members of the camp, Spiritualists: Maria Ruland, and Krista Wright. Both mid-fifties, both fairly new to camp. An impertinent, lasting heat had crept into the wind and we fanned our faces. We were not in a hurry. We rocked, took turns swinging the pendulum, cracked some jokes, and then Ernie suggested we use the dowsing rods to read one another's auras.

I'd heard the words countless times before, and a few friends of mine had had their auras photographed before, but I didn't know what it truly meant.

The campers came to a general consensus: the aura is an electro-magnetic energy field that surrounds a person—a shell-shaped ball of energy that encompasses a body and consists of seven "auric bodies," or seven interrelated layers: the astral, the physical, the lower, higher, spiri-tual, intuitional, and absolute planes. Each auric body affected the oth-ers, and each one resonated at its own unique vibration, or frequency, positive and negative energies, and positive and negative polarities.

The physical aural plane is the closest layer to us, and for it to be in balance, we need to be in good health, and to be physically comfortable.

"If a person's physical aural plane is imbalanced," said Ernie, "if someone is sick and in bad health, the physical aural plane would appear smudged." To heal your physical aura, someone added, just meditate and try visualizing the color green.

The next plane, the astral plane, is our "emotional layer," which stores our emotional history. Following that is the lower plane, which relates to our thought patterns and reason and how we construct our own individual realities. This is the one, added Ernie, in which most people spend their waking hours.

Above this is the higher mental plane, where we store our more spiritual beliefs and are of a higher mind. This is where our self-love is stored, as well as our selfishness, our gratitude, and unconditional love. Next is the spiritual plane, which solely has to do with your own personal spirituality. This plane connects us to both our immediate environment and the world at large.

After that is the intuitional plane, or the celestial plane. This is where we store our intuition, or instincts, our spiritual awareness, and our dreams. And finally, there is the absolute aural plane—the big glowing red bow on top of your head; the tip of your energy field. This plane works to balance the others. It is the plane that, when in balance, harmonizes the other planes, and, I was told, it contains the blueprint for each person's spiritual destiny.

I volunteered to go first. I stood and backed up until my spine was pressed against the outside wall of the Camp Etna Inn. Everyone else rose and spread out perpendicularly from where I faced, making a line like a firing squad. Upon James's cue, the group of Spiritualists lifted their rods to chest-level and took slow steps toward me. Once they reached the outermost plane of my aura, their rods would part open.

"Go ahead," said James, and they walked. I waited. No rods parted. The group took another step forward, and another, and another. Apparently, my aura was currently quite small, and out of balance. Upon seeing this, I shrunk a little then stepped to the side.

"My turn!" said Ernie.

Aura reading, water witching, spirit photography, ghost hunting, levitation. All of this stuff had a reputation for being woo-woo, for being silly, misleading, or nonsense. The people on the porch knew this. There have always been skeptics of their faith, critics and devoted opponents, resolute on squashing such metaphysical beliefs and incorporeal practices, those determined to bury Spiritualism even before Houdini came along and who will continue to appear long after his body has turned back into soil.

"My objective in writing this book is to present an explanation of so-called occult phenomena concerning which credulity is still as busy as in the days of witchcraft," writes Dr. Millais Culpin, in his 1920 book *Spiritualism and the New Psychology.* "The producers themselves—mediums, clairvoyants, water-diviners, seers, or whatever they may be—are sometimes of such apparent honesty and simplicity that disbelief seems almost a sacrilege; therefore, part of my aim is to show how a man believing firmly in his own honesty may yet practice elaborate trickery and deceit."

Dr. Culpin goes on to explore Freud's theory of the unconscious, and lists practices like dowsing, table tipping, pendulum swinging, automatic writing, and thought reading as examples of "psychological automatism"—a type of behavior that occurs in a number of neurological and psychiatric disorders and resembles simple repetitive tics or may be a complex sequence of natural-looking movements. "The agent is conscious neither of their muscular movements," states Culpin, "nor the mental processes producing them. They can be cultivated to provide amazing results in tapping the memories of the unconscious, and if the agents remain in ignorance of their true mechanism, a systematized delusion is built up and accepted as proof of the supernatural."

Skeptics claim that there is nothing mystical or magical about dowsing: the motion of dowsing rods (or sticks or pendulums or branches or whatever tool the dowser uses) has also been attributed to something called the "ideomotor response" or ideomotor reflex, or IMR. Derived from the terms "ideo" (the idea, or mental representation) and "motor" (muscular action), IMR is a most often used to refer to the process whereby a thought or mental image brings about a seemingly "reflexive" minor automatic muscular reaction, often outside of the awareness of the person doing it. Essentially, IMR is a person unconsciously deciding to take action.

"My turn," said Ernie, and we swapped places. I stood in line with the rest of the Spiritualists while Ernie stepped forward to the wall then turned to face us.

"Go ahead," James called out, and our line took one step forward. By the second step, every dowsing rod opened up and flew apart like a can-can dancer. This was followed by a chorus of oohs and ahs. Ernie had a really big aura.

"I mentally pushed it," said Ernie, gushing. "I pushed it out."

In her epic reportage "The Dowser Dilemma," Kate Daloz recounts the story of Edith Greene, a dowser in Vermont, and how, in 2004, despite her ability to locate fresh drinking water for her town, the town snubbed her, solely on their criticism of the legitimacy of Edith's methodology, mainly out of the fear that endorsing Edith would be read as an endorsement of witchcraft.

"Interrogating Edith about her methods," writes Daloz, "or even watching her at work, does not lead to what one might call an explanation." So when the tips of the dowser's rods fly apart, seemingly of their own accord, asks Daloz, what exactly is going on? "For Edith, there's no question about what is physically causing the rod to move: she is." And when I asked James and Ernie what they thought about it, they said the same—that it was probably just their subconscious doing it. They didn't stop to ponder it too much, other than to suggest that our bodies have an innate sensory ability. That sometimes, our bodies just *know*.

Hans-Dieter Betz, a physicist at the University of Munich who conducted a research group on dowsers offers a similar explanation, albeit more complexly, that subtle electromagnetic gradients may result when water and natural fissures create changes in the electrical properties of soil and rock, and dowsers somehow can sense these changes, causing them to respond by moving their wire rods. Their subconscious sensed the water.

I put my rods down on a purple picnic table, slightly confused as to what my own mind was doing and feeling somewhat defeated by the size of Ernie's aura compared to mine. I sat down next to James and harrumphed, loud enough for him to hear me.

James patted me on the back. "It's simple," he said, "and also it's not."

"We possess several subtle bodies interpenetrating the physical body," writes Stephen A. Herman. "The individual soul, or consciousness, is enveloped by several covers the densest of which is the physical body followed by the mind, intelligence, and false ego. The mind may be compared to a computer, the intelligence is the program, and the false ego is the identification with a temporary role."

"You got your conscious," Arlene had said to me the other day before I had left Loyalty Lodge. I'd asked her how one accesses the part of their mind to sense beyond what was in front of their eyes. "You got your subconscious," she explained, extending one finger to her forehead, "and then up here," she said, tapping on her temple, "you got your God conscious. And you shove that into your subconscious and you forget about it." Her shoulders slumped, as did mine. "But," she continued, "you can access it through meditation. At camp, it's what we taught, what we worked on. It's what we did."

It's simple, and also it's not. If there are 121 subtle states of consciousness, how could one ever access another person's truth? How could I, or anyone, prove the validity of the dowsers? Or for that matter, the truth of these Spiritualists and the other mediums at camp— how could we ever truly see exactly what they could see, what they could hear, what they could sense or could feel? I wasn't here to clarify or verify. What good would it do me—a personal conquest to prove something wrong and me right? The question of whether these Spiritualists were "making all this up" was much more complicated than it at first might seem, because it was an impossible one. Truth and reality had a different meaning to every person at camp, and there was no way to tell if the truth began in their bodies or their minds or a part of their mind or from a voice in the heavens above. Nor did it matter to them, because it felt real. Each reality and each doorway was different—it could begin with a single thought or a feeling or a sight or a sound, a nudge or a taste; it didn't matter as much as what it was doing for them—it was leading them forward, moving them ahead. The question wasn't whether I believed them; the answer was that I believed in them.

For all I cared, the Spiritualists could have been showing me how to walk on my hands, because what I soon began to see, whether I was upside down or right-side up, were two very blatant things: their faith, and my own lack of it. What was happening was an exercise in faith, and I had failed. I'd failed to loosen my grip, failed to get out of my own way, failed to have faith in what might happen if I stopped trying to control everything. The Spiritualists and mediums I had met had all told me that while they considered themselves skeptics of Spiritualism and that it was a healthy thing, more than anything, the one thing they valued and trusted fully was their instinct, their intuition, their deepest consciousness, and the importance of exercising it daily. They had faith, and these Spiritualists were showing me that faith doesn't just happen—it requires action, and it requires some level of commitment, some bit of devotion. With my sagging brass rods and incessant mental chatter storming down my own path, blocking my clear view and silencing my own voice of instinct, I realized that my state of consciousness was a shallow one, and I had failed the point of this exercise. There had been so much chatter going on inside my head that I hadn't paid attention to what was really happening, or what had been for some time.

The mental chatter we hear questioning our every move is the voice of the ego, and if I'd learned anything from my time at Etna thus far, it was that ego is louder than intuition, far more dangerous, and could really cause one to walk around in circles, or to circle the drain. With my dowsing rods, I had wanted certainty from someone else; with the Spiritualists, the certainty came from within—a nudge. Listening to that nudge was an act of faith. Faith was action, and I was starting to realize that it was my own job to find the meaning for myself. It wasn't about finding proof; it was about welcoming one's intuition, not shutting it down. It was about opening up and letting go. I'd become quite good at listening to the unabating jabber in my head, but perhaps it was that quieter voice, the subtle nudge and not my louder thoughts, that had always brought me to all the places I needed to be, and so effortlessly. Looking back on it, I'd always been told that I was a sensitive person, and that this was a bad or weak thing. But it had always been this sensitivity that had led me to the moments that mattered, the moments where I dug deeper to understand life—for instance, to write about funeral homes, or to explore death. Maybe it had been this inner voice that had led me to Maine and to Camp Etna in the first place, and maybe it was time I started following this part of me much more fully. Perhaps it was time to wake up. This is what I discovered after Dowsing for Answers. This is when I decided to stop thinking so much, and to start to slow down and listen more instead. I took a breath, picked up my dowsing rods, and did my best to catch up with the rest of the group.

CHAPTER 7

The New Generation

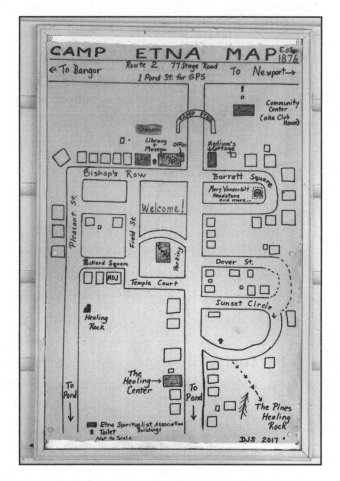

A hand-drawn map of the campgrounds. *Mira Ptacin*

"Nonsense," Diane told me eagerly, clutching my arm and smiling wildly. "We have to embrace what doesn't quite make any sense—the non-sense—if we are ever to begin to understand the other dimensions, and life after death." Or life after *life*, as Dr. Raymond Moody had told her and the rest of the full house that had come to see him speak that day. It was July, the heat was searing, and, Camp Etna's small size notwithstanding—the Spiritualists of Lily Dale, for example, have a year-round population of approximately 275, with an estimated 22,000 visitors attending each summer—the Big Kahuna had indeed arrived.

Dr. Moody was old, and he was famous—a combination as fragile as a Ming vase. Completely bald and covered in age spots, Moody had warm and curious eyes, a kind face, and skin the color of a Band-Aid; he looked a bit like Elmer Fudd and had a Southern drawl. Approaching eighty, and despite his credentials (two PhDs, one MD, one World Humanitarian Award, eleven books and counting), despite the subject of his scholarship (the experience of death), and despite his fan base (millions—plus he'd been a guest on *Oprah*), Dr. Raymond Moody still remained down-to-earth, and was without gloom or doom as he told the crowd this: "We have to train our brains to think outside the box and examine what doesn't make any sense. Only then will we be able to expand our vision and see what lies beyond this life on Earth."

While some say death is an annihilation of consciousness, others believe it is the passing of the soul into another plane. To come up with something closer to an answer, Moody spent years gathering and studying the stories of people who had been medically pronounced "dead" but then came back to life. Out of these testimonials, the doctor came to identify several similar phases that occurred shortly following each person's passing: their hearing the news of being pronounced dead; feelings of peace and quiet; unusual auditory sensations (in one account, a woman tells how, as she lost consciousness, she heard "a loud ringing. It could be described as a buzzing, and I was in a sort of whirling state." Others describe it as a shrill whistling sound, a severe humming, or something that sounded like the wind). Next came the dark tunnel and the out-of-body experience, where the newly dead could see their old body below, being resuscitated or sprawled out on the road following a car accident, or wherever they'd died. This was followed by "meeting others," or becoming aware of other spiritual beings in their vicinity to ease the transition of death. And finally: the being of light, then the end-of-life review. After this, the "border" or limit, like a gray mist or a fence across a field, and then the decision to keep going, or come back to life. Their old life.

Dr. Moody himself had died briefly after attempting suicide in 1991 (a death that Moody claims was the result of an undiagnosed thyroid condition that had severely affected his mental state). Two years after this, Moody was hospitalized again—this time by family, who claimed he'd been spending too much time locking himself in dark rooms and talking into mirrors, but in Moody's defense he was conducting a study in "scrying"—a practice inspired by ancient Greek psychomanteums, where the living would gaze into a mirror in a dark or dimly lit room in hopes of communicating with the dead. Shortly after this, Moody built his own psychomanteum in Alabama. This week at Camp Etna, he planned on teaching his students how to build their own.

"When I was in my own altered states of consciousness, I recovered a reliable method from the ancient world where many people can come out and converse with their departed loved ones." This is what Dr. Moody had told Diane as she videotaped him earlier in the week. As per usual, Diane was doing what she could to bring in more warm bodies to her beloved camp, and she took it upon herself to put together a promo video for Camp Etna's Facebook page. Diane was a Raymond Moody superfan, and still had her original copy of the *Reader's Digest* issue from 1975 that excerpted bits of *Life After Life* when it first came out. The book went on to sell 13 million copies worldwide.

Life After Life entered the spiritual waters in the wake of the subcultural pioneers of the 1960s. With the decline and steady break-down of the majority of hippie communes, counterculture metamor-phosed until the 1970s birthed a new spiritual revolution: New Age.

Many former members of the counterculture movement of the '60s, including Timothy Leary, became adherents of the New Age move-ment, and while its exact origins still remain under debate, the purpose of New Age was clear: to bring together the wider "fluid and fuzzy cultic milieu" of American society.

In 1970, an American theosophist named David Spangler was feel-ing this pull too. While Moody was compiling his research to prove that we don't actually die, and five years before the publication of his findings, Spangler put a pin in his own idea: a central notion was that our world was entering the Age of Aquarius (which happens roughly every 2,150 years, when the sun's position at the time of vernal, or the March equinox, moves in front of a new zodiac constellation) and as the Earth was moving into a new cycle, a simultaneous release of new waves of spiritual energy was initiating a new change in the current of our world. Spangler preached that people should channel and make manifest this new vitality in what he declared was the beginning of the "New Age" movement.

People embraced other terms for the era ("esotericism," the "light," "alternative," "holistic," and "spiritual" (with a small s) just as freely as they embraced other spiritual concepts, practices, and philosophies. Spiritualism, Theosophy, and New Thought percolated through the new movement, as did the ideas of earlier occult influencers like Franz Mesmer and Emanuel Swedenborg (two theorists who had persuaded Mr. Andrew Jackson Davis, one of the forefathers of Spiritualism). Some people joined Spiritualist churches and attended Spiritualist camps. Some found other outlets. Traditional witchcraft, Paganism, and Wicca meshed and mixed with the techno-shamanic movement, the Goddess movement, neo-Druidry, Celtic revivalism. People were joining the Temple of Set, and members of the Church of Satan were less reluctant to come out of hiding. It was a cocktail of belief systems and sacraments, "a synthesis of many different preexisting movements and strands of thought." The possibilities were endless.

The possibilities took shape: New Thought churches. Transformational training courses. Helen Schucman's *A Course in Miracles*. Raymond Moody's *Life After Life*. Shirley MacLaine's *Out on a Limb*, in which the actress, singer, dancer, and sister of Warren Beatty shares her theories on life after death, belief in meditation and mediumship, trance-channeling, and UFOs. A miniseries soon followed. Soon came the birth of New Age music and the rebirth of the study of astrology and planetary-alignment courses and crystal healing. With the New Age conferences and workshops came videocassettes, audiotapes, jewelry, clothing styles, haircuts. The New Age movement, which evolved into a practice focused on self-reliance, brought with it an abundance of self-help tools, metaphysical bookstores, and literature genres. By the 1990s, esotericism had morphed into a frenzied "enterprise culture," and the term "New Age" was more of a marketing tool than a practice. I could see why Arlene could be so opposed to even letting the two words enter her camp.

But there has always been a thin line dividing popularity and selling out, a compromise between dissemination of information and vending. Entrepreneurialism and consumerism had given New Age a bad rep, and yet, if you look closely, evidence shows that New Age has managed to seep deep into the wet soil of our culture. Or perhaps it has always been there but was resurrected—the ancient wisdom and timeless practices, ideas and beliefs proving incapable of extinction.

Diane had placed her prized copy of the 1975 *Reader's Digest*, now yellowed and crinkled like a dried dahlia, on top of a table in her museum to display for all the visitors who'd come to listen to Moody's lecture. The topic of today's talk: embracing the nonsense. Lesson number one: you must think outside the box. The event was held inside the Gladys Laliberte Temple, and it was filled to the brim with visitors. Outside the perimeter of the congregation, Gladys's granddaughter was walking her cat.

The woman was middle-aged and medium-height—strong, thick, like it'd take a lot to knock her down. She was wearing a T-shirt and beige cargo shorts. Her hair was short and white with a natural kick-flip to it, and she was holding the end of a thin leash that was attached to the collar of a Norwegian forest cat.

"Bezoar," said the woman. "That's his name. It's the medical terminology for 'furball.'" Down by her flip-flopped feet on a path of pebbles, the gray-and-black feline wrapped around her legs like a thick curl of smoke. The cat bellowed a bit, then rubbed its gums on his human's ankle. The human's name was Karlene Tanner.

Like Arlene Grant, Karlene was a kind of camp elder, too, except that when Arlene joined Camp Etna, around 1964 or 1965, Karlene had been just a child, summer-camp age. With her father's mother being the great Gladys Laliberte, Karlene and her brother Morgan hitched onto her like baby opossums and, from the time they were small kids, joined Gladys each summer when she was at camp; Camp Etna and everything within its gates had been home to Karlene for the better part of her life. When not at Camp Etna, Karlene was raised Episcopalian, Baptist, and a little bit Catholic, so when Gladys would bring her to the Spiritualist community, they'd have to fib about it to Karlene's grandpa and the rest of her Christian family, saying they were just going to a regular old Maine summer camp. (Gladys did eventually divorce her husband, and came out about Spiritualism.)

Karlene pivoted in a spot on the lawn where violets grew in profusion, then invited me to her cottage, which was up the road and near Harrison D. Barrett Square and Mary Scannell Pepper Vanderbilt's grave, and was, of all the homes, closest to the entrance of camp. It was a white bungalow with a screened-in porch from which hummingbird feeders and wind chimes swayed. Like most cottages at camp, hers was not fancy. Unlike most cottages, Karlene's didn't have a name.

"We've always been in this corner," she said, unlatching Bezoar's leash. "From May fifteenth, when we turned the water on through

October fifteenth when we turned the water off. The campground would be teeming."

As I stepped onto the porch, Karlene lifted her limbs toward the landscape behind me—her arms were pinkish and pale, strong and muscular, the arms of a person who knew how to throw a curveball. With broad strokes of her hand, she painted a memory of Camp Etna in the '70s that was similar to Arlene's: the two-oven restaurant in which Loretta did all the cooking with the help of Pierre, who had a voice "of pure, pure tenor, and had sung on Broadway," the truckers who would stop by for pies on their way to the interstate. She told me about the message circles, the walks in the woods, the packed church services, the Camp Etna thrift store and bingo nights, and how the older mediums would always want to win so they could buy toilet paper.

"Back in the day, mediums would stay through the winter even without insulation, because they couldn't afford anything else," she said. "That's how they lived. Living here is cheap, and people tried to buy houses for cheap living." To purchase on the grounds now, you have to be a Spiritualist, and you had to be a member of a Spiritualist church for at least a year.

Inside Karlene's nameless cottage, a fan and television were running, with a cool breeze blowing on my skin as Ellen DeGeneres danced in the aisles with her audience. We sat down, and Bezoar leapt up into Karlene's chair and perched himself, taking temperature of things. The cottage was an inheritance—the place had originally belonged to Gladys, and after everyone in the family died, it was passed on to Karlene. All summer long, Karlene herself had been doing construction on the cabin, winterizing it. The last surviving member of her family, Karlene had just moved back to Camp Etna after recently retiring and was living here full-time. She was in-between: part of both the old generation and the new.

Like the women who raised her, Karlene was a psychic and she was a medium. Clairvoyant, clairaudient, she had it all—could see the dead, hear them, feel them, smell them—she'd always been able to, never had to try hard. As a kid and growing up, she'd walk from cottage to cottage, visiting her spiritual aunties and picking up tips and training. Karlene absorbed it all; she got to be good at it. Real good. Then one of the women on the grounds helped Karlene discover her career—she told her to go into nursing.

"Thoughts are things," said Karlene. "I went into the ICU because I could read thoughts, and I always knew what the patient wanted. If someone has got a tube in their mouth and they're throwing out thoughts, I could pick them up. I could hear a voice loud enough to make me turn around and look. Thoughts are tangible, and if someone is sensitive enough to put it out there, I can pick it up easily."

As a psychic nurse, Karlene knew things ahead of time. She knew when a code red was coming in. She knew if someone's heart rate was at 220. She knew she could do a body scan of a patient with her third eye and physically identify the problem. She knew she could do hands-on healing to mend it. As an ICU nurse, Karlene could also help people cross over from life to life after death. "If somebody was dying, I could help them transition. Plus, I'm comfortable with death because I know what's there—or what comes after it. Most nurses are scared of death, and they don't want people to die."

She helped her brother Morgan pass too. He had AIDS, was in the ICU with a tumor in his lungs, and didn't want to go to a nursing home. He asked to be taken off the ventilator. "The most visceral thing I've ever seen in my life was watching Morgan walk into a lawn with trees to meet my parents, my parents hugging him, bringing him in, and them all waving back to me. I waved back at them, but I also said, 'Yeah, yeah, yeah. You're all fine, but I'm still here!' And this is the way people should pass. I tried to help people die with dignity."

After leaving nursing, Karlene traveled a lot—Pennsylvania, San Francisco, El Paso, Vermont. She married and divorced. She came out as a lesbian. She did construction, worked in the Dartmouth College infirmary, did labor on a tomato farm, and took a job at a chiropractor's office for a while before retiring at age sixty-three. "All my family died young, so I said *the hell with that.* I retired and I've been here ever since." The prodigal daughter.

"Sometimes it can be a lot. Being able to connect with so much. So you gotta protect yourself. For instance," she continued, "my grandmother Gladys. She was an alcoholic. My assumption was that she heard voices and she couldn't handle it. Luckily, and eventually, she found this religion. But back then you couldn't tell people you heard voices."

Karlene was facing me, but her eyes shifted to the space behind me. She was distracted, trailed off, and then she said, "OK, like, right now, right now there is a man standing behind you."

My body went stiff like a sharpened pencil—as far as I could see, Karlene and I were the only people in the room. "He's some kind of grandfather figure," said Karlene. "Your father's father, or uncle?"

She spoke quickly, flipped her hands around in front of her like she was folding a sheet. Long ago, Karlene had set her boundaries and conditions—told spirits how to appear and with what patterns. *Some are new to this, too,* she'd said. *They're learning to communicate with you as well.* To make it easier on the spirits as well as herself, Karlene set certain patterns: if a spirit comes in and the spirit is from the sitter's mother's side of the family, Karlene would see it on her right side. Dad's side of the family were on her left side. Aunts and uncles step out to the side, friends stand behind the sitter. She waved her hands to indicate which generation and how far back the spirit went —one generation, then two.

"He's around you all the time," she continued, cool as a cucumber. "Fairly tall, six-foot-two, broad-shouldered, narrow waist, rolled-up sleeves, strong head of hair. Similar facial structure to yours too. Had all his teeth too." Karlene laughed. "He was very proud that he had all his teeth. A T-shirt under his shirt, nice pair of pants. Small circular glasses. He worked with his hands, can build anything and so can your son. He's around your son all the time too." Next, Karlene pressed her hands together like she was washing them. "Tactile," she said, "and always has to touch things."

I had no idea who Karlene was talking about, but it was the same spirit bio I'd gotten from Barbara when I'd asked her on a whim if she could see my spirit guide—she'd described a man from my father's side, same "shirt-sleeves rolled up," same framed glasses. Also, I had not offered any information about myself to Karlene—I'd never told her I had a son. I sat perplexed, but Karlene simply moved on, as if a passerby had waved through the window then disappeared, which, I supposed, had just happened.

"Tell him I said hello?" I didn't know what else to say.

Karlene bowed her head, laughed, and with that, we moved on.

Karlene wiped her hands onto the smooth fabric of her long shorts. "Mediumship can be a gift," she said, "but it can be dangerous too. When I was here as a little kid, most people on the grounds were in their sixties, seventies, eighties. There weren't a lot of young people, and that's still an issue today. But in the 1960s and '70s, however, there were a lot of older mediums, and they were a bunch of egotistical mediums. Strong mediums, but egotistical mediums, like my grandmother. It made my head want to blow up." Because of this, Karlene almost didn't return to Camp Etna.

She separated herself from the camp around the time when New Age had really peaked, because the camp started to feel infected. The energy had turned dark, almost too much for her to bear. Starting in the 1970s, mediumship became less about being a channel and more about competition. Camp Etna mediums were contending with the ubiquitous access to New Age, and they were also contesting one another. There were a lot of mediums on the grounds, and mediumship was how each one of them made their money—how they fed themselves, bought toilet paper, heated their cottages.

"Clients would drive on and they had to pick their medium, and the competition to get clients, and of 'who was the best' took over. It was bad," said Karlene. "The higher you go up, the better you get as a medium, the more you are tested spiritually." She placed her hands over her abdomen, then moved them up toward her chest. "As you go through your chakras, you have your root for survival; your gut (fear-based); your heart, which can lead you to lots of places; your throat (so you can speak your mind without holding back) . . . the higher up in the chakras, the higher up in the spiritual realm." Karlene placed her index finger firmly on her forehead. "When you reach the third-eye chakra, you're doing readings. You're in the realm of telling people things and guiding them in their lives—or spirit is telling them this through you. And if you start to say, Oh, I'm so good, then your ego is not in check. You have to check your ego. You have to be cognizant about what you're taking. A good medium shouldn't need any kudos."

While Karlene's talk of the chakra system sounded New Agey, it was actually older than the religion of Spiritualism itself. According to the Bhagavad Gita, as well as Sufism, Taoism, Tibetan Buddhism, Kriya yoga, and Hermeticism, within a human's physical body is what is known as the subtle body (also referred to as "the most sacred body," "true and genuine body," "the diamond body," "the light body," "the rainbow body," "the body of bliss," or "the immortal body," depending on the belief system), which is composed of mind, intelligence, and ego. Within the subtle body are invisible energy centers known as chakras—whirling, spinning vortices of energy and vibration that correspond to the massive nerve centers in the physical body. The chakras are powerhouses of vitality that, in order to function healthily, a person must keep in balance. To those who believe, this system is as timeless as the soul.

"I'm sure she already made it clear," Karlene said reticently, "that Arlene doesn't want this place to be New Age."

I nodded.

"I hear that. But what folks don't realize is that to get the young people in, you gotta do more. For example: Tarot cards aren't Spiritualist. That's not what the church does. At the church, we live by the principles. If you start to bring in other stuff, that's not what Spiritualism is. Tarot cards are considered a crutch. And that's fine—just don't use it in the church. People get all hung up with what is being done in the church. Maybe the old-timers feel threatened. When you're being praised all the time, it's called the you, you, you as opposed to thank you, spirit. That's where the ego comes in."

The cat meowed, making a low-pitched, menacing sound. Karlene reached around and pulled Bezoar from the top of the chair behind her and put him on her lap. "Thoughts are things," she said again, looking at Bezoar. "People on these grounds who are ill, there are reasons."

Bezoar cried again, prompting Karlene to roll her eyes, stand up, and carry her cat to the porch. As she opened the aluminum door, Bezoar twisted from her arms, dropped to the ground, and scurried outside, most likely on a hunt for chickadees.

"All the ladies here have their little things," said Karlene. "Some will call themselves historians when they're still pretty new to this place and completely off in their historical facts, while others will go off on 'the old Spiritualist' ways and rant about how things *used* to be." She shrugged and smiled. "When you get all the Spiritualists here, it's like getting a bunch of politicians together." She brushed the fur from her T-shirt and sat back down. "And yes, I can talk to animals."

It was the inside opposition and butting of egos that had driven Karlene away from Camp Etna, but after enough time as a medium in the wild, something compelled her to return. And as far as she was concerned, this was her last stop for a long time.

"When I finally came back, I did it so I could continue to find out who I was, and now my role here is to be present. When you come through the gates of Etna you go into another world. Here at Camp Etna, time stands still. The grounds are healing. It is protected. And we are building it back up to be protected. Like right now, we have new people coming in, new mediums, younger ones, and they are coming in because they have found their people. And maybe that's the reason I'm here now. I'm here to help change the energy of this place. There is a whole group of us right now doing it. We are bringing in the new."

The act of bringing also meant propulsion, clearing out old energy.

Just down the street from Karlene's cottage and a few yards away from Loyalty Lodge sat Heart Song, a white, LEGO-shaped cottage, which was now occupied by two younger Spiritualists new to camp, a medium named Angie and her husband, Washian, a shaman. Not long after Karlene moved back to Camp Etna, Angie and Washian, along with Barbara, had helped her get rid of Gladys—or really, the four of them released the ghost of Gladys Laliberte.

Even after she died, Gladys would wander the camp. "She was dead but she was still earthbound," said Karlene. "The dead can come back and show themselves, but the others still in limbo will stay and wander." According to Karlene, you can recognize a ghost because it has a different energy; they have more human emotions. Ghosts are full-on ego, and they become possessive of what they think is theirs and they're not going to give it up, so some can stay earthbound forever unless someone crosses them over. "There is no time on the other side. Twenty or thirty years can be a second. We're the linear ones."

One night, on Barbara's suggestion, Karlene, Barbara, and Angie got together in Heart Song and offered to release any trapped spirits into the white light. They sent Washian back to Karlene's cottage to make sure Gladys didn't try to get in and hide out inside.

"We're doing a circle, and my grandmother doesn't want to go—I mean, it's been since 1978—that's a long time. She loved these grounds. I swear, these grounds were *her being*. But they were also her ego. We asked anybody who was on the grounds that wanted to go, to go, and they all went into the circle and you could watch them go up and into the light. I recognized a lot of people from the 1960s that were still here that went. And then we opened it up to a fifty-mile radius: *If you want to pass, now's the time. Go into the light. Your family will meet you on the other side.* It was fabulous."

"And what about Gladys?" I asked. "Did she go into the light too?"

Not without a fight, Karlene told me. As they were doing the circle, Gladys went to Karlene's cottage. Washian was upstairs brushing his teeth and heard someone pounding on the back door. He went downstairs to check but there was nobody there. Then he heard more pounding on the back door and realized it was Gladys. He told her that he was not letting her in, scolded her, and instructed her to go down to the temple, that they were trying to help her. After that, she retreated back to the temple to be released, but reluctantly.

"My grandmother Gladys went kicking and screaming," said Karlene. "And now it's a totally different thing—she's different. And she is happy that she fully transitioned. But I had to set my limits."

I, too, was headed to Heart Song, now on my way from Gladys's former cottage to meet with the new generation of Camp Etna Spiritualists. Just as Karlene and her troupe were releasing the old, they were bringing the ancient to the grounds as well: today, under the guidance of Angie Butler Welch, we would be tapping into the Book of Life.

"The Akashic record," said Angie, "is the energy domain that holds the recording of the journey of your soul." I asked her to repeat it again, and slowly. "The Akasha," she said, "is your soul energy. In traditional religions, it's known as the Book of Life."

Angie had swooping eyelashes, a narrow nose, and sported a strand of hot pink that snaked through the rest of her caramel-colored hair, which she raked back with long nails that sparkled and were painted the color of emeralds. Her voice was as soft as a cotton ball, and I couldn't help but think of the Disney princesses of my youth: exquisitely feminine. Her diction was flawless and very graceful, which could be said of the woman in her entirety. She was a decade older than me but looked a decade younger, bloomy and floral, as if the beads of sweat on her temples smelled naturally like bergamot and vanilla.

From outside the screen door to the small porch of Heart Song, a summer breeze pushed through, offering relief and making the wood-and-chrome wind chimes flutter. Beyond that, I could hear what sounded like applause coming from the Gladys Laliberte Temple—Raymond Moody's lecture on death and nonsense was wrapping up.

Visitors loaded into their cars and drove off, their tires kicking up dry gravel and leaving temporary clouds of dust in their place.

"Basically," said Angie, "everyone has their own individual records, and we've all had previous incarnations. Let's say you have Tom Cruise, and he's doing his thing—he's acting. He's in *Top Gun*, and he's playing the character of Maverick. But underneath that, he's still Tom Cruise. And then you have Tom Cruise in *Mission: Impossible*. Still Tom Cruise, but he's wearing a different mask."

"He's a Scientologist," I countered. "Doesn't he believe he's an alien?"

"Perhaps he's not the best example," Angie responded, "but you get what I'm saying. *Reincarnation*. Each movie is a different lifetime, same soul. When I read your Akashic record, think of me going to a card index in an old-school library. I can go into a section of the library, open it up, all things about you in all incarnations of your life, past, present, and future, all of the things that are possible, all that is there and accessible for me to read."

The Sanskrit term *akasha* was introduced to the language of theosophy through Helena Petrovna Blavatsky, a Russian occultist, philosopher, and author who co-founded the Theosophical Society in 1875. Blavatsky characterized the akasha as a sort of life force, the "indestructible tablets of the astral light" recording both the past and future of human thought and action. In 1883, Alfred Percy Sinnett, a British scholar, author, and theosophist living and studying in India, published his book *Esoteric Buddhism*, in which he further expands on the idea of the Akashic record by citing the first president of the Theosophist Society, Henry Steel Olcott, the first well-known American of European ancestry to make a formal conversion to Buddhism. Olcott wrote, "Buddha taught two things are eternal, viz, 'Akasa' and 'Nirvana': everything has come out of Akasa in obedience to a law of motion inherent in it, and passes away. No thing ever comes out of nothing . . . Early Buddhism, then, clearly held to a permanency of records in the Akasa and the potential capacity of man to read the same, when he was evolved to the stage of true individual enlightenment."

"*Akasha*," Angie continued, "is the Sanskrit word for atmosphere, and the Akashic record is like an enormous supercomputer encoded in the ether, or etheric plane, which is a nonphysical plane of existence, that catalogues the compendium of all events—every human thought, emotion, word, intent, action, karmic natures, all our desires—of every human unit throughout time, every dream, plan, and movement that has ever occurred in the past, present, and future."

"That's"—I coughed—"quite a lot."

"I know," said Angie, and smiled pleasantly.

It wasn't until 2010 that she found Camp Etna, via the invitation of Dr. Barbara Williams, whom she refers to as her spiritual mother. Angie first met Barbara and Steve in 2008, at a lush chunk of woodland called Acres of Wildlife. Self-described as a "Camper's Paradise in Southern Maine," the place was an isolated three hundred acres of rustic recreation devoted to nature and good old-fashioned family fun. Still in existence, Acres of Wildlife has a general store with penny candy, fishing poles, and soft-serve ice cream. The grounds have sandlots and rusted metal playgrounds that probably don't pass current safety inspection standards but do have plenty of large things to climb up and jump off—the best kind. It has horseshoe tosses and putt-putt golf, a gemstone mining stream, taxidermy displays, motorhome grounds, rentable cabins, pop-up tent areas, and is surrounded by an additional three thousand more acres of state-owned pine. At Acres, you're outdoors more than you are in.

Every year, worn out by the exhaustive duties and absurd psychic garbage that women are forced to lug around, Angie would round up her squad of lady friends to abandon the menfolk and drive down the long sandy road to the gated entrance of Acres for their homemade retreat weekend and a particularly earthy strain of girl time. The objective: to refresh and regroup. During Angie's retreat in 2008, she was in a particularly potent place of trying to access and understand her truth, because she wasn't finding it through traditional religion, and she wasn't feeling it in her marriage, either. It happened to be October at Acres, and coincidentally, just after Heavy Metal Weekend and right before Halloween (Zombie Weekend), the campground was hosting its annual "Mediums Weekend." For Angie, that's when everything changed.

Barbara was giving a psychic development class, educating the curious and recruiting newbies, when their paths crossed; upon meeting Barbara and upon first glance, Angie felt an uncanny and deep connection to her, more than she had with anyone for years, and it couldn't be undone. She immediately signed up for Barbara's development class. Barbara's teachings clicked. The women clicked, and Barbara took Angie under her wing. Before long, she and Steve invited Angie to Camp Etna, told her to stay at Peacefull Solitude, to walk around, get to know the camp, and that's where Angie's world unfolded for her in a way that finally made sense.

Back then, Angie was still married to her first husband, and together they were raising a daughter. But at Etna, Angie began to meet new people, *her* people, people like her who believed in a grander scheme, bigger than the religions she was used to. "People who walk the line spiritually," was how Angie described them. "I found the religion of Spiritualism, and even though Spiritualism is a religion, I found it wasn't within the confines of 'you are a sinner and you will never achieve greatness.'"

To Angie, Spiritualism wasn't a religion led by a handsome man with brown shaggy hair and a sexy brown beard who was born in the Middle East but happened to be presented as Caucasian as a cowboy, a religion that was judged by a white man with a white beard on a white cloud, a religion that came served with a side of fear and the hot topping of "you'll never be good enough," she explained. "I couldn't wrap my head around the idea that if I'm made from God, why would I be 'bad'? When I found Camp Etna, I was *seeking*, and I was seeking *love*."

Like the majority of the mediums at Etna, Angie had always had intuitive gifts, had always been able to see the dead. Earliest memory: being four years old and being sent downstairs at a friend's house to go retrieve kitchen towels out of the dryer and coming upon a billiards party of dead people having a pretty good time. But Angie was raised in the Baptist church, and as she grew up, she pushed her special sight back, and back some more. Despite the world telling her the dead didn't exist, her sight of spirit, she says, still stuck.

"And yes," said Angie, "I did the whole Ouija board thing. Once, when I was younger and didn't know about protection, hadn't learned the White Light Protection Prayer, I was playing with a Ouija board and my friend said the thing you're never supposed to say: *'If you want to use my body . . .'* And something went in, something came in."

Angie's voice shimmied a little bit, and she drew her hands into her lap. "Suddenly, my friend was not herself. My friend stabbed me on my hand—*stabbed* me. Right then and there. I was speaking to her and she wasn't responding and then she stabbed me with a butter knife, right in the center of the palm of my hand." Angie extended her slender arm, then opened up her hand to reveal the scar. It looked like a piece of risen yeast. A wedge of moon.

"It was one of the scariest moments of my life," Angie continued. "She stood there after she stabbed me, laughing and laughing and laughing in a voice that just wasn't hers, and then she peed her pants. Right there, just peed her pants, and then she dropped to the floor and passed out. I never touched the board again. I tried burning it, it wouldn't burn. I gave it away. It was a matter of not protecting our-selves. I still won't say the name it gave us." Angie inhaled for a spell before sighing heavily: "I dare not speak its name because I know to speak it would call it in."

Angie married young, a man who was traditionally religious, but she didn't hide her mediumship from him, and he believed in her—said she had what the Bible calls "The Spiritual Gift of Discernment." "But dead people scared him. To him, there was no way to differentiate between a spirit or a demon." So Angie kept her mediumship at bay, or at least she kept it under the radar. She'd slip into the New Age and Occult sections of the bookstore, searching and studying, starting with *The Encyclopedia of Divination of Prophecy*, by Walter B. and Litzka Gibson. It was the 1990s, the age of neon. Now it was 2017. Angie was in her early forties, had divorced, then married a shaman, was hiding nothing, and owned her first cottage at Camp Etna.

"I've got this gift," said Angie. "I know I'm supposed to use it to help people. But I only use it on the energy vibration of love."

"How do you know it's the energy of love?" I asked.

"I trust fully," said Angie. "Can you tell the way you feel differently with your child coming up to you than anyone else? It's how it *feels* to you. When I am on the energy vibration of love, I start talking a mile a minute. The vibration is faster. If you're going to be working with someone from light, someone from love, that's what it feels like. And if you find something that isn't, it's usually because it's someone that has not crossed over. There are negative things out there."

Angie stood up, sauntered into her kitchen, and came back with a small wooden bowl of trail mix and offered it to me. I grabbed an almond and popped it into my mouth.

"When you read my Akashic records," I asked, "what does that look like to you?"

"It's more of a feeling," said Angie. "And it depends on the person I'm connecting with." The place where she goes to find the connection, to read my personal card catalogue that exists in the ether, is in her own mind. "I bring my soul there. When I open the records, I can feel the differences in vibrations when I'm there. Together, we can go in and rewrite something that has happened in your past, like a traumatic event. Through deep meditation, I take you back in time to that event so that you can understand it in a new way, remove yourself from it, forgive yourself for whatever happened. Or we can take you to before the event happened and clear out all the energy of the incident. We are looking at the incarnation of the soul as you, and we are reading why things are happening or not happening, why we can't break certain patterns. It's like a spiritual counseling session. I feel humbled that I'm allowed to do this. I feel honored that somehow I was chosen and allowed to pass on that message and inspire some sort of healing and hope and confirmation and belief, and to me, it is just as amazing to sit back afterwards and say wow. And I don't say, *Wow, I did that.* What I'm saying is, *Wow, that person is changed.*"

I grabbed another handful of nuts while Angie lit a candle. "And what does it feel like when you're connecting to someone who has already passed?" I asked. "When you're connecting to the spirit of a dead person?"

"It depends on the person I'm connecting with," said Angie. "I'm allowing myself to almost merge into their energy, the spirit's energy. What is it they want their loved one to know? It's like whatever they are is me. I can feel their sadness, happiness, ultimate love, sorrow, joy . . . I feel it all because it feels like it's me. I'm not sure if I'm stepping into their energy or if they're stepping into me. And it took years of practice to understand it."

Here are her two most important teachers: Barbara, and meditation. When you are in meditation, Angie explained, your brain waves are different than when you are fully awake. When you meditate and you're good at it, you go to the same place that you go to when you're asleep as far as brain waves are concerned, awaken a part of your brain that's normally asleep—the right brain. The left brain is reading, writing, arithmetic, languages. The right side of your brain is images, music, art, poetry, creativity.

"Before I get ready to do a reading," said Angie, "I dump all my junk." Angie meditates and leaves behind anything that would stop her from connecting—things like fear, doubt, judgment—centers herself.

"Next, I raise my vibration to meet Spirit, because Spirit is at a higher vibration."

I asked her what spirit vibration feels like. The only vibration I knew and was familiar with was a strong one—an obvious one, like when I turn my cell phone on vibrate. "But it doesn't feel like that, does it? Is it that strong of a feeling?" I asked.

She described the feeling as subtle, sometimes refined, sometimes slight, light and tingly. It could be different for everyone—hair-raising, goose bump–inducing. It could be a whisper or a wind, and many times you don't notice it, unless you are paying attention.

"Next," said Angie, "I visualize colors as I count up. Then, in my mind's eye, I go up this little set of stairs, and then I come to a door, and that's what will allow me to enter, to be connected. I always see a big picture window and I make sure that's clean, and that's my third eye. I have a little computer in my little spiritual room, and I make sure that that's on. I have a telephone in there and I always pick it up and make sure I have a dial tone so that I can hear them. I look over and I have a book. I make sure my book is open, and that's where I have my Akashic records."

"How long does it take you to get to that place?" I asked.

"Thirty seconds."

Angie and I sat in silence for a few beats, and with no further questions, she told me to relax, and that we'd begin with the reading. She closed her eyes and took a breath as I looked down at my knees and waited until she spoke again or moved.

And then: "Your records are now open."

To describe what an accurate psychic or mediumship reading is like inevitably strips the moment of any magic. A truly accurate read by a psychic or medium feels not at all how one might expect: there are no fireworks. It's more akin to a gentle ahhhh or a feeling of connectivity— not so much a blinding truth, more like a crack in the curtains letting in the light, or the singing of a song or a short jingle that you thought only you knew.

"You need to keep your mind clear and organized. Things will continue to get busier and if you don't have your schedule in place, it will stress you out. Keep yourself focused. If you don't, it's going to cause you anxiety, and your anxiety is going to come out in different ways and different ways around your family. You will have a big sense of relief when you finish your book. And then you'll be on to your next thing, but please give yourself a break. You have a fire underneath you but please take a little time for yourself."

When Angie shared with me what she saw in my Akashic records, I remained grounded on a synthetic couch cushion in Maine. I didn't hear or see or feel anything celestial—no long-tailed comets flying past through the heavens. It felt more like a flashlight cast on a knowledge that only I knew, with specific examples of my idiosyncrasies, my temperament, my daily small bad habits and specific personal things that stand in my way, and obstacles that were being called out by a complete stranger. Basic things—work advice, marriage, health. Shortly after Angie started, she was up and running with my truth.

On money: "The energy that they put around you is that you're still holding on to some kind of fear, but you've always had enough. Your passion is already leading you there. It's just a matter of time before you get the payback. You haven't tapped into the opportunities available to you."

On marriage: "Just because he is a math person doesn't mean you can't have a blast having him by your side. You are here to teach each other lessons. And you need to reinstate a date night. They're telling me *reinstitute*."

It came fast, and I sheltered myself into it. Angie brought forth a soft, pleasant bundle of nagging, critique, encouragement, and instruction. It was quietly astonishing. Astonishing, because it was information that I'd been waiting for my own cognitive therapist—one whom I'd been seeing for over four years, talking at and paying weekly sums of money—to tell me to do. But in therapy, my counselor would ask, and I would answer. With Angie, it was not like this. I didn't share or have to say a word.

Almost anyone would find some resonance with a message about being organized and focusing and making time for self-care. There was really nothing in her reading that was incredibly specific to me—it could have applied to a lot of women—but it really *felt* specific to me.

It was like both a résumé and a to-do list that I'd already been keeping in the back of my head but had been denying and neglecting. What Angie said mattered to me. It felt personal and clarifying, and made *me* feel verified.

Karlene had told me that as a medium, if you're 60 to 70 percent accurate, then you're very good. You're being told something from Spirit, and you're interpreting it. "If the person is not getting it immediately, we say, 'Take it with you,'" she'd said. "So just take it with you. You may find out later and it will resonate later." She'd said that when people go to see a medium, they usually go in with a specific intention in what they want to hear—a set idea of what's not necessarily going to come through. And that's where the funky stuff happens. "I've had readings where I was not matching at all, so I say, 'Go take your money back and try a different medium.' Before I read, I ask for my highest and best. To let the truth be seen. Ask yourself: Is it true? Am I getting this right? Is this my shit or their shit?"

"With mental mediumship," said Angie, "that's all we're doing. We're increasing your awareness." It is our job, as the sitter, to find the meaning in whatever form it comes in. And the purpose had remained what it always had: to help heal people. Mediums were here to heal, to give a new perspective. Angie was bringing out something I'd forgotten existed, and this was doing something that no other drug or therapy had. "It's validation to what you already know," said Angie.

This is more than my therapist has accomplished in years—Angie gets that line a lot: Perhaps that's why she was getting so popular among the circuit and slowly getting to the point where she could quit her day job and go full-time as a medium. This was the prophecy she'd been given by Barbara: Angie, if you come to Etna, they will come to you.

At Acres of Wildlife, soon after the two women had met, Barbara told Angie this: Your mediumship is going to take off. You're going to draw pictures and give messages and that's how your skill will take off.

And Barbara was right: Angie was now putting more into her time as a professional medium and tapering off from her day job as a domestic-violence advocate.

"I totally believe in it and am all about supporting and empowering women, but domestic-violence advocacy takes its toll," she said. "People leave their abusers and come back, leave and come back. And as much as I'd like to fix that with a magic wand, I just can't. I get so much joy—it's just, it's just *joy*—doing the mediumship work, the *spiritual* work, and with the support of Barbara, I finally made the decision that this is what I should be doing."

Not long ago, Kelly Purington invited Angie to join her on some gigs she'd been getting from nearby restaurants. Then they brought Karlene Tanner on board as well. The ladies did mediumship readings, but they called them "Psychic Dinners" because the word "psychic," Kelly had explained to me, was more mainstream than the word "medium." Because sometimes it's about the advertisement, said Kelly, just as the phrase "life coach" was sometimes code for "intuitive," and they had to be business-savvy. They were ambitious but they were not vain, and they were getting booked all across the state. I'd even come across Kelly's business cards tacked up to the bulletin board in my own neighborhood. The new generation of Camp Etna mediums did house calls, had websites, Facebook pages, Twitter accounts, Instagram. They were using social media and studied with business coaches (one coach in particular was Barbara's daughter Nadia) to make sure they were taking the right self-respecting entrepreneurial steps to ensure their businesses remained a success. Mediumpreneurship. Or, soulpreneurs, said Angie. That was what they called themselves.

"When you are a potential client, a person pining for someone who is not around anymore, the more improved [the medium's] techniques and the wider the variety, the better it is for everyone," Angie stressed. She and her entourage were continuously refining their techniques, emphasizing how what they did had the elements of healing, of artistry and sophistication, and that what they did was conducted in an

An advertisement for a psychic and medium fair, where Angie first
met Barbara and soon after became a Spiritualist. *Mira Ptacin*

upbeat and inclusive manner, for both the living and the dead. Regard-
ing the way we approach the culture of death, Angie and her colleagues
were thinking outside the box. They even had hot-pink sparkly pens
that advertised their services. I used mine all the time—I swear it
improved my handwriting.

In addition to giving psychic readings, mediumship readings, and
reading Akashic records, Angie teaches intuitive-development classes
to people who are where she used to be and want to learn how to get to
where she is now. She leads a course entitled "Creating Etheric Sacred
Spaces." She teaches intuitive angel-painting classes, art scrying, candle magic ("using the elements of fire and spirit and wind and sometimes water and sometimes earth to bring about things you want"),

fairy house–making, and manifestation courses. Come autumn, she herself would be taking a pranic healing certification course.

I asked Angie if some of those classes are what some of the older Spiritualists clump into the category of "New Age bullshit." This tension between old versus new was not a secret on the grounds. In a small community of women who were psychics and mediums, it had to be impossible for thoughts to be off the radar, or clandestine.

"Look," said Angie, "the world is changing. Perceptions are changing. There are people looking for purpose and understanding of why we are here. You have to keep your backbone, but you also have to be willing to go out and meet people where they are at. Yes, there is controversy in stepping into the metaphysical stuff, but I know I see a lot of people who are slowly opening themselves to 'spiritual' types of things—and if you can reach them where they're at, whether you do it through old-school or New Age practices, then from there you can start to introduce them to the concept of Spiritualism."

With both hands, Angie brushed back her *golden* hair, took a long breath, and, harnessing a bit of frustration, took a sip of water. "Everywhere you go, there will always be crappy politics. Everyone will be looking at the same exact thing, but they all will be looking at it differently. Their emotion will create a perception that creates their version of reality."

Just then, a colossal charcoal-colored truck pulled up to the rocky patch outside Heart Song and turned off its engine. The driver's-side door opened, and a man the size of an acrobat jumped out. "That's my husband," Angie said. "Washian."

Washian was shorter than Angie, had furniture-brown hair, a round face, and wore wraparound polarized sunglasses, pleated khaki pants, and a collared polo shirt with the Home Depot logo stitched onto the heart. He opened the porch door and stepped into the living room. Angie kissed his palm and placed it upon her cheek as her husband's face relaxed into a smile. Upon Angie's introduction, Washian and I exchanged a short, awkward hug, and then we sat down. Angie stood behind him, gently drawing small circles on his back with the nails of her index finger as he began untying his work shoes.

"This man is an amazing cook," she said. "And a great baker, does his own laundry, cleans up after himself, makes me coffee every morning and breakfast every weekend. And he makes a mean sour pickle." Washian sat up and nodded. The recipe had come from his grandmother.

Just as she'd met Barbara, Angie met Washian at Acres of Wildlife at a mediums fair, not long after she'd steeped herself fully into Spiritualism and divorced her first husband.

In life, Angie explained, you travel in soul packs. "When I refer to Barbara and Steve as my spiritual family, it's because we are—we've been together in past lifetimes. They're part of my soul pack." Before she met Washian, Angie had a dream, a vision, and a visit that told her it was time for her life to take a dramatic turn, and that she was soon going to be reunited with another member of her soul pack, a past-life person she'd spent many lives with many times before.

"I remember wondering, *How am I going to know you?* because he wasn't going to look like he had in the past lifetimes. What I'd heard in my dream was 'You'll know by his eyes.' Soon after, I went to Acres and there was this guy named Washian giving a presentation on shamanic practices—he talks to trees—and we were out doing a drum circle and I just happened to look over at him and it hit me—that was him. He was the one. And I was like, *Oh my God, REALLY? He's shorter than me. Really?*"

Angie and Washian got together in 2012, purchased their summer cottage at Etna in 2014, purchased their home in 2015, and then they got married in 2016. Washian reached out for his wife's hand and she gave it. "When I was with my ex-husband," Angie explained, "we were in a state of considerable despair. We tried to make it work, but it was more like living with a friend. It just wasn't where I was supposed to be. But now, there's something different about having the person that you are with be your complete partner."

"What if your partner doesn't believe in mediumship?" I asked.

"Then you explain it with science," said Angie. "Everything is energy."

She tapped on the coffee table in the middle of the three of us. "This was a tree at one point. This was energy. Everything is going to have a different vibration. When your flesh piece dies, there is still some energy and it has to go somewhere. Energy can't be destroyed. This is a scientific fact. The energy has got to go somewhere."

Washian had his arms crossed over his chest and nodded as he listened to what Angie had to say. He'd recently been ordained as a pastor at the Healing Light Church, which was renting space in the wintertime in Camp Etna's temple. In addition to working at Home Depot, he also had a shamanic healing business called Rollin' with Spirit. From her husband's neck hung a pendant the size of an eyeball. I glanced down at it and Washian crossed his legs.

"Washian calls his motorcycle his modern-day horse," Angie chirped.

"As a shaman, and a medium," I asked Washian half-jokingly, "does this mean you see through me right now?"

"We don't do readings without someone's permission," he replied. "Shamanic practice is all about helping other people heal." He said that his healing work differed a bit from the traditional Spiritualist practices—that he was a musical healer, and cured others by playing what he referred to as "intuitive music" on his flute.

"I play what Spirit asks me to play," said Washian, and that although he was self-taught, he learned how to make his instruments under the direction of a gentleman from the Penobscot nation.

Washian stood up, went to the side of the room, and came back with something small in his hands. He raised his hands toward my face then uncupped his palms.

"Is that a turtle shell?" I asked.

"Yes," Washian answered. "This is a rattle I just made. I made it myself."

Washian and Angie also taught classes together. One was called "Awakening the Spiritual You," a beginner's class of oracle cards, energetic protection, and testing out different ways to get messages. The next-level class was called "Awakening and Expanding the Spiritual You," which was a weekly intermediate that offers hands-on practice, tools and methods of mediumship, intuitiveness, and protection. "It's this class—Awakening and Expanding," said Angie, "where you find your tribe." The couple teaches spiritual classes at two different locations—Brewer and Ellsworth, Maine. Their youngest student was twenty-one and their oldest was over eighty. Currently, their target age group is the young twenties.

Each soulpreneur has a typical clientele for their mediumship too: more often than not they are women. More often than not they are within the age range of thirty to sixty, but Angie had a special niche with older men. She wasn't sure where that came from or why, but often her clients were elderly men who came to her wanting to connect with their deceased spouses.

I asked her why consulting with a medium was something most people today considered taboo, or silly, and not to be taken seriously. "Especially men," I added. "Your situation being an exception."

"A woman came to me and she had lost her brother," said Angie as Washian exited the room. "She came with her husband. We had a very powerful session, lots of confirmation, lots of details, and in the end of the reading, the woman turned to her husband and said, 'See? Now do you believe me?' And he said, 'Yes, yes, now I do.' But afterwards, he still had no interest in booking a session for himself. He said he didn't want to know who was around him that he couldn't see.'"

Angie stretched out like a cat, arching her back, then inhaled deeply. "But later, the gentleman did book an appointment for his mother-in-law." She exhaled and regained her posture.

I asked her if maybe it had something to do with privacy, and the fear of appearing vulnerable, of not knowing.

"I think it's about the female and male energies," Angie answered. "Scientifically, the feminine brain is more emotional, and spirit energy is typically more of an emotional energy. And the male energy," she continued, "the male vibration, the masculine is more factual than emotional. Like, *If I can't see it, it's not real.* But for women, it's more *If I can FEEL it, then I know it's real.*"

About 70 percent of Angie's clients come to talk to dead people, and the other 30 percent come for life guidance (for example, Akashic record readings).

"Just like you," said Angie, "I've had more than a handful of clients tell me that sitting with a medium once has done more for them than their grief counselor has done for them in years, because I give them closure and absolute confirmation that that person is still around energetically. I'm not saying counseling is bad—not at all! What I'm saying is that when you add the mediumistic piece to grief counseling, the clarity and the healing comes like lightning." She snapped her fingers and made a pop. "I used to be so scared to have people cry in front of me, but now when they do, it's a feeling of fulfillment, because maybe for the first time, maybe in this moment, they finally have peace."

Here's what Angie thinks about traditional American grief rituals: something is missing. They're incomplete. Our current culture is too black-and-white when it comes to grief. Angie believes that when a person is grieving, the Kübler-Ross stages all apply, but something is still missing: the spiritual component. The energetic component. Because if you go back to the fact that we are energy, and that we are spiritual beings living in energy within a different density of energy, there is more than just the death of the body, says Angie. "We have this idea that when someone passes, that's all, that's it, and all you have are memories. But when you add in the spiritual component, the death of the body is not the end. When you add in the spiritual aspect, the mediumship aspect, you can still grieve their physical presence being gone, but you can have peace knowing that energetically, they are still around and still accessible. But you're supposed to move on."

Angie paused for a moment, looked down at the air near my shins and my feet, then looked back up at my face and into my eyes.

"If I'm bringing forth a child," she said, "a small child that has passed away, I will see her small energy below you."

This comment came out of nowhere, and it knocked me off my

feet, so to speak, because I had lost a child. It's not that she couldn't have known this—Angie could've Googled me and read about my first book. I'd written a memoir about the experience. My story was no secret. Ten years ago, during the ultrasound that was to tell us the sex of our baby, my husband, Andrew, and I had learned that the child had severe chromosomal abnormalities and defects—a malformed brain, collapsed skull, broken heart, spina bifida—and had zero chance of survival outside my womb. They told us this, and that the child wasn't going to live, and then, on a small piece of paper, they wrote down the sex of the child: a girl. Shortly after this, we named her Lily. Within ten days of the ultrasound, she was gone. The procedure to remove Lily's body from my body was painful, humiliating, and lasted three days. One month later, Andrew and I got married, and life moved on. But I didn't. I was diagnosed with post-traumatic stress disorder and it took me almost a decade to acquire any semblance of joy, control, mental homeostasis, or even a glimpse of inner peace. To dig out of the quicksand of sorrow took work, and it felt like work. I hated it. I saw therapist after therapist. I exercised like crazy with the intention of feeling a sense of control of my body, as well as the feeling that endorphins brought. I even trained for and ran a marathon. Then I started taking medication. But nothing seemed to lighten my load. My marriage was falling apart, too, so finally, and pretty spontaneously, Andrew and I decided that if our partnership was going to survive, and I was going to get better, we had to get out of New York City and start the kind of life we now needed. In retrospect, it was a move to save not just our marriage but to save our souls.

A few years after that, I became pregnant and gave birth to my son, Theo. It made me feel like my body was, in fact, *not* broken, and for the most part, the sorrow from losing Lily seemed to dissipate, but not completely. But then, just now, after hearing Angie's words—*a small child that had passed away*—my sorrow got blown away. Actually, it felt more like something opened up within me, blossomed like an orchid, and then that feeling lifted.

I will see her small energy below you. It seemed to me that Angie had acknowledged Lily and her presence, and this made a deep part of me not only acknowledge Lily, too, but feel validated for the realness of the grief I still harbored. I had been hiding from this grief because up until now, I didn't think whatever grief still existed was legitimate enough to still exist. Because up until now, I'd gone along with the logic that Lily was never really real in the first place.

In the ultrasound, doctors had referred to Lily as "it." They used words like, "it has no chance of survival outside your womb." Everything after that became procedural, and I went with it. My sadness became procedural, too. The stages of grief. I went through them all, checked them all off, but anxiety persisted, and this didn't make sense to me. Why was it so easy for everyone else to move on but not me? Somewhere in my mind and maybe my heart, there was heartache and there was grief, because, even if she hadn't lived a "full" life, she had been my daughter. And it wasn't until Angie said those few words that this realization came to my head, and to my heart. When she said this, it opened up the possibility that the grief that stuck with me and that I had pushed deep down and tried to hide, was justified.

As I sat, Angie didn't break my stillness. When I finally lifted my head, looked back up and into her eyes, she spoke. "It's amazing what two minutes of silence can do for you."

Whatever had just happened, whatever had just come through, whatever we'd experienced together, whatever Angie had seen or hadn't seen, whatever had gone on between us was nothing old or new. It wasn't religious or human or even something palpable or tactile but was rather timeless and weird and absurd and totally illogical and could only be described as nonsense. But to me, that didn't matter. Because whatever had just happened in that brief exchange, in that small moment between me and the medium sitting in front of me was the first time in a very long time that I came to an understanding of one particularly painful thing I'd buried deep inside me; under a hard shell of things was a tenderness that I'd been trying too long to protect. A sorrow that finally, at long last, made perfect sense.

CHAPTER 8

The Powwow

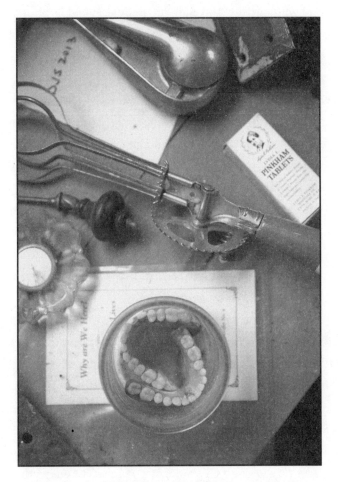

Ephemera and relics from Camp Etna's past. *Greta Rybus*

The powwow was big and busy.

Animal antlers and turtle shells. Deerskin hides and sixteen different sizes of dream catchers. Gray-haired couples walking hand in hand and sporting matching fringed black leather motorcycle jackets. Bright-red or white-and-yellow flocks of feathers and then that one head, as hairless as a white onion but for the maroon streak of Mohawked hair cutting through its middle. Vendor booths selling tomahawks. Vendor booths selling sage, sweetgrass, cedar, and bells. Vendor booths selling walking sticks. Moccasins were not out of the question.

Today marked the first day of the 2017 annual Attean Family Powwow. Barbara had invited me and encouraged me to bring my kids, and I'd agreed to both. It would be my first powwow, and I knew little about powwows, no more than I knew about, say, a rain dance, which was to say my familiarity amounted to practically nothing, save for several ounces of flaky, false, and engrained stereotypes. Barbara had told me that the word "powwow" came from the Narragansett word "powaw," which could be translated into the phrase "spiritual leader," and said that whatever else I wanted to know about the event I could go ahead and find on the event's website.

All are welcome, declared the website for the event. *Tribal representatives from Maine, New England & around the country will be at the park with native dancers, drummers, craft vendors, singers & traditional food booths. Host drum is Split Feather Singers, guest drums are Black Hawk Singers, Grandmothers Tears, and Walking Bear Singers. Also, Joseph Fire-Crow will be returning, make sure you check out his show . . . . His CDs will be available for sale . . . His performance is always a great time not to be missed . . . Also, Wolf Cry Singers, a wonderful woman's hand drum group, will be performing.*

With my one- and three-year-old fighting for space in their shared stroller, we rolled through a full and sandy parking lot toward the entrance of the event, which was being held in the town of Gray at an expansive outdoor center called the Maine Wildlife Park. Formerly known as the "Game Farm," the Maine Wildlife Park served as a permanent home for feral animals that could not be returned to their natural habitats—kind of like a zoo, but for animals who had come to the park primarily because of their problems rather than their majesty and wonder. But still, they were there for people to look at. The park was its own entity and depended on outside revenue for its funds to keep it running; in 1992, the Maine legislature implemented a mandate requiring the original "Game Farm" to become financially self-sufficient.

As we stood in line to buy our tickets, a sign: *All proceeds go to the park and used for the care and upkeep of the local animals that have been injured and can't be released back into the wild as well as the care and release for the ones that can.* A swarm of coolers on wheels and band of torsos clad in beige leather and black, of aquamarine fringed shawls and slim beaded arms—the cluster of humanity lurched forward, bit by bit. I wheeled the stroller ahead, then stopped. Wheeled another inch, then stopped. I could hear, in the distance, the deep, deep sound of the great drums booming, coming from a place we were hoping to be.

A powwow refers to a gathering—sometimes public, sometimes private—in which the First Nations People of North America (the natives of this great land) convene to drum, dance, sing, socialize, and honor their dead, their living, and their culture. The Attean Family Powwow of today still resembled powwows from the late nineteenth and early twentieth century, a time when, in its rabid quest for land and ruthless economic exploitation, the US government did whatever it could to destroy the Native communities that they believed stood in their way.

In 1923, a man had a fear of dancing. His name was Charles Burke, he was white, and he was the US commissioner of Indian Affairs. Like his counterparts in the government, Burke wanted to suppress and eradicate anything that prevented the assimilation of Native Americans into white culture. Burke suggested that Native American dancing was especially suspect—those movements were the opposite of the polite waltzes of sedate white society. The Natives were exhibitionists! They moved all their body parts! The work of the devil! A threat to Christianity! That's when Burke passed a bill he hoped would further eradicate Indigenous Americans—their past and their future—by limiting the number of times a year in which they could gather to engage in traditional dance and embrace their culture and their people. Even though the bill was passed without a hitch, it didn't do what Burke had fully hoped—the Native Americans didn't disappear completely, and the powwow never died.

Customarily, a powwow consists of dancing, drumming, and singing. But each of those acts is incredibly rich with an astonishing amount of depth and meaning, reverence and etiquette, complex rules and guidelines. The powwow wasn't savage; the powwow came from a sophisticated culture that flourished on these lands before Europeans showed up. However, a general summary or outline of the events of a powwow could be billed as this: upon commencement, there was the Grand Entry, followed by the men's tradition dance, followed by the men's grass dance, followed by the men's straight dance, followed by the men's fancy dance. This was followed by the women's traditional dance, the women's fancy shawl dance, the women's jingle dress dance, and in some gatherings, the couples' two-step. All powwows are nuanced, and every single one is going to differ from the previous or the next, each belonging to a different genre and regional variation, not to mention the unique and flawed and beautifully individual humans who breathe life into each individual powwow of which they're a part. Nonetheless, at all powwows, one thing always remains consistent: drumming is the central symbol of each sacred gathering.

The drum is thought of as its own being, and is to be regarded and respected as such. Drummers are expected to be ready to sing at a moment's notice. Drummers are expected to remain at their drum at all times, and in most regions it's considered disrespectful to ever leave the drum completely unattended. Some drum groups do not allow women to sit down at their drum but did welcome them to stand behind the drummers and sing backup harmonies. At some point in most powwows, the drum would be offered gifts, like tobacco, and musicians acknowledged this by standing up reverently. Bottom line: the drum was the pulse that kept the entire community alive. When it was heard, the drum made the people live in the moment; the rhythm of the drums was meditative. Empirical evidence shows that when we meditate, it triggers a self-repair mechanism in our bodies. It enhances the production of endorphins and serotonin and stops the production of cortisol and adrenaline. So the drumming does the same thing that antidepressant medicine did—it produced selective serotonin reuptake inhibitors (SSRIs). How ironic that the difference between the words "meditation" and "medication" is one letter.

A powwow takes months of planning. Typically, there is a planning committee, which, among an endless list of tasks, is in charge of securing the master of ceremonies and an arena director. There is the PR and communications team. There are the sponsors to recruit (colleges, tribes, wildlife parks, campgrounds), vendors to organize, traders, food, layout to arrange, the setup, the rentals, takedown, shelter, rain dates, EMS, first-aid stations, you name it. Plus, there is the procurement of a live bald eagle, the majestic creature that always makes a cameo in the opening ceremony of essentially every Native American powwow.

The Attean family were members of the Penobscot tribe, and, together with the Mi'kmaq, Maliseet, Passamaquoddy, and Abenaki Indians, had once been members of the old Wabanaki Confederacy. Nowadays, there are approximately 3,000 Penobscot Indians, most of whom live in Maine. The Attean family had lived both on and off of Indian Island, as well as in and around Old Town, Maine, not far from where the powwow was being held.

Once in the park, my children and I entered a sea of vendor booths, concessions, and warm bodies. The majority of people didn't appear to be Native American, and most of these non-natives seemed to know one another too. Attending powwows was part of their lifestyle. This was their subculture, and these were more or less their people. Many of them carried lawn chairs. My son asked me if there were any deer. There was still about thirty minutes before it was time for the opening ceremony, so before tracking down Barbara and Steve and staking a spot on the lawn, we took a walk.

Sidestepping goose poop, I pushed my kids in the stroller down a smooth concrete path for about a quarter of a mile until we saw the cages. A blind albino raccoon. Two beavers in a shallow murky pool. A faded red-tailed fox. It was daytime; some of them were nocturnal creatures. A sad porcupine paced back and forth in a small rigid cage along a track of soil, an indentation of the path the creature paced day and night. These were supposed to be rescued animals, but rescued from what? My children squealed with delight at what appeared to be a muskrat, but my stomach churned and I said nothing to them about how the poor creatures looked less like they'd been saved and more like miserable prisoners locked in a tiny cages, cooped up and on display, and that this was not a good thing. A lynx pacing her cage. A bear pacing her cage. A cougar, a coyote, a moose. I swear I could feel their defeat in my bones. My daughter, still a baby, cooed as a red-tailed hawk slept, unable to fly. Soon my son found the deer, and with pellets from a 25-cent vending machine, stuck his palm through a fence and handfed a doe. She seemed OK, and while she nibbled, she looked back at us with the same half-curious, half-unamused expression.

The powwow would be starting soon, and my son toddled back to the center of the grounds as I followed him with my daughter in the stroller. There was a breeze blowing through the trees spreading a fairground bouquet of smells: French fries, corn dogs, and other American fried foods, the hallmarks of obesity. A solemn and stoic-looking man—a Native American in khaki-colored leathers, beaded moccasins, and a vibrant headdress—appeared on the path in front of my son, and I asked if I could take this man's picture, and he replied in a hushed but heavy tone that seemed to make his words last longer.

"If you hadn't asked, I would not have let you," he told me. "You shouldn't take without asking. So thank you for asking my permission." I captured his image, thanked him, and then I chased my children to the central spot of the event: a circle. The actual ceremony of the powwow would be taking place inside a circle. In the Native American culture, it was not the pyramid but the circle that represented the paradigm of life. It was the shape of eternity, the figure of a ring, a reminder that all the people were linked, not ranked.

On the outer rim of this ring, in a roped-off perimeter adjacent to a buckskin and knife vendor booth were Steve and Barbara Williams, mediums in the wild. They sat in the lawn chairs they'd brought, with Barbara sporting large sunglasses and a royal-purple dress that draped over her long legs and stopped short just above her sandals, and Steve clad in his uniform of brightly colored tie-dye shirt and light-blue jeans. It was almost noon now, which meant the opening ceremony would begin any minute. Drums thundered for the warm-up. Barbara motioned my kids over to sit with her, and my shy daughter crawled into Barbara's lap without a second thought.

"I came to the realization that when you step back from this cacophony of sound," said Barbara, "especially during a drum circle and even no one is in rhythm, what you are hearing is truly the heartbeat of humanity." Barbara began attending powwows regularly around 2009, shortly after she became a member of Camp Etna. At the Spiritualist camp, Barbara initiated and led drum circles, incorporating them into the camp's itinerary and practices. "That's what the drumming appeals to," said Barbara, stroking my daughter's cheek and looking down at the top of her head. "It appeals to the heartbeat in all of us, the commonality."

Several beats boomed low. Instantly, the crowd on the lawn responded by quieting down. "I get mesmerized from the drumming,"

Barbara whispered. "I look around at everybody and everybody is look-ing on with the same eyes."

As she quietly pontificated, several people approached at different times seemingly to pay reverence. It appeared that Barbara had clout, a little band of disciples, or maybe they were just some scattered mem-bers of her soul pack. Whoever they were, these folks were extraor-dinarily responsive to Barbara's presence. Her influence seemed to reach well beyond the lines of Camp Etna. As more and more people approached and before they departed, they seemed to be thanking her for something. Maybe it had been for a reading she'd given them, maybe Reiki or pranic healing, or her advice with Ayurveda or homeo-pathic medicine. Perhaps it was for a cleansing or clearing or a ghost hunt. Perhaps it was for a deed she'd done or perhaps for her acu-men, but unquestionably, these people had approached Barbara with gratitude.

"Some of us seek out cultures that are like-minded to find what is missing—it can be a lifelong search to find your own tribe. But that's what we're all searching for: our own tribe. And whether it be reli-gious or family or intellectually, your tribe is where you fit in. Catholic, Christian, Jewish, Muslim, it doesn't matter. We are all trying to seek out our tribe. And when you have your support system, it's easier to be inclusive than exclusive."

Again the drums resounded. Tribal elders had gathered and formed a line outside the entryway to the central circle of the soil amphitheater as the emcee spoke into a microphone, first asking everyone to stand, then something about not taking photographs. The Grand Entry was sacred and should not be filmed, and as we were pushing our bodies up to stand on our feet, another person approached Barbara. Barbara lifted up my daughter and handed her to me, and, with the assistance of Steve, stood, turning halfway to face both the central arena as well as the woman. Clearly, it was another fan, gushing and fanning herself with a folded-up program. She hugged Barbara. Barbara returned the embrace and blessed the woman then and there. The woman nodded down toward Barbara a few times quickly and walked away backwards as the ceremony finally commenced.

Without being asked or reminded, and in unison, anyone wearing anything on their head removed it ("unless it contains an eagle feather," whispered Steve, leaning into my ear). As dancers in bright garb followed a color guard into the ring, Barbara picked up the narration: groups entering the circle were arranged by category (veteran, elder, tribal royalty, age), and the group's place on the totem pole, so to speak, determined who entered and when. The rhythm of the drumming picked up speed, and that's when the bald eagle entered the picture—a living, breathing, injured yet rescued bald eagle, a resident of Acres of Wildlife. The bird of prey was carried into the center of the ring on the arms of a uniformed park employee, and she held the eagle cautiously with two massive mustard-colored suede gloves. Once the pair had made it to the center of the arena, the ranger slowly lifted her arm and perched the bird. The crowd that watched made not a sound. Some people bowed their heads. The moment stood still.

"Sometimes they have to call it short if he gets too nervous," Barbara whispered to my children, whose eyes, too, were locked on the majestic spectacle within the ring. "We are honoring of all the elements today," she told them. "Mother Earth, sky, wind, fire. Everything is represented there. Before people went into the circle to dance, they were smudged with ashes."

By now, the patriotism and valor of the spectacular rainbow of humans was palpable. The place felt sacred. The air felt sacred. The sand and soil beneath us made the pulpit. An older man in the powwow circle—a veteran, maybe?—held a large banner aloft. His hair was dark and untrimmed, and his face was just as beautiful as the wood he held that had mellowed with age. There was a blessing, some kind of prayer. And then they danced. It was a soft, slow dance—meditative. Shuffles and a hop, a dance that had been passed down and down again like a story.

"Each dance represents something different," Barbara explained. "There are the grass dancers—those who went out and cleared the field.

There is the honoring of the animal spirits, the honoring of veterans, the males, the female. And if you listen to what they're calling out, you realize they call out everybody. It doesn't matter if you're native or not, adult or child. It's absolutely an inclusion. They dance for all of us."

I asked Barbara if she would be getting up there today, if she was going to dance too.

"I would love to," she replied. "But haven't been able to. It'd be hard not to get winded." She tapped the sole of her foot with a walking stick and grimaced. "Foot injury."

The women were strong-jawed and ruddy. The men like willow trees. And the children tougher-looking. My kids were calm and observant. The heartbeat of the drums had slowed us all into the same speed, and the outdoors atmosphere fell into a feeling where it seemed we were floating around, not in our own individual worlds but rather all in the same womb.

"You see?" said Barbara. "Just a coming-together for the same goal: reverence and honoring."

Time passed and the dances changed. After a while, my daughter put her head onto the bare ground and curled up into a deep nap, while my son alternated between imitating the dancers, piling up stacks of pine needles with the other children near him, and drawing with his finger in the sand. Overhead, a cloud passed by, placing a cool shadow onto his face. I planted my elbows into the earth behind me and leaned back. Even though my roots were eastern European, right now I felt like I was in a very familiar memory. I looked over at Barbara and we both smiled.

"It's from that community, that spirit—this is why we come here," she said. "It's in the honoring. The honoring of everything. And not just the dead. When they dance, they're honoring the dead absolutely. But they're also honoring those who have lived through so much."

Even though everything Barbara was saying made sense to me, even though everything that was happening around me at the powwow felt completely natural—that it was alive and real and fresh, making it effortless for me and everyone here to get out of our own heads and stay fully present with the pulse of the drums and the language of the dancers' bodies—I still started to feel the bulge from the inside pressure of my mind. I didn't resist it. I broke off from the present moment, fed into my mind's chatter, and saw who I had become: a sad little porcupine. I had caged myself in, and for decades had been pacing back and forth back and forth on the same pathway of thinking, over and over again. I wanted to have control over my life, but I never seemed to be able to maintain it. I kept losing things. My brother shouldn't have died. I shouldn't have lost a baby. I identified myself through what had been taken away, through what I didn't have, goals never reached, wishes not fully realized, et cetera, et cetera—life had been brutal and would continue to be ruthless. I'd been with these thoughts for as far back as I could remember, and so this way of thinking had been deeply ingrained in those pathways in the cage of my brain. I'd thought that because of all that hadn't gone the way I expected it to go, that I was a victim in life who still was waiting to be the victor. This is what I thought, and if thoughts were things, then my way of thinking was preventing me from being the victor. If I didn't get off this deep path, the cycle would continue. Life wasn't fair—this was what I'd been raised to believe, and this was what I, most likely, would be passing on to my children. I didn't think I was committed to any one particular faith or belief system, but this whole time I actually had been: being a victim—powerlessness—had been my quiet religion this whole time.

What was it that Diane had told us that day, back during her tour of her Camp Etna museum? That it was the Native Americans who were the first mediums in the United States, not the Fox sisters. Within the several hundred distinct American Indian languages, there has never been a single world that could be translated as "religion." For the indigenous peoples of America, religion has never been a distinct category of one's culture, it was rather something that always been closely integrated with the culture. This is what the Native Americans thought about death: Death was a transition between two worlds. At the time of death, the soul would leave the body and join the souls of relatives and friends in the world of the dead. They believed in reincarnation, that there was a cyclical nature to life rather than in the concept of heaven or hell or judgment, supernatural rewards or punishment after death. Indigenous author and historian Shirley Muldon writes that her tribe believes in "reincarnation of people and animals. We believe that the dead can visit this world and that the living can enter the past. We believe that memory survives from generation to generation. Our elders remember the past because they have lived it." For many American Indian cultures, the focus of religion, particularly the ceremonies, was on maintaining harmony with the world. Yes, the awareness of death was there, as was the vague concept of something happening after death, but none of this was dogmatic. They'd find out what happens during death when they die; therefore in the meantime, they should not waste time thinking about it. The concept of religion was less focused on death but rather focused on living a life of grace and harmony, not control and power.

I looked down at my own flesh and blood—my son and daughter, now both awake and participating absolutely as they watched without judgment a young child in the circle in front of them who was dancing and staring upward with a soulful expression and not saying a word. Despite all that had been destroyed and taken from them, the Native Americans still lived in reverence with Mother Nature, still celebrated their ancestry, still survived. I thought about all of the animals in the cages and the trees surrounding us and how we all currently listened and breathed, all as one heartbeat. And all of this, all of it set up this moment like a bear trap for my brain and I felt so very, very small. As the drumbeats firmly stomped, I stayed separated from the moment. This ancient ceremony became a scene while I turned fully inward—the moment was now about me, back in my head, growing more and more suspect that there was something profoundly shameful about the way I had been living. What if power really was gained by loosening up, rather than gripping tightly? What if wisdom was attained not by know-ing, but by being able to sit with the unknown? Stand tall like a willow tree swaying with the winds that came and went rather than hard and calcified as an obelisk like the Washington Monument. It really was true—in order to let go, you had to let go. It was impossible to escape the suffering of life, so why not suffer proudly and with dignity rather than miserably?

I suspected Barbara had picked up on my extended silence by now, on what it meant and what it was doing to me, so she broke it up and spoke: "I can't say for all cultures, but in a true religious culture, you have a cohesive honoring of greater wisdom than ourselves. Although some have fallen through with that. Even in Indian cultures, some have fallen through with that."

I blinked, breathed, turned to Barbara. "Why do we do always do that to ourselves?" I asked.

"It's just the human parts," she said. "The human parts come out, and that's what screws us every time." Ahead of us, a dance ended just as another seamlessly began. "Come on, Steve. Help me up here." Barbara motioned to her husband and then to me. "You stay here and sit, little mama. Take a rest." She then turned to my children. "Hey, kids, how about we go check out the toys?" Their ears perked up. "But no iPads and Game Boys or whatever electronic doohickeys you kids nowadays play with." It was beneath her dignity to compete with machines, and she didn't mind saying that. "Today it's going to be hand drums and dream catchers!"

"Go for it," I agreed, standing up for the gesture as they loaded up into the stroller and turned to make their way to the vendor shanties. I waved my crew off then sat back down in the soil. Soon, a gray moth fluttered over and landed on top of the denim at the bend of my knee. I looked down at it and did not swat it away. The creature lacked nothing. It was more than enough.

CHAPTER 9

Church

Greta Rybus

It was Sunday, the tenth of September, in Maine, and just approaching ten thirty in the morning. Below me, a breath of cold air whistled through a crack in the painted plywood floor. I slid my foot over the top of the gap then up looked up at the pulpit.

Members of the Healing Light Spiritualist Church were silently reflecting on what had just been recited moments before, after Pastor Washian had asked the congregation to read aloud a prayer, which was located in the binders under their seats.

I ask the Great Unseen Healing Force
To remove all obstructions
From my mind and body
And to restore me to perfect health.
I ask this in all sincerity and honesty,
and I will do my part.
I ask this Great Unseen Healing Force
To help both present and absent ones
Who are in need of help
and to restore them to perfect health.
I put my trust
In the love and power of God.

Their God was defined as the infinite intelligence. Their God was everything, and in everyone. Their God was ultimately what they called love. Church was a full house today, made up mostly of comfortably dressed women and middle-aged men, a few young couples and a couple of teens, plus one baby—maybe forty or forty-five people in all. Maybe the number seemed minimal, but considering the religious landscape in Maine, it was pretty good. Protestant (Baptist, Episcopalian, Methodist, and so on) and Roman Catholic churches in Maine were struggling to fill their pews. One by one, churches were closing their doors and shutting down, reselling their insides to thrift stores while their buildings were bought by developers who repurposed them into expensive condos or fusion restaurants. It reflected what was happening around the country.

Healing Light Church held services every Sunday at ten thirty in the morning at the temple and would continue to offer its weekly Sunday services throughout the winter, even after camp shut down for the season. They paid rent for use of the temple, money that went straight to the board, which then decided what to do with it and how to spend it. Despite camp having so many expenses, sometimes the board used Healing Light's rent money to pay for heating the church they rented from the board over the wintertime.

Fall equinox was still twelve days away, but you could go ahead and call it autumn now. It was cold outside. Sweater weather, L.L.Bean gear on every other person. Camp Etna campers were packing up, pulling out wood to board up cottage windows as the 141st season drew to a close. Soon, water would be shut off and pipes drained so the frigid cold wouldn't burst them and flood abandoned summer homes during the off-season.

The energy of the summer events had died down and ended too. In the last couple of weeks, the last handful of classes trickled off: Orb Photography at the end of August, Washian Welch's "Creating a Sacred Energy Bag," Candle Manifestation with Angie. Two of the very last listed events were visiting medium Sue Dhaibi's "Psychomety," in which she would uncover facts about a person by touching inanimate objects associated with them. And then, little over a week ago and on the first of September, the camp closed off the summer season with a talent show (free and open to the public). Regrettably, I'd missed it, but Diane reported back that the talent show had been good for camp morale. There had been a Three Stooges skit, but the rest of the few acts were mostly songs, including the one she'd performed. "It was for opening up the chakras," said Diane, and it had been sung to the tune of "Do Re Mi." "But we used Sanskrit names instead," she said, then joyfully demonstrated it for me: *"Lam, the root of my pure soul. Vam, the spot that's just above. Ram, the power to drive myself. Yam, my heart that's just above. Ham, I speak therefore I am. Om, the sound of all mankind. Sri, the crown of one and all, and that will bring us back to Lam!"* Cathymac suggested they establish the tune as Camp Etna's new theme song.

Now no one was singing. Instead, and only momentarily, was the audio of the syncopated waves of human breathing (and one cough) as the congregation sat facing the altar of the Gladys Laliberte Temple. Washian sat on what you might call stage right. His church uniform was casual—a short-sleeve black button-down collared shirt, and his hands were folded into the lap of turmeric-colored pants, his head bowed down, eyelids lightly closed. To Washian's left and all the way on the other side of the rostrum was Barbara, also seated, her body folding inward. Her clothing shimmered, long hair grazed her shoulders then fell to the floor, each strand held down by the force of gravity. To me, Barbara looked like a stallion, or Stevie Nicks.

Typically, the general format of a Spiritualist church service has three parts: the healing, the lecture, and the spirit communication. The first—the healing portion—runs for about fifteen minutes. After an opening hymn, a brief welcome, and general weekly announcements, today's assigned healers were summoned to the front of the sanctuary. Relaxing digital music, calming and somewhat celestial, like Enya or Yanni, streamed from a boombox plugged into black rectangular speakers.

"And now," said Washian as he lifted his head to face the congregation, "if anyone would like, you are welcome to come to the front of the room to take part in the hands-on healing." He motioned to the two empty chairs that had been separated from the rest and moved up to the front of the temple, between the altar and the first row of seats.

Two people approached the front of the room and sat down in two chairs. Then two healers stood behind them and set their hands upon their shoulders. I recognized one of the women—her name was Marcia Ruland and she'd seen my aura, measured it after James's dowsing class. Beneath her hands, Marcia's "sitter" melted like an ice cube into her chair.

The healers closed their eyes and seemed to concentrate with an enormous yet serene effort as they steadily and slowly moved their hands on or above different areas of the sitter's body. Once the healer felt that the healing was complete, that the energy had been channeled or shifted or got unstuck, they then tapped the sitter, indicating that the job was complete. No one flinched; it was rather immaculately smooth, like a mother's special touch. The healing portion of church went on for about twelve minutes—the sitters would sit, receive healing, go back to their seats while another Spiritualist would take a seat, heal, condition, repeat. Heal, condition, repeat.

There have been countless studies and extreme attempts to prove that both life after death exists and that it does not. The list is expansive and unending—from scientist Duncan Macdougall's attempt to weigh the soul (concluding that the soul's index of infraction was zero, and since all substances except "the ether of space" give some refraction of light, the soul was therefore made of ether) to Dr. Ian Stevenson's 2,268-page opus, *Reincarnation and Biology: A Contribution to the Etiology of Birthmarks and Birth Defects*. This list goes on and will continue to grow, but really, in my opinion, being swayed by someone else's proof of truth or fraud was beside the point. What mattered was that you chose what you believed in, and you stuck with it.

The Vajrayana Buddhists of Mongolia and Tibet have the belief that there is a soul that lives inside the body, and once a person dies, the soul leaves the body and the body becomes an empty vessel that should be returned to the Earth. So the flesh is chopped into pieces and placed high upon a mountaintop and exposed to the elements—the wind, the rain, the sun and her heat, the soil and the worms beneath it, eagles and vultures and any animal that is in need of food and nourishment. For the Tinguian culture, mourners dress the deceased in their best clothes, prop them in a chair and place a (lit!) cigarette between the lips of the corpse, or the deceased is placed in a *tabalang*, or raft, along with a live rooster before being set adrift on a river. In the Benguet culture of northwestern Philippines, when a family member dies, those who remain place a blindfold over the eyelids of the corpse, then place the body next to the main entrance of their house. Hindus believe that the soul, or the atman, is continually cycling through different bodies, and so in Hindu culture, death is not grieved so much as an end of life but as a change in the atman's journey. The mourning rituals are quite complex and long-lasting (up to 31 days): the bereaved wear only white, bathe twice daily, and eat only vegetarian meals, and when they reach the thirteenth day of mourning, a ceremony called *shraddha* is performed, which involves a fire sacrifice and offerings to all the gods as well as the deceased's ancestors. It is only after this assigned griev-ing and honoring period that the family then resumes the day-to-day grind of the living. After her mother died and was placed in a simple pinewood box and buried in the earth, my own Polish mother, still so young at the time, dressed in black for an entire year, embracing her sorrow for 365 days. Acknowledging her grief helped harness it, helped her move through it.

It was almost time for the second portion of church—the lecture—something I'd grown up calling "the homily," but instead of a robed father, today's visiting was Barbara. Despite living on Etna's grounds throughout most of the summer season, Barbara and Steve weren't members of Healing Light. They belonged to a Spiritualist church in Portland, Maine, which made Barbara today's visiting medium. Barbara drew a crowd; even Arlene said she might attend the service. I turned my head, scanning the crowd for the presence of Arlene, but did not see her. Perhaps she was just completely out of my view. Perhaps, like Barbara in an airport, Arlene knew how to make herself invisible too. Or maybe she'd torpedoed her own boat, maybe Arlene was still in bed.

Washian lowered the volume of the music, rubbed his hands together, then coughed a little, hinting that the healing portion of the service would be ending now, which meant that Barbara would be going on. From her seat, Barbara shuffled some papers, and after the last hand had hovered and the sitter returned to their family, Washian took to the stage to introduce Dr. Williams. When Barbara reached center stage, she bowed slightly to Washian and he did the same to her. Next, she took a deep breath, gripped the podium, and steadied herself a little. It was the first time I'd ever seen her shy.

"I get nervous," she said, addressing the crowd with a masked smile. The lines of her dress formed a shape like armor over her body.

"Believe it or not," Barbara continued, "I'm an introvert that's lived as an extrovert." She set down her stack of lecture notes on the floor below her and kicked them aside. "I always bring something written, but today I'm going to just talk. Today, I'll just let spirit take over and guide me. I operate best when I'm in that space."

And thus, the lecture began.

"Recently," said Barbara, speaking from down in her stomach, "my topic has changed. What I've been focusing on has changed. Sometimes things like this—internal changes—are voluntary, and sometimes we go kicking and screaming. But nonetheless, the world is always morphing, and we must do the same. Change is like weather—we cannot help it. Who asks for hurricanes? Fires? Earthquakes? The same can happen with us inside. Like anything, when a change is happening, we worry. We are always worrying. Why is that? Why do we fight the current? Why do we fight and swim upstream?"

A few members of the congregation agreed with her aloud. Several clapped. Barbara had a certain pertinacity to her. She stood tall with a reflective glow of amber in her eyes and pressed on.

"We are very, very powerful spiritual beings," she continued. "We cannot always change someone's path. If someone is meant to go through something, we can't always change that. We can tap into the power of ourselves, and we can bring about more positive change. Challenge yourself to be that very powerful force for good." Her face was stern and luminous. "And withdraw from negative-speak! Everybody is allowed their own opinion. People are allowed to think. There are so many times that we mirror other people. A couple of years back, I became a Heyoka. Do you know what a Heyoka is? Heyoka is a Native American word that means 'sacred clown' or 'fool.' I became a Heyoka, which meant I was an empath to the max. It wasn't an expression of my emotions. I was an expression of the room or the persons."

Most people have a small opinion about death. They examine it with barely a glance and say, "No, this isn't for me," then move on or away. We want to avoid talking about it, when it's near we step around it, and when we are confronted with it, we want to control it. But the way we think about death influences the way we think about life. To me, American death culture is, for the most part, underdeveloped, unfledged.

When my brother Julian died, my family was still members of the Catholic Church. Even though Jules's death was sudden and tragic, my parents only had about three days to pull themselves together and organize his funeral. One of the minor details to be worked out was the funeral procession music. We had to pick a song to play when the casket was carried in by his best friends, young kids in junior high, and our cousin Mark. The morning of the funeral came quickly. We all lined up in the back of the church, dazed, confounded, sleep-deprived, dehydrated, and still unable to eat anything. Just as the boys were starting to walk down the aisle with the heavy container carrying the body of my younger brother, the musical director of St. Philip's Catholic Church stopped us. She stopped everyone, in fact, the entire funeral ceremony, even the priest, and she was outraged. Apparently, we had violated a church rule when we'd picked the Beatles song "I Will" for the funeral procession. It wasn't a musical number plucked from one of the church's songbooks, nor was it a Catholic hymn. We'd overlooked this (hadn't even known the rule existed), and the musical director refused to let the service go on until we changed the music to a song from the church hymnal. This was so important to her, our abomination, I remember this vividly. It's one of the strongest memories that remains from the time surrounding my brother's death.

In this country, it takes a lifetime to save up for a funeral. Over a decade ago, when I was early in my career and writing about funeral homes in Maine, I saw caskets that cost as much as college semesters. There were even pricier ones, chrome and gold-laced, that advertised a guarantee that the body inside wouldn't decompose as fast as the corpses in the less-expensive caskets. We cling to this body. But with death and in life, despite our advances, our common American culture still doesn't have an effective set of practices that deal with death, or that make any real sense. Like Angie said, we still haven't nailed down the spiritual component of grieving. Current grief culture in the United States is a brief and perfunctory ceremony with no follow-up. Everyone is expected to have closure and move on. We have the stages of grief, we have endless distractions, but we don't have much checking back in. Instead, we have: move on, be productive. And unless you're crazy, you don't talk to the dead.

Barbara was on a roll now and the Spiritualist congregation was right there with her, leaning forward in their seats, aching for an answer to their own personal question and pulling in each of Barbara's words to make them work for their own interior worlds. After a steady drive, she reached the thesis of today's spiritual lecture: that we should gracefully accept our gifts, whether we asked for them or not. Washian snapped his fingers twice. People in front of Barbara nodded. The women. The men. Young and old, they all nodded heartily. The energy inside the temple began to rise and swirl.

"When something happens," she continued, "we all have choices: victim, or victor. Will you be a victim or a victor?"

"Victor," said the congregation.

"I can't hear you," countered Barbara. "Victim? Or victor?"

"Victor!" the congregation cheered.

"So, where to start?" asked Barbara. "How you gonna start?"

No one said anything.

"Well, then I'll tell you where you're gonna start. And it's simple. It's so very simple! You start your day with a blessing. A prayer. You start your day, every single day, with the White Light Blessing. It can be elaborate, or it can be very simple. And it takes seconds. Seconds!"

By now, the congregation was jazzed, and she kept going. "Would you like to hear it?"

"Yes!" The churchgoers applauded, and, following Barbara's lead, everyone lowered their heads.

"The White Light Blessing goes like this: *I ask you to encircle me in the white light of love and divine protection, compassion and wisdom. I ask if there is any negativity or lower energy within me or around me that it go out of me and is rendered harmless. I ask this for twenty-four hours. Amen.*"

There were a few seconds of nothing, and then Barbara spoke. "It is that. Simple. Thank you." And with that, everyone clapped until she returned to her seat as the congregation stood to recite the most recently updated Declaration of Spiritualist Principles, now nine in total:

1. We believe in Infinite Spirit and that God is Infinite Spirit.
2. We believe that the phenomena of nature, both physical and spiritual, is the expression of Infinite Spirit.
3. We affirm that a correct understanding of such expression, and living in accordance therewith, constitutes true religion.
4. We affirm that the existence and personal identity of an individual continues after the change called death.
5. We affirm that communication with the so-called dead is a fact, scientifically proven by the phenomena of Spiritualism.
6. We believe that the highest morality is contained in the Golden Rule: "Whatsoever ye would that others should do unto you, do ye also unto them."
7. We affirm the moral responsibility of the individual and that they make their own happiness or unhappiness as they obey or disobey Nature's physical and spiritual laws.

8. We affirm that the doorway to reformation is never closed to any human soul here or hereafter.

9. We affirm the precepts of prophecy and healing are divine attributes proven through mediumship.

"Great Creator," said Washian, "Infinite Intelligence, we have so much to be grateful for. Thank you. Thank you. Thank you." He pressed Play on the boombox, and, being the sad broken monsters that we were, we sang, "Let There Be Peace on Earth." Our voices filled the church, reverberating off the hardwood floors, the cold white stucco walls, and the smattering of framed photos and framed newspaper clippings and the centuries-old framed Spiritualist programs; the tattered flags, sunflower banners, the vases of silken sunflowers and carnations. *To take each moment, and live each moment, in peace eternally! Let there be peace on earth and let it begin with me.* We sang and we sang.

It was now the final segment of the service, the part that set the Spiritualist church services the most apart from other Western religious ones. It was time to communicate with the dead.

"And while there is only enough time during a service for a few people to receive messages from their deceased loved ones," said Washian, "everyone present will benefit from this morning's messages by witnessing proof of the continuation of life. Today," he continued, Barbara now at his side yet towering over him, "we are very blessed to have Barbara for the mediumship portion of our service."

Washian walked backwards with his hand extended to her as she stepped forward deferentially, off the stage of the temple and into the seated congregation, Moses parting the sea.

"May I come to you?" Barbara asked a man seated in the fifth or sixth row. He was in maybe his late fifties, slim, Caucasian, gray hair, handsome. He looked worried, like a shaken can of seltzer water, and there was a mute sadness to him, but he agreed to Barbara's advance by nodding quickly and emphatically.

"It's your mother," said Barbara immediately. "She has been here with you the entire time."

"Oh," said the man. His voice wavered. "She's the reason I came today. This place. It was my last resort." He began to cry softly.

"Yes," Barbara assured him, "she is here with you. She's here, and she's showing me that she was very frail towards the end of her life. Does that make sense?"

The man agreed rapidly.

"And here she is, she's sitting here fixing you, making sure you're OK, petting your hair." Barbara paused, cocked her eye to the side slightly. "Oh wait, she is asking something. Do you have a brother? Because she's asking about him too."

The man cried once more and nodded again. Yes, yes.

"When you are consumed with your worries, the outdoors is where you should go to find peace. Do you do that? Because your mother wants you to know that when you do that, this is good for you. She wants me to tell you that she loves you. She didn't say it to you enough, or hardly ever, but she wants you to know that she loves you."

Now mutely weeping, the gentle man lowered his head and nodded again and again and again, collapsing into himself then wiping his face with a flannel-clad left arm.

"Bless you," said Barbara, "and I'll leave you with that."

Barbara moved to the other side of the congregation until she reached a woman, mid-forties, her spine erect. She was petite and dressed in pastel colors and sat in the second row just in front of me. Her hair was frizzy, pulled into a ponytail.

"May I come to you?" asked Barbara, pointing at the woman, and then flicked her finger to a woman seated beside her. "Actually, you have a lot of people in spirit behind the two of you. So many people talking—it's like the entire Sprint network is standing behind you two right now. You ladies are definitely related. Are you sisters?"

The women nodded and then looked at each other, their skin like powdered sugar. First, a message from their grandmother. Next, from their stepfather. "He's come in for both of you," said Barbara. "He's saying that you are both very strong women, and that you don't rely on others to do things for you. He's very proud of that." She studied the slim space of air between the backs of their two chairs. "He's standing right in there, so I know he's definitely part of the family. Looks younger than he was when he died. You have so many people here for you but they're talking all at once and it's hard to hear anyone." Barbara closed her eyes for a breath then shook her head rapidly in frustration. "One at a time, people! One at a time!" she exclaimed, and after delivering their messages like they were Christmas presents, she walked to the back of the congregation.

There, she came upon a woman quietly seated in one of the last chairs of the church who seemed to be hiding.

"Your energy preceded you," Barbara told her. "It's your first time here, isn't it?"

The woman confirmed nervously, yes.

"You made a good choice coming here," said Barbara, and proceeded. "There is a woman here. She was like a mother to you. You were a little girl. This was a parental figure that raised you. I'm seeing you with her as a young girl. She had something in her chest area, and it affected her lower extremities." From where I sat, I heard the hidden woman huff for air.

Barbara continued: "There are times when you think about her and you go back to being a little girl; this was a time when you were carefree, had no worries, and you knew you were loved. That energy surrounds you. Her energy now surrounds you and she is so proud of you—the minute you walked in, your energy was so big, such wonderful energy. I could feel it. And she is with you. She is absolutely with you. And she wants you to know she's OK. She's glad that you came here today. It was the right thing to do, and the right time. I'll leave you with that." This was followed by a whimpering, a sob.

Recently, my husband, my sister-in-law Kerri, and I took our kids to see the movie *Coco*, a Disney-Pixar film. By the end, I sat crying, not merely in tears, but bawling, and probably scaring or at least confusing most of the audience, kids *and* their parents. The movie was about Mexico, and the Día de Muertos, the Day of the Dead. It was a story about celebrating our ancestors and the importance of not forgetting them, of remembering them. In my home, I didn't participate in the activities of Día de Muertos, and not because I'm Polish-American. It was because my desire for Crate & Barrel–catalogue perfection and stylish décor had taken precedence in the rooms and on the walls of my home over the mismatched frames of my goofy relatives and photographs of deceased ancestors. Having a symmetrical, picture-perfect house made me feel safe. It made me feel like I had control, and that with everything in order and in its place, neither harm nor entropy could not reach me there. And then I went and saw that movie, and during the car ride home, with my husband glancing at me oddly and handing me tissues, I cried because our house didn't have any pictures on the walls of my deceased brother, and that was my own doing; I could blame no one else. I cried because in my quest to conquer chaos, I had disrespected my brother, had almost erased him, not to mention my ancestors who came before him. I cried because I was a complete fool—my house was not my home base. My house was storage space. What the hell had happened to my notion of faith?

"Unfortunately, we are running out of time." It was around eleven in the morning when Washian returned to the center of the stage. "This will be one of the last ones," he announced as Barbara wrapped up the last of the spirit messages, and, after accepting the embrace of one more churchgoer, made her way back to the front of the temple to close up today's service.

"*Dear God,*" Barbara prayed, "*we thank you for this day and the blessings that ensue. May we all go forward in our day in peace and in comfort, thinking of everything we have learned and experienced. With prayers in*

Etna Pond, Camp Etna, Maine.

Come to Camp Etna, we have a message for you.

A train would deposit an overflowing vessel of eager visitors
right in front of the Etna Pond and they'd make their way up
a forest path leading them to Camp Etna.

*our hearts for those who are less fortunate, let us uplift those so that it may
be a better world. So be it.*"

"*So be it,*" the congregation repeated, and with that, the Spiritualist
church service expired.

Before I left camp to return to my life and family, I decided to stop
by Peacefull Solitude one last time to thank Barbara and Steve for
the warmth and openness they'd shown me throughout the summer
season. When I'd first arrived at Camp Etna, and knowing nothing
about me, they'd opened up their lives without hesitation and ushered me into all the quiet corners of their world, despite the fact that
I was coming to their community as a journalist, not a Spiritualist.
All the while, they were never vague or guarded. We'd become friends
in the process.

Their cottage was a nest so open that no matter what time of day you showed up, you'd never be interrupting. I walked in and found the couple sitting on the couch, resting. I sat down next to Barbara, the comfortable cushions enveloping me. Spirit jumped up onto my lap, and I stroked him. The dog's breath was a bit labored, a bit smelly. Both their beloved animals were in their golden years. I pet Spirit some more and kissed him on his small head.

"Nice sermon today," I told Barbara, "You mentioned something about certain changes going on in your own life. What did you mean by that?"

Barbara sighed and rolled her eyes. "Oh, that." She went on to explain that she simply just needed to rest, because, as usual, she'd been over-doing it. In a cautious yet unwavering tone, Barbara explained that she'd been reevaluating her life lately, and wondered if it might be time for her to move on from Etna, or at least slow down, maybe take a step down from her post among the Spiritualist camp. She'd brought in and trained a lot of good young mediums. She'd been organizing it so much, creating the programs and pamphlets, curating the events and teaching classes and spinning so many plates all at once that it had gotten her weary and was taking a toll on her health. Her back had been killing her, her legs, knees, feet; her body ached. Something was telling her that it might be time for a change.

But what about camp? Was it strong enough without her? They believed they would live forever. Would Camp Etna survive? This is what I thought but didn't ask Barbara, because I realized it no longer was the right question. Despite the initial impression the camp made on me last winter when I first arrived to table-tip with Janice—that it was a marginal cluster of ramshackle cottages occupied by a quirky subculture of mystics and members of a religion that most people hadn't heard of—Camp Etna was way more than that.

I'd been worrying about the fate of Spiritualism, about Camp Etna and its inhabitants, sentimental that their shared purpose had expired. But by looking around, not only at the women of the camp but at the women in my life, I realized that Spiritualism had done what it had meant to do: It had given people power. It had given women an opportunity, a safe place to use their voices, and made it acceptable for them to speak from their gut, from their intuition and instinct, from their minds as well as their hearts. The feminist spirit of Spiritualism wasn't dead; it was a ghost living among us. Plus, the new guard had arrived at camp—the new generation of Spiritualists holding down the fort, advancing the story once again. Things don't die if there is a will by those left behind to remember—things that live forever do so by devotion. No longer was it a question of whether or not Camp Etna would survive. Camp Etna would always exist, whether in physical form or through its artifacts and photographs hanging on its walls, through stories and legends and memories, or from the vivacity that the Spiritualists breathed into every soul who came through the iron gates of 77 Stage Road. And because of this, Camp Etna would live forever.

As I was on my way out the door, Barbara insisted that I swing by the temple that I'd just left. A mediumship-development class was taking place—Karlene was teaching it, and I might find it interesting, she said, and then, just like that, she pushed me out the door.

The temple was unlocked, so I let myself in. Slick as a sardine, I slipped into my seat without turning any heads or making any waves. Karlene didn't introduce me or make a fuss; the only acknowledgment of my bungled presence was the short beat when she raised her eyebrows, otherwise the class continued on seamlessly in her grandmother's temple.

". . . so they will be *excited*," said Karlene, "but your boundaries are important," They students wrote this down. I opened my notebook, too, and I turned on my audio recorder. Other than Karlene, no one in the group knew that I was a journalist and not a student like them, that I wasn't writing down Karlene's lessons but rather what I was scribbling down my observations of her, and of them.

There were four of us in the room, which was a small, sectioned-off sanctuary in a corner of the Reverend Gladys Laliberte Temple, just to the right of the front entrance. I sat on the right side of a smooth oak bench, sharing it with a woman whom I recognized from today's church service—one of the two women with alpaca-colored hair, the Sprint-network sisters who'd gotten a reading from Barbara.

"I recently lost my husband," the Sprint woman offered to the class. "He died, and so I started to come here." She pulled a tissue out from under her sleeve. "I had a feeling I had to let go. The other day, I took off my ring so that he could move on. So he could do what he needs to do." She sniffled and dabbed a fat tear from her cheek.

"Yes," Karlene agreed. "He's here. He's telling me, 'I stayed around because you needed me. I stayed around but now you realize you don't need me as much.'" The woman began to sob, and Karlene leaned toward her and placed her hand on the woman's shoulder in a gesture of *there, there.*

"I've done fine with all my own family passing," said Karlene. "But we still need to grieve. We all need to have closure. Even if you're a medium, you're still human. You still have to be able to go through these human things."

"My cat understands it," said the widow.

"Cats think we're stupid because we haven't gotten it yet," said Karlene.

The other student in the room laughed. She'd been relatively quiet up until now. Her name was Deane, and she was the woman who'd tucked herself into the back of the temple during the church service—the camouflaged one who'd blended into the temple until Barbara approached her with a message from her late grandmother—that she was proud of her granddaughter, that she was on the right path, and that Deane had made the right choice in coming to Camp Etna today.

"Not only are these spirits coming in with love, they're coming in excited because they're going to be used," Karlene continued. "They're saying, *I get to help you.*" She hammered her clenched fist onto her palm in emphasis, and as she spoke, both the widow and Deane fervently scrawled out each sentence the instant it left Karlene's lips. "So let them help you!"

The class was good. The instructor's timing was good, her rhythm was good, the way her words fit together so soundly—she made something so hard to wrap one's head around seem so simple, so basic, so obvious.

"These spirits get to help progress you, but you are also helping progress them," said Karlene. Some of them are young souls, and you're helping them advance."

By now I was familiar with this concept: how different souls are at different stages in their development, and that by assisting those living on the earth plane, some of these souls, or spirits, were earning their stripes to advance to their next stage of soul development. And by letting them help us, we were also helping them evolve. It was a pretty profound notion, but that was essentially the gist of it.

"There are a myriad of spirit guides around that you can tap into," Karlene explained. "Whispering little things like 'Don't go down that road' or 'Let's just wait for five minutes.'" She crossed her arms and shook her head no. "Also, those are not your guardian angels. Angels are from a whole different dimension. When people die, they don't become angels! *People will never become angels,* and *angels have never been people!*"

The widow sitting next to me chimed in on this, explaining that she'd taken a class earlier this summer at camp with visiting lecturer Dr. Louis Gates called *How to Meet Your Spirit Guides.* "I met my gatekeeper," she said, then listed off the others, counting them on elegant narrow fingers. "And the doctor, the chemist—I call him the alchemist—and, and, and I can't remember the other one we're supposed to have . . ."

"That's because they're all different," replied Karlene. "Different depending on what we need at the time. I mean, your gatekeeper has been there your whole life, but the other ones? I just find them fleeting." She brought up a brief anecdote to illustrate her point further: there was a day recently when she was working on the plumbing in her nameless cottage, and she got stuck. "So there I was, under a puzzle of pipes, and I called out, 'I NEED A MASTER PLUMBER! I can't get this to copper to solder, can you come in and help me?' And know what?" Karlene patted her hands together as if she were shaking off a layer of dust, or otherwise congratulating the situation. "They sent in a master plumber! I got my master plumber. You call upon what you need! Because they're available, they *want* to help."

She paused for a moment and sat back in her chair, putting both hands behind her neck. With one booted ankle resting atop the opposite knee, Karlene waited for our pens to stop looping and for us to look up. "You pull in what is necessary in your life. But you can also just *ask* them for help. Ask for a master car mechanic! Did you know you can do Reiki on your car?"

Outside the temple, a leaf blower whined sourly, emitting the stink of exhaust, gasoline from the machine. Above Deane's head, a ray of sun shined inside the temple through stained glass, imprinting the silhouette of a large bird, perhaps a raven or a crow, resting on the other side of the window.

"You gotta release," said Karlene, her voice like a camp counselor. "Release and trust. Do your part, and trust. Let go, and trust. You're lost and you get the sense you are supposed to take a left, *take it*. Trust that they're going to take care of you."

It was two p.m. now, and I began to wonder if my family was wondering where I was. I'd planned to leave earlier but hadn't, and I hadn't called to tell them about my change in plans. Maybe they were anxious about where I was, or if something had happened to me. Maybe they wondered if I had gotten into a car accident, was injured badly. What if they were worried that I was dead? It was an epic notion, but this was the kind of dramatic thinking I jumped to immediately whenever a person I cared about hadn't shown up or hadn't called. I cast a sidelong glance at the women in my group as if that could give me the answer, and that's when I noticed an enormous shift in the energy of the room.

It was Deane. Nearly paralyzed, Deane had hunched over in her chair, her arms crossed, making an X over the front of her chest. She was shivering too, and breathing heavily but otherwise frozen like a mannequin in a department-store window. The skin on her face was damp, and the color had gone pale, almost translucent. She sniffed in hard through her nose, quickly glanced up at me, then immediately put her head back down. Just as Karlene was about to pick up where she left off in her lecture, Deane's voice broke.

"I'm getting really anxious right now," said Deane, quivering. "I'm getting really anxious right now because I'm a psychic, I've been a psychic my whole life, my grandmother was a psychic and she raised me that way and I was very comfortable being a psychic." The words came out of her mouth in small bits and rapidly, as if they'd been shaken out of her. "I am *not* a medium," she continued. "I am *not* a medium, I'm a psychic and I'm comfortable being a psychic, but, but . . ." She paused. By now Deane was shaking, and then she shouted, "But, but does anybody else see this man standing right there?!"

The widow glanced around and shrugged. I did the same. Other than Karlene, Deane, and the widow, I saw no one else in the temple. To make sure, I turned completely and looked behind my chair, but saw no man there either.

"I am NOT a medium," Deane cried, nearly yelling now, "and this is happening to me and it's been happening to me for a year now and it's freaking me out!" She covered her face and began to sob. I'd never seen a panic attack before and was pretty sure that's what was materializing.

"It's OK," said Karlene calmly. She was completely unfettered. "*Breathe*. It's OK. Just breathe." She placed her hand on Deane's knee and then said, "There *is* a man standing there."

By now Deane was nearly hyperventilating. She was hugging herself tightly, with her head sloped downward. "OK," she said quickly, and stared hard at the ground by her feet, holding her gaze firmly down, too petrified to look back up.

"You're OK," said Karlene. "You're OK."

"Phil?" Deane said quickly. "His name is Phil. He said his name is

Philip? Phil?" With trepidation, she lifted her head and sort of shaded her eyes with one hand, and with the other, pointed toward me. "He's touching your shoulder."

"Whose shoulder, my shoulder?" I asked.

"Your shoulder, yes. Or like the back of your chair or something." Deane looked up briefly to the space behind me then quickly returned her focus to the floor in front of her. "This is just FREAKING ME OUT," sobbed Deane again, and as she was starting to come more unraveled, Karlene jumped in.

"Stay with us, now, stay with us. You're OK. He's not going to do anything with you. How tall is he, Deane? Just talk to us."

Deane whimpered like she'd been defeated. "I'm in my sixties. Why is this happening to me now?"

"Because *it's time*," Karlene told her. "Because *it's time*, Deane. It's time. Like you said, you've always been psychic. It's the medium part that scares you, because you can see things. Ask him—"

"I'm afraid to talk to him," Deane interrupted, "because when you do that, when you talk to them, they take you over." She wiped her nose and sniffled. "That's what's been happening to me. When you acknowledge them, they take you over!"

"*Noooo*," said Karlene. "Noooo. Not OK!" She muted herself momentarily and bit her lip. "So that's why you were asking about boundaries earlier." Karlene thought about this for a second and then jumped back in to walk Deane through whatever was happening. "You say to him, 'You cannot attach to me,'" said Karlene. She sounded like a hostage negotiator. "Say it! Say it out loud, Deane."

"YOU CANNOT ATTACH TO ME," Deane demanded, looking up boldly, then promptly dropping her head back down.

"Say to him, 'You can be here and you can be present,'" Karlene continued, "and that's OK because he is here to present to someone—"

"Do you know a Phil?" Deane said again. She was now looking directly into my face. A cold sweat ran across her forehead. "Or a Philip? Do either of you know a . . ."

"That's my dad's name," I answered, because it was true. My father's name is Phil—Philip Courtney Ptacin—but as far as I knew and as of that morning, my father, Phil, was alive and well.

"Oh," said Deane. And then, "Is he dead?"

Before I could answer her, Karlene cut in. "I'm here with you," she reminded Deane. "Stay with me. I can see him with you."

"I'm not crazy," Deane called out.

"You're not crazy," Karlene answered her.

"And guess what the talk was about today in church?" said Deane, sniveling. "How to accept gifts you don't want."

"So he's fairly tall?" said Karlene. "Phil?"

"Yep," said Deane. "And he's got brownish hair." She was much calmer now and she blotted her eyes with a tissue. "Did he keep it real short?" she asked me.

"It's not your father," said Karlene. She rotated her wrists in the air a couple of times then said to Deane, "Go back two generations."

"He's lighter now," Deane told her.

"Because he stepped further back," said Karlene.

Deane seemed to be feeling safe, secure, and not crazy, and without further instruction, she began voluntarily listing off what she saw: what Phil looked like, how he had appeared to her: he had little tiny spectacles. He had rolled up the sleeves of his button-up shirt, and was wearing pants. He had tall, skinny, prominent cheekbones, and he didn't seem menacing. "I've seen dead people, also people who are menacing," she added. "Or just assholes. They're not nice just because they're dead."

Karlene jumped in. "Phil's not going to do anything to you. He's just coming to say hi. That's all."

"Yeah," said Deane, "he wasn't menacing at all. But he kept saying, *My name is Phil, my name is Phil, my name is Phil,* and he just keeps saying it and won't go away until I acknowledge him. They won't go away."

"It's because they get so excited that they're finally recognized," said Karlene. They're excited that they're finally being seen. A lot of people go over—they die—and they don't believe all of this, just like we, the living, might not believe all of this, either. They're like an exuberant child." And as she said this, I recognized something: the shirtsleeves rolled up, the round spectacles, a tall man with brown hair, an ancestor from my father's side of the family—it was the same description that the other mediums at camp, spontaneously during interviews, had given me. Phil, my spirit guide, had been making cameo after cameo during my time at Camp Etna. And here he was again.

Deane turned to me. "Are you a teacher?" Her brow was crinkled. "He's talking about teaching now, Phil. He says you're about to make some changes and go into something . . . are you going to start teaching somewhere? A college?"

Before I could answer, Deane started to pick up speed and kept delivering whatever message she was hearing from Phil. She said he was also mentioning something about a project. Was I writing something, working on a report? Maybe a book? Whatever it was, Phil told her that I'd be doing both at once—the teaching and this writing project.

"He's saying something about how in about eight months' time, you're going to be in a completely different place. And that it's going to pull a lot more out of you. It's going to be harder to do it. And you're going to have to throw your whole self into it. And he's really happy about it. Like, he was on the path, he was on that path but couldn't finish it. And Phil is here to help you. Phil is here to help you with this new endeavor. It's going to be way more demanding than you expected. But stick with it. Throw yourself into, and—HALLELUJAH, now he's gone!" said Deane, cheering in relief, then nearly keeling over in exhaustion.

Here's what I didn't tell Deane: that I was writing a book. That that's why I was in that room to begin with. Or that the day before, I had just been offered a teaching position at a university in New Hampshire. Nobody knew about this; I hadn't even told my husband yet. I was a mother to two small children with a new job that involved a significant commute, plus a book deadline that was fast approaching. The eight months' time that Phil had told Deane to tell me marked the date of both this manuscript's deadline as well as the last day of my semester of teaching. As for who this spirit Phil was, I wasn't sure. Honestly, I thought my dad had been named after a Philip from the Bible. I wasn't sure if there even was a Philip mentioned in the Bible, but when I got home that evening and called my father to ask him why his parents had named him Phil, my dad said he didn't entirely know the origin and that he would have to ask his siblings, who would later tell him that my father had been named after a relative. An uncle, or great-uncle named Philip. I did indeed have an ancestor named Phil from my dad's side of the family. But out of all of this, the most pertinent bit was the message that I took with me out of all this—that it was about to get hard and if I stayed deeply rooted and just went with it, all would be well. Because after I started the new teaching job, between the book and teaching and kids and life, things did get almost unbearably exhausting. And when they did and I wanted to quit and collapse in a heap, I thought about Phil and Deane, and I swayed like a willow tree instead.

Here's what I didn't know about Deane: I was her first. She had never done something like that before, had never stuck around to see what a spirit had to say. In fact, it wasn't until the end of the class that she revealed to us that it was her very first time at Camp Etna, she didn't know a single person at Camp Etna, nor had she ever met any Spiritualists, and that she'd only come to the class in the first place because she wanted someone to teach her how to turn it off, how to make it stop. Deane had done some research on places where she might be able to find a medium who might be able to teach her how to turn off whatever had been turned on and keep it off for good. Eventually, she came across Karlene's class, which was being offered every Sunday immediately following the ten-thirty Healing Light Sunday Spiritualist Church service. Deane lived in Connecticut. One day, she found out her friend was coming to Maine for a class reunion, so she decided to hitch a ride and finally check out this strange Spiritualist camp. She could check out the mediumship development class, but would first sit through the church service that went before it, plant herself near the back of the temple and closest to the door in case it turned out these people were a bunch of wackadoos and she needed to slip out and make a run for it. But then out of nowhere Barbara came to her of all people and delivered a message from the spirit of Deane's grandmother. The message was unexpected and perfect, in alignment with all the questions she'd been having and answered just what no one but Deane knew about and needed to hear. And now here she was, sitting in class, having just delivered her first mediumship reading and almost convinced not to shut off her clairvoyance as she'd planned, but to embrace the gift instead.

"Once they get their message across, they leave." Karlene assured her and Deane pushed back.

"What kind of life am I going to have if this just happens whenever?"

"No," said Karlene. "That's why you're going to set up boundaries."

"Because when I'm doing my psychic readings, I *schedule* my readings," Deane continued. "My clients don't just come in whenever. I schedule when they're going to happen. But this? I don't know how to handle this. This just *happens*."

Karlene placed the tips of her fingers back on Deane's knee again and leaned toward the distressed woman. "You accepted it by coming here," she said. "You opened yourself to Phil by coming to this class. It is a mediumship-development class, isn't it?"

Deane's lips made a thin and tentative smile and then she nodded. Karlene pressed on.

"You say, *Only good come can come to me*. If they start making you anxious, say, *Back up. I'm not ready to talk to you now. Bring it in in a gentler manner which I am able to accept.* They're learning this too," said Karlene. "The minute you accept all of this, Deane, and once you can set your boundaries, it will become easy. It will flood in. They're shifting energy, they're walking through. And it's amazing how fast it will come in." Feverishly now, both Deane and the widow were writing down everything Karlene said. "Your life will go so much smoother. You can ask questions and get answers. If you open up and accept it, you get more and more information. You can have fun with it."

"*Have fun with it*," Deane mouthed as she penned it in her notebook. It was obvious that Karlene had brushed away any bitterness, and the woman was not afraid anymore. Later, Deane would describe it: when she discovered that she was seeing dead people, that she was a medium, it felt like as having just been told she was going to have vertigo for the rest of her life, but after leaving Camp Etna, she'd finally been given a prescription.

After class on my trip back home, I kept the radio off and drove in silence. I thought about faith. What is it? I wondered if I should have faith in what had just happened back at the temple and whether what had happened was real. The whole idea of reality is that it is fact, and what makes something a fact is that it's reproducible, it can be proven. But nothing would last if we all gave up so quickly on things we were unsure of, if we gave up believing in something when it was harder to stand by it and easier to just let it go. Back in the temple, what was said and delivered to me through Deane—was that enough proof? Did that count? I kept driving ahead and sitting with the fact that, my entire life, I'd avoided defining and distinguishing my faith. What *did* I believe? We pass down stories. We honor the dead and remember our ancestors. A person is gone, a moment dissipates, but the memory remains, and memory is a vehicle to get to know who you are inside. But often, we are programmed not to look. We are programmed not to see God. But the truth to me is that we are God, watching God.

As I reached the end of my drive, I got a glimpse of some kind of answer: it was time to participate. I'd been waiting for someone to tell me what to do, but what would I tell my kids? A lot of us go through life wondering, and waiting, and wondering, and waiting, but maybe it would be healthy to make a choice. Why not decide what you believe in instead of just wondering? When I finally reached home, I went inside and hugged my family.

"It's your life," Karlene had insisted, moments after Deane had delivered her first spirit message and shortly before class was dismissed and we all went our separate ways. "You're on this plane, and what do you want? But instead of saying, *I'm in control*, you can say *I'm choosing to do this.*"

Karlene looked into the group of us and repeated her words. The grieving woman, the new medium, and I all nodded in agreement, accepting them. She continued: "You can say, *If this is the path God has chosen for me, then let me choose what I need to do, and how I need to accept it.* Because the choice is yours. The choice is yours."

Acknowledgments

First and foremost, always and forever, I am in gratitude for the love and support given so endlessly by my wonderful parents, Philip and Maria Ptacin. Every good thing about me comes from you. You keep me grounded and sound in mind and spirit. Thank you for helping me take care of (or taking over the care of) one sick kid, two antsy dogs, and one broken toilet that wouldn't stop overflowing that one ridiculous morning that my manuscript was due. I couldn't have done this without you.

A hearty shout-out to the publications where excerpts of this book first appeared: *No Man's Land*, *Lenny Letter*, and *Tin House*. And with that, I thank the most excellent editors that spearheaded them: Michelle Legro, Deidre Dyer, Jessica Grose, and Emma Komlos-Hrobsky. You are powerhouses and your encouragement gives me vital soul fuel. Emma—without you, my fascination with Camp Etna would have never blossomed into a book, or an article, and possibly might not have ever gotten out the steel trap of my monkey mind. And to Chelsea Conaboy—you were there from the book's birth to its last word at one a.m. on a Tuesday morn. A particular note of gratitude to the scholars Ann Braude, Wyatt E. Brumfield II, and Todd Kay Leonard for unearthing all the artifacts into an abundant and comprehensive history of the earliest years of Spiritualism.

Lisa Bankoff, my stalwart agent, literary mama bear, powerhouse, and calming voice of reason: I love you very much. Thank you, thank you, thank you.

It was a true honor to work with the best of the best team at Liveright: Marie Pantojan, Cordelia Calvert, Rebecca Homiski, Don Rifkin, Rachelle Mandik, Jessica R. Friedman, Beth Steidle, Steve Attardo, and Kelly Winton. In particular, I'd like to thank Katie Adams for having faith in *The In-Betweens* before it manifested into a book, and whose wisdom, insight, and grace literally created feminist history.

To the Spiritualists and *magnificent* women and men of Camp Etna, past and present, who make up this story: I am beyond grateful and still stunned by your willingness and openness, your kindness and transparency, enthusiasm and selflessness. If I could make this paragraph glow in the dark I would, but you people already bring in the light. In addition, thank you to Deane Driscoll for including me in your enormous shift and evolution.

Thank you to my lifelong mentors Nancy Hood, Jim Butler, Claire Ott, Suzanne Hoover, Jo Ann Beard, Vijay Seshadri, Vincent Lyon-Callo, Jason Roberts. To my scattered squad, whose friendship, conversations, enthusiasm, research, and straight-up help gave me the freedom to do this (roll call): Celia Blue Johnson (always!). Michelle Koufopoulos (my shero). Amanda Angelo (Cream Team). Ellen O'Connell Whittet. Katie Devine, David Daniels, Barbara Sueko McGuire, Christina Cooke (since Salt and until forever), Cathrin Wirtz, Sarah Hempel Irani, Kitty Gilbert, Jamie Herndon, Abigail Raminsky, Koren Zailckas, Chelsea DeLorme, Rebecca Falzano, Sarah Arrand Heeley, Cate Marvin, Emily Flake, Laura Mazikowski, Alison Devers, Re Gibson, Jess George, Niki Taylor, James Walsh, Judy Fitch, Alexis Raymond, Courtney Farr, Agata Czyzewski, Seri Gilliam, Sam Duckworth, Steven Jackson, Caitie Whelan, Nancy Marshall, and Diane Ricciotti. Big ups to Emily Russo, Josh Christie, Rose Heithoff, Steph, Alex, and my big brilliant family at Print Bookstore in Portland, Maine. Gratitude to Donna Galluzzo, as well as my family tree of the Salt Institute for Documentary Studies. To Linda Holtslander: you are a treasure, and how lucky I am to share the rock with you. To Ned: my buddy, my cheerleader. Thank you, Greta Rybus, for your generosity! Hugs to Lisa Lynch and Ellen Huston at the café for feeding and pampering me, particularly though the inexhaustible tail end of the Maine winters. Thank you to the teachers and staff at the Peaks Children's Workshop and Brick School—it takes a village. And thank you to my village for all your love—my Peaks Island family.

I have an incredible tribe: Sabina and Alex (and Juliette); Maya and Maddie and Mary; my mother-in-law (and deadline coach), Evelyn Jackson; Kerri and Brian and Annabelle, and of course Huck and Maybe—thanks for being the fire. But most of all, thank you, Andrew Michael Jackson. Andrew, you are my number-one friend, my number-one partner, my number-one Excel worksheet, father of my babies, hiker of rescued doggies, dish-doer, compost maintainer, she-shed builder, sidewalk shoveler, best dad. You are so good to me, so patient and so kind, a true feminist and an ocean of compassion. I love you so very much, and I thank you. And finally, to my beautiful children, Theo Julian and Simone True: I love you as much as infinity times infinity.

Notes

CHAPTER 1: OPENING SEASON

2 **by 1897 would spread across the United States and Europe:** Emma Hardinge Britten, *Nineteenth Century Miracles: Spirits and Their Work in Every Country of the Earth* (New York: William Britten, 1884).

3 **I asked the noise:** Todd Jay Leonard, *Talking to the Other Side: A History of Modern Spiritualism and Mediumship* (Lincoln, NE: iUniverse, 2005), 225–28.

4 **One tap meant yes. Two taps, no:** Barbara Weisberg, *Talking to the Dead: Kate and Maggie Fox and the Rise of Spiritualism* (New York: HarperCollins, 2005), 19.

4 **"the state of railway stocks":** Arthur Conan Doyle, *The History of Spiritualism* (Newcastle Upon Tyne, UK: Cambridge Scholars Publishing Classic Texts, new edition, 2009), 37.

5 ***Spiritualism will work miracles:*** Ann Braude, *Radical Spirits: Spiritualism and Women's Rights in Nineteenth-Century America* (Bloomington: Indiana University Press; 2nd edition, 2001), 17.

6 **"rapid journey":** Leonard, *Talking to the Other Side*, 58.

9 **"emancipation of women from all legal and social disabilities":** *Spirit Messenger and Harmonial Guide,* October 18, 1851, 127; *Banner of Light*, September 17, 1859, 7.

9 **"Spiritualism has promoted the cause":** *Spirit Messenger and Harmonial Guide,* October 18, 1851, 127; *Banner of Light*, September 17, 1859, 5.

10 **"The first conditions to be observed":** *The Spiritual Magazine* 4 (1869), 197–99.

11 **In 1852, *The Spiritual Telegraph* began circulation:** Leonard, *Talking to the Other Side*, 216.

22 **"Declaration of Rights of the Women of the United States":** The site of the papers of Elizabeth Cady Stanton and Susan B. Anthony, Rutgers, The State University of New Jersey: http://ecssba.rutgers.edu/docs/decl.html, accessed March 1, 2019.

23 **"Even if it was acceptable to us":** *Herald of Progress,* February 4, 1860, 4, and March 31, 1860, 4.

23 **"The Banner shall continue to wave":** Braude, *Radical Spirits,* 79.

24 **only one woman engaged:** Ibid., 164.

24 **seventeen of them men, and one woman, a non-medium:** Ibid., 164–69.

25 **"This is man's work":** *Banner of Light,* November 11, 1865, 8.

25 **only one woman:** Braude, *Radical Spirits,* 169.

26 **"under a tent":** Clarence A. Stewart, *A Short History of Camp Etna* (self-published and found in the Camp Etna museum), 1.

27 **"with few implications"** . . . **"gracefully mingled":** Braude, *Radical Spirits,* 174.

27 **"painted by a medium":** *American Spiritualist,* August 7, 1869, 113.

31 **Margaret stepped forth and demonstrated:** Weisberg, *Talking to the Dead,* 241–42.

CHAPTER 2: BRIGHT EYES

44 **"I had retired but was wide-awake":** M. E. Cadwallader, *Mary S. Vanderbilt: A Twentieth Century Seer* (Chicago: The Progressive Seeker Publishing House, 1921), 4.

45 **"There was something about it":** *Lewiston Journal,* 1908, sourced from http://www.campetna.com/mary-vanderbilt.html.

46 **"You squaw in de corner":** Cadwallader, *Mary S. Vanderbilt,* 6.

49 **a readership of 30,000:** The International Association for the Preservation of Spiritualist And Occult Periodicals, www.iapsop.com/archive/materials/banner_of_light/, accessed March 4, 2019.

50 *Why hello Mister So-and-So*: Ibid., 7.

50 **"There is at a Spiritualist camp"**: Cadwallader, *Mary S. Vanderbilt*, 40, 44.

52 **"[He] takes a deep interest"**: "Head of the Spiritualists in U.S. and Canada a Maine Man," *Bangor News*, December 12, 1904, sourced from https://www.campetna.com/harrison-d.-barrett.html, accessed March 18, 2019.

53 **"Ten years ago, Mary Pepper was considered a good platform medium"**: Cadwallader, *Mary S. Vanderbilt*, 14.

53 **"Tall, with the massive frame of women of mountain regions"**: *Australian Town and Country Journal* (Sydney), March 15, 1905, 35.

53 **"Mrs. Pepper's prayers"**: Cadwallader, *Mary S. Vanderbilt*, 19.

53 **"Hundreds of people go to hear Mrs. Pepper"**: Ibid.

54 **"[In Germany] I was taken to the castle"**: Quoted in Ibid., 27.

54 **"unconsciously believe in the communication"**: Ibid., 28.

55 **"the sympathy and cooperation of her husband"**: Ibid., ix.

55 **"a woman of unscrupulous habits"**: *New York Times*, June 11, 1907.

56 **"SPIRITUALIST FAITH SIGN OF INSANITY"**: *New York Times*, September 4, 1907, 2.

56 **"except for his belief in astrology"**: Kerry Segrave, *Women Swindlers in America: 1860–1920* (Jefferson, NC: McFarland and Company, Inc. Publishers, 2007), 16.

56 **"Spiritualist Bishop of Brooklyn"**: *New York Times*, November 12, 1908. 2–7.

56 **The verdict . . . Later that year:** Segrave, *Women Swindlers*, 15–17.

57 **"I like large audiences"**: Cadwallader, *Mary S. Vanderbilt*, 44.

57 **"a lecturer of no mean repute"**: "America's Most Distinguished Spiritualist Succumbs After Long Suffering," *Bangor Semi-Weekly*, January 17, 1911, sourced from https://www.campetna.com/harrison-d.-barrett.html, accessed March 18, 2019.

58 **"some day the silver cord" . . . "as if a procession"**: Cadwallader, *Mary S. Vanderbilt*, 46.

58 **"spirit emerged from earth conditions"**: Ibid., 47.

CHAPTER 3: GHOST HUNTING 101

64 **"one whose organism is sensitive"**: National Spiritualist Association of Churches, "Defining Spiritualism," https://nsac.org/what-we-believe/definining-spiritualism/, accessed March 4, 2019.

65 **"the dematerialization of physical objects"**: Stephen A. Herman, *Mediumship Mastery: The Mechanics of Receiving Spirit Communications* (Amherst, MA: Atendriya Press, 2016), 6.

65 **"Physical is not dependent upon the spirituality"**: Ibid.

65 **a substance to produce physical manifestations**: Ibid., 4.

67 **"Mental mediumship . . . is also dependent upon attunement"**: Ibid., 3.

86 **"The bell tower flickered in flames"**: R. F. Johnnett, *Bates Student: A Monthly Magazine* (1878), 164, Edmund Muskie Archives, Bates College, Lewiston, Maine.

CHAPTER 4: ROSABELLE, BELIEVE

96 **"Initially, regular mediumship"**: Leonard, *Talking to the Other Side*, 125.

96 **"Sitters in a séance"**: Ibid.

97 **"gagged and blindfolded"**: Braude, *Radical Spirits*, 177.

98 **a new type of feminism:** Estelle B. Freedman, "The New Woman: Changing Views of Women in the 1920's," *Journal of American History* 61, no. 2 (1974), 372–93.

99 **"In the wake of the war"**: Jeremy C. Young, "Empowering Passivity: Women Spiritualists, Houdini, and the 1926 Fortune Telling Hearing," *Journal of Social History* 48, no. 2 (December 2014), 343–44.

99 **14 million in faith:** Mental Floss Staff, "Houdini's Greatest Trick: Debunking Medium Mina Crandon," Mental Floss, http://mentalfloss .com/article/53424/houdinis-greatest-trick-debunking-medium-mina -crandon, accessed March 3, 2019.

100 **"angel upon earth"** . . . **"guiding beacon"**: Joe McGasko, "His Lost Sweetheart: Harry Houdini and His Mother," Biography, www.biography .com/news/harry-houdini-mother-cecilia-weiss, accessed March 4, 2019.

100 **"Rosabelle, sweet Rosabelle"**: William Kalush and Larry Sloman, *The Secret Life of Houdini: The Making of America's First Superhero* (New York: Atria Books, reprint edition 2007), 539.

100 **Cecilia remained his number one:** McGasko, "His Lost Sweetheart."

102 **"The great day of the Fire-eater"**: Harry Houdini, *Miracle Mongers and Their Methods: A Complete Exposé of the Modus Operandi of Fire Eaters, Heat Resisters, Poison Eaters, Venomous Reptile Defiers, Sword*

Swallowers, Human Ostriches, Strong Men, Etc. (New York: E. P. Dutton, 1920), 97–98.

102 **"I was willing to believe":** John Cox, "The Real Story of Houdini and Doyle," Wild About Houdini (blog), www.wildabouthoudini.com/2016/04/the-real-story-of-houdini-doyle.html, accessed February 11, 2019.

102 **"meant to me an easing of all pain":** Ruth Brandon, *The Spiritualists* (New York: Knopf, 1983), 173.

103 **"My sainted mother could not write English":** Troy Taylor, "A Haunted Friendship," The Haunted Museum (blog), www.prairieghosts.com/doyle_houdini.html, accessed February 11, 2019.

103 **"Vultures who prey":** Harry Houdini, *A Magician Among the Spirits* (1924; reprint, New York: Arno Press, 1972), 190.

104 **straight for Margery's séance:** David Jaher, *The Witch of Lime Street: Séance, Seduction, and Houdini in the Spirit World* (New York: Crown Publishers, 2015), 183–87.

104 **"I've got her!":** Stefan Bechtel and Laurence Roy Stains, *Through a Glass, Darkly: Sir Arthur Conan Doyle and the Quest to Solve the Greatest Mystery of All* (New York: St. Martin's Press, 2017), 205.

104 **"Houdini, you goddamned son of a bitch":** Kalush and Sloman, *Secret Life of Houdini*, 430.

105 **"Margery Passes All Psychic Tests":** *New York Times*, July 22, 1924, 19.

105 **"as low as one can imagine":** Houdini, *Magician Among the Spirits*, 282–83.

105 **"I am an author":** Kalush and Sloman, *Secret Life of Houdini*, 481.

106 **"curse . . . leaving in its wake a crowd of victims":** Houdini, *Magician Among the Spirits*, 180.

107 **"Do you know how many crimes" . . . "[If the medium] is a colored man":** House Committee on the District of Columbia, Fortune Telling Hearing, February 26, and May 18, 20, 21, 1926 (Washington, DC), 18–19, 139.

108 **"great soul and a good Christian" . . . "This man Houdini":** Ibid., 73–75.

108 **"the talented political operative" . . . "asking his 'girl'":** Jeremy C. Young, "Empowering Passivity: Women Spiritualists, Houdini, and the 1926 Fortune Telling Hearing," *Journal of Social History* 48, no. 2 (December 2014), 354.

109 **"but one more year to live":** John Cox, "Margery's Curse," Wild About Harry (blog), https://www.wildabouthoudini.com/2014/06/margerys-curse .html, accessed March 4, 2019.

109 **"Would you mind":** Jaher, *The Witch of Lime Street*, 382.

110 **"I can't fight anymore":** "The Life and Death of Harry Houdini: Magician's Bravado May Have Played Role in Halloween Demise," National Public Radio, *All Things Considered*, October 30, 2003, https://www.npr .org/templates/story/story.php?storyId=1485266.

110 **"This is a Houdini night" . . . Another newspaper reported:** John Cox, "Halloween 1936, The Final Séance," Wild About Harry (blog), October 2014, www.wildabouthoudini.com/2014/10/halloween-1936-final -houdini-seance.html, accessed February 11, 2019.

111 **"Mrs. Houdini. The zero hour has passed . . . It is finished. Good night, Harry":** Kalush and Sloman, *Secret Life of Houdini*, 557.

112 **"Ten years is long enough":** Allen Spragett and William V. Rauscher, *Arthur Ford: The Man Who Talked with the Dead* (New York: New American Library; distributed by W. W. Norton, 1973), 246.

CHAPTER 5: LOYALTY LODGE

114 **"As the twentieth century unfolded":** Darryl V. Caterine, *Haunted Ground: Journeys Through Paranormal America* (Santa Barbara, CA: Praeger, 2011), 10.

115 **Era of Great Mediums:** Leonard, *Talking to the Other Side*, 62.

115 **She'd even written a book:** Barbara Williams, PhD, *Psychic Self Defense* (self-published, 2016).

127 **"blend with the medium's aura":** Tracie Delysia Wolter, "What Is Trance Mediumship?" The Other Side Press Online (blog), October 27, 2015, https://theothersidepress.com/what-is-trance-mediumship-2390.

128 **"You start relaxing" . . . "You don't have a physical mind":** "Trance Medium Elaine Thorpe Shares Her Story and Allows Her Guide Jonathan to Answer Questions," YouTube, February 27, 2018, https://www .youtube.com/watch?v=073U46anPWI, accessed March 4, 2019.

133 **"Just four years after":** "The History of Morris Pratt Institute," Morris Pratt Institute, www.morrispratt.org, accessed February 12, 2019.

CHAPTER 6: WATER WITCHING, OR DOWSING FOR ANSWERS

145 **At one time there were more than twenty:** Dayton Martindale, "The Stolen Children of Maine," In These Times, July 18, 2015, http://inthesetimes.com/rural-america/entry/18201/stolen-children-maine-native-wabanaki-truth-reconciliation-genocide, accessed September, 2019.

148 **"The surface is quite broken":** George J. Varney, *A Gazetteer of Maine* (Boston: B. B. Russell, 1881), 223.

156 **"both Moses and his son":** Lloyd Youngblood, "Dowsing: Ancient History," American Society of Dowsers website, https://dowsers.org/dowsing-history/, accessed March 4, 2019.

157 **German miners:** "Faust" website: https://www.faust.com/legend/divination/dowsing/, accessed March 4, 2019.

157 **Queen Elizabeth's royal mines:** John Weidhofft Gough, *The Mines of Mendip* (Oxford: Oxford University Press, 1930), 6.

157 **Martin Luther declared:** "Dowsing," Christian Research Institute (CRI), July 10, 2009, https://www.equip.org/article/dowsing/, accessed March 18, 2019.

157 **declared satanic:** Arthur J. Ellis, *The Divining Rod: A History of Water Witching* (Washington, DC: Government Printing Office, 1917), 17.

157 **more than half the domestic wells drilled:** Kate Daloz, "The Dowser Dilemma," *American Scholar* (March 1, 2009), 91.

161 **"strongly opposes the use of water witches":** National Groundwater Association, "Water Witching," http://wellowner.org/basics/planning-for-a-water-well/water-witching/, accessed March 4, 2019.

161 **analyzed the successes and failures:** "Finding Water with a Forked Stick," *Popular Mechanics*, December 7, 2004, https://www.popularmechanics.com/science/a3199/1281661/, accessed March 4, 2019.

164 **"My objective in writing this book":** Millais Culpin, *Spiritualism and the New Psychology: An Explanation of Spiritualist Phenomena and Beliefs in Terms of Modern Knowledge* (London: Edward Arnold, 1920), 1.

165 **"psychological automatism":** Ibid., 98–99.

166 **"Interrogating Edith":** Daloz, "The Dowser Dilemma," 90.

166 **a research group on dowsers:** Evon Z. Vogt and Ray Hyman, *Water Witching, USA* (Chicago: University of Chicago Press; 2nd edition, 2000), xxvii.

166 **"We possess several subtle bodies":** Herman, *Mediumship Mastery*, 9.

CHAPTER 7: THE NEW GENERATION

173 **"a loud ringing":** Raymond Moody Jr., MD, *Life After Life* (New York: HarperOne; Anniversary, special edition, 2015), 20.

174 **"fluid and fuzzy cultic milieu":** Olav Hammer, *Claiming Knowledge: Strategies of Epistemology from Theosophy to the New Age* (Leiden and Boston: Brill, 2001), 14.

174 **the Age of Aquarius:** David Spangler, *Explorations: Emerging Aspects of the New Culture* (Traverse City, MI: Lorian Press, 1980), 78.

174 **Earth was moving into a new cycle:** Wouter Hanegraaff, *New Age Religion and Western Culture: Esotericism in the Mirror of Secular Thought* (Albany: State University of New York Press, 1996), 94.

175 **"a synthesis of many different preexisting movements":** James R. Lewis and J. Gordon Melton, "Introduction" in *Perspectives on the New Age*, eds. James R. Lewis and J. Gordon Melton (Albany: State University of New York Press, 1992), xi.

175 **"enterprise culture":** Paul Heelas, *The New Age Movement: Religion, Culture and Society in the Age of Postmodernity* (Cambridge, MA: Blackwell, 1996), 168.

181 **the subtle body:** "Nature, the Enjoyer and Consciousness," Bg 13.6–7, Bhagavad Gita, www.vedabase.com/en/bg/13, accessed February 12, 2019.

181 **The chakras are powerhouses:** Michelle Fondin, "What Is a Chakra?" The Chopra Center, https://chopra.com/articles/what-is-a-chakra, accessed February 12, 2019.

185 **"indestructible tablets of the astral light":** H. P. Blavatsky, *Isis Unveiled: Secrets of the Ancient Wisdom Tradition* (Wheaton, IL: Quest Books; new edition, 1994), 178.

185 **"Buddha taught two things are eternal":** Quoted in Alfred Percy Sinnett, *Esoteric Buddhism* (Boston: Houghton Mifflin, 1884), 127.

CHAPTER 8: THE POWWOW

206 **dancing was especially suspect:** Clyde Ellis, *A Dancing People: Powwow Culture on the Southern Plains* (Lawrence: University Press of Kansas, 2003), 14–15.

207 **when we meditate:** David Michie, "How to Invoke the Medicine Buddha," *Lion's Roar Magazine*, September 2018, 52–55.

207 **approximately 3,000 Penobscot Indians:** "Penobscot Nation," AAA Native Arts, www.aaanativearts.com/penobscot-tribe-of-maine-index, accessed February 14, 2019.

214 **"reincarnation of people and animals":** Quoted in "Traditional Native Concepts of Death," September 1, 2014, posted by "Ojibwa," Native American Netroots Forum, https://nativeamericannetroots.net/diary/1726, accessed March 4, 2019.

CHAPTER 9: CHURCH

218 **struggling to fill their pews:** Kelley Bouchard, "A Changing Landscape: Where the Spirit Moves in Maine," *Portland Press Herald*, May 22, 2016.

221 **attempt to weigh the soul:** Duncan Macdougall, "Hypothesis Concerning Soul Substance Together with Experimental Evidence of the Existence of Such Substance," *American Medicine New Series* 2, no. 4 (April 1907), 240–43.

221 **The Vajrayana Buddhists of Mongolia and Tibet:** "After Death, Tibetans Still Prefer Sky Burial," *New Kerala*, September 1, 2005, The Buddhist Channel, http://www.buddhistchannel.tv/index.php?id=1,1614,0,0,1,0#.XH4XHi2ZOL9, accessed March 4, 2019.

221 **For the Tinguian culture:** Faye-Cooper Cole, *Traditions of the Tinguian: A Study in Philippine Folk-Lore* (Chicago: Field Museum of Natural History, Publication 180, 1915), 19.

222 **In the Benguet culture:** Zoë Byrne, "The Unique Funeral Customs of Various Filipino Ethnic Groups," June 4, 2015, SevenPonds, http://blog.sevenponds.com/cultural-perspectives/the-unique-funeral-customs-of-various-filipino-ethnic-groups, accessed March 5, 2019.

222 **a ceremony called *shraddha*:** Pramod Kumar Agarwal, "Hindu Death Rituals and Beliefs," January 30, 2017, Speaking Tree (blog), https://www.speakingtree.in/blog/hindu-death-rituals-and-beliefs, accessed March 5, 2019.

Further Reading

Blum, Deborah. *Ghost Hunters: William James and the Search for Scientific Proof of Life After Death*. New York: Penguin Books, 2007.

Brandon, Ruth: *The Spiritualists*. New York: Alfred A. Knopf, 1983.

Braude, Ann. *Radical Spirits: Spiritualism and Women's Rights in Nineteenth-Century America*. Boston: Beacon Press, 1989.

Deane, Lady. *The Mystical Card Reading Handbook*. Epping, NH: ACS Publications, 2016.

Dickey, Colin. *Ghostland: An American History in Haunted Places*. New York: Viking, 2016.

Doyle, Alfred Conan. *The History of Spiritualism*. Newcastle Upon Tyne, UK: Cambridge Scholars Publishing Classic Texts, new edition, 2009.

Estés, Clarissa Pinkola. *Women Who Run with the Wolves: Myths and Stories of the Wild Woman Archetype*. New York: Ballantine Books, 1992.

Herman, Stephen A. *Mediumship Mastery: The Mechanics of Receiving Spirit Communication*. Amherst, MA: Atendriya Press, 2015.

Jaher, David. *The Witch of Lime Street: Séance, Seduction, and Houdini in the Spirit World*. New York: Crown Publishers, 2015.

Leonard, Todd Jay. *Talking to the Other Side: A History of Modern Spiritualism and Mediumship*. Lincoln, NE: iUniverse, 2005.

Manseau, Peter. *The Apparitionists: A Tale of Phantoms, Fraud, Photography, and the Man Who Captured Lincoln's Ghost*. New York: Mariner Books, 2018.

Moody, Raymond, Jr., MD. *Life After Life*. New York: HarperCollins, 1975.

Owen, Alex. *The Darkened Room: Women, Power, and Spiritualism in Late Victorian England*. London: Virago Press, 1989.

Roach, Mary. *Spook: Science Tackles the Afterlife*. New York: W. W. Norton & Company, 2005.

Ruiz, Don Miguel. *The Four Agreements*. San Rafael, CA: Amber Allen Publishing, 1997.

Simone, Natalie. *Supernatural Entertainments: Victorian Spiritualism and the Rise of Modern Media Culture*. University Park: Penn State University Press, 2017.

Tadd, Ellen. *The Infinite View: A Guidebook for Life on Earth*. New York: TarcherPerigee, 2017.

Underhill, Evelyn. *Mysticism: A Study in the Nature and Development of Spiritual Consciousness*. New York: E. P. Dutton, 1911.

Weisberg, Barbara. *Talking to the Dead: Kate and Maggie Fox and the Rise of Spiritualism*. New York: HarperCollins, 2005.